IEG WORLD BANK | IFC | MIGA
INDEPENDENT EVALUATION GROUP

Results and Performance of the World Bank Group

IEG Annual Report 2010

Volume 1: Main Report

2010
The World Bank
Washington, D.C.

1818 H Street, N.W.
Washington, D.C. 20433
Telephone: 202-473-1000
Internet: www.worldbank.org
E-mail: feedback@worldbank.org

1 2 3 4 13 12 11 10

Cover: Top: Children in Bhutan look over terraced fields. Photo by Curt Carnemark, courtesy of the World Bank Photo Library. Center right: © S. Oskar/Corbis. Bottom: Ceramic tile manufacturing plant in Brazil. Photo by Jouni Martti Eerikainen; used with permission.

ISBN-13: 978-0-8213-8577-7
e-ISBN-13: 978-0-8213-8607-1
DOI: 1596/978-0-8213-8577-7

Library of Congress Cataloging-in-Publication Data have been applied for.

World Bank InfoShop
E-mail: pic@worldbank.org
Telephone: 202-458-5454
Facsimile: 202-522-1500

Independent Evaluation Group
Communication, Strategy, and Learning
E-mail: ieg@worldbank.org
Telephone: 202-458-4497
Facsimile: 202-522-3125

Printed on recycled paper

Table of Contents

Appendixes

Boxes

Figures

Tables

Volume II Management Response to Recommendations

Abbreviations

AAA	Analytic and advisory activities
ACP	Agreement at Completion Point (International Fund for Agricultural Development)
ACS	Activity Completion Summary
ADB	Asian Development Bank
CAS	Country Assistance Strategy
CRG	Credit Review Guidelines
DOTS	Development Outcome Tracking System
DPL	Development Policy Loan
ECG	Evaluation Cooperation Group
E&S	Environmental and social (effects)
ESW	Economic and sector work
FDI	Foreign direct investment
GTFP	Global Trade Finance Program
IBRD	International Bank for Reconstruction and Development
ICR	Implementation Completion Report
IDA	International Development Association
IED	Independent Evaluation Department (Asian Development Bank)
IEG	Independent Evaluation Group
IFC	International Finance Corporation
IICCR	Institutional Investor Country Credit Rating
M&E	Monitoring and evaluation
MIGA	Multilateral Investment Guarantee Agency
NLTA	Nonlending technical assistance
PER	Project Evaluation Report
PPAR	Project Performance Assessment Review
PRSC	Poverty Reduction Support Credit
QAG	Quality Assurance Group
XPSR	Expanded Project Supervision Report

Acknowledgments

This report was prepared by a core team led by Anjali Kumar, Independent Evaluation Group (IEG)–World Bank; Stephen Francis Pirozzi, IEG–International Finance Corporation (IFC); and Stefan Apfalter, IEG–Multilateral Investment Guarantee Agency (MIGA), with contributions from Anahit Aghumian, Andaleeb Alam, Marianne Ellen Anderson, Unurjargal Demberel, Sidney Edelmann, Jouni Martii Eerikainen, Cheikh M'Backe Fall, Jean-Olivier Fraisse, Hiroyuki Hatashima, Beata Lenard, Brett Libresco, Albert Martinez, Bidjan Nashat, Garima Sahai, Cherian Samuel, Janardan Prasad Singh, Aurora Medina Siy, Aida Tapalova, Jesse Torrence, Yoshine Uchimura, and Victoria Viray-Mendoza. Contributions were also provided by consultants Luis Lopez-Calva, Osvaldo Feinstein, Linda Morra, Ray Rist, Joanne Salop, and Suleiman Wasty. The team appreciates support from Ismail Arslan, Monika Huppi, Soniya Carvalho, Nischint Bhatnagar, and Melvin Vaz.

The evaluation greatly benefitted from constructive advice and feedback from many persons. Nils Fostvedt and Bruce Murray served as peer reviewers to the report. Valuable commentary was also provided by Martha Ainsworth, Amitava Banerjee, Hans-Martin Boehmer, Daniela Gressani, Ali Khadr, Aart Kraay, and Andrew Warner. William Hurlbut and Heather Dittbrenner provided editorial support, and production assistance was provided by Yvette Jarencio. Yezena Yimer supported all aspects of document delivery.

The evaluation was conducted under the guidance of Mark Sundberg, Cheryl Gray, Stoyan Tenev, Marvin Taylor-Dormond, Christine Wallich, and Vinod Thomas.

Director-General, Evaluation: *Vinod Thomas*
Director, IEG–World Bank: *Cheryl Gray*
Director, IEG–IFC: *Marvin Taylor-Dormond*
Director, IEG–MIGA: *Christine Wallich*
Manager, IEG–World Bank, Corporate and Global Evaluations and Methods: *Mark Sundberg*
Head, Macro Evaluation, IEG–IFC: *Stoyan Tenev*
Overall Task Coordinator, IEG–World Bank: *Anjali Kumar*
Task Manager, IEG–IFC: *Stephen Francis Pirozzi*
Task Manager, IEG–MIGA: *P. Stefan Apfalter*

Foreword

The Independent Evaluation Group's (IEG) annual report—*Results and Performance 2010: The World Bank Group*—covers the content previously included in three reports: the World Bank's *Annual Review of Development Effectiveness*, the International Finance Corporation's (IFC) *Independent Evaluation of IFC's Development Results*, and the Multilateral Investment Guarantee Agency's (MIGA) *Independent Evaluation of MIGA's Effectiveness.*

Recent activity at each World Bank Group institution has been dominated by the global financial crisis, yet response patterns have been markedly different. New commitments at the World Bank more than doubled in fiscal 2009, exhibiting a strong countercyclical pattern in public sector support. New investments at IFC have shown a procyclical pattern, with strategic prioritization of portfolio protection over the generation of new business; this was caused in part by resource constraints. New IFC business activity, which had more than doubled from 2005 to 2008 and had been expected to increase, fell by 18 percent in fiscal 2009.

MIGA responded to the crisis by adopting the financial sector initiative of 2009, which focused on supporting financial institutions in Europe and Central Asia. This resulted in an expansion of MIGA's already significant exposure to the financial sector. A question is whether the sharp contraction in activity at the World Bank and the vigorous resumption of growth at IFC that took place after the Asian crisis will occur again.

The World Bank and IFC have increased resource transfers to International Development Association (IDA) countries over the decade, and transfers were sustained during the crisis. At the Bank, IDA commitments increased by a third in fiscal 2009, compared with a 25 percent increase in fiscal 1998–99, relative to the three preceding years. IFC's rapidly growing Global Trade Finance Program is an increasing source of IFC commitments to IDA countries. There are also common areas of risk across the three institutions: relatively high levels of client and country concentration, high deficits in some borrowing countries, and increased levels of exposure to the financial sector.

Project performance as measured against stated objectives has declined somewhat among projects exiting the World Bank portfolio in the past three years; outcomes, however, remain higher than a decade ago. At IFC, project performance measured against market-based benchmarks has been stable, but a lagged impact of the crisis is emerging, as in past crises. At MIGA, just over half of recently evaluated projects had satisfactory or better development outcome performance—unchanged compared to earlier evaluations. The performance of World Bank infrastructure projects exiting the portfolio remains better than the other sectors; outcomes of the recent expansion of infrastructure projects are awaited. Development outcomes in Africa remain a challenge. And a review of the implementation of evaluation recommendations by management points out how the World Bank Group's and IEG's tracking systems must go beyond compliance to accountability and learning.

Among the selected issues related to development results, the report analyzes outcomes of World Bank projects that have been decentralized. Although data are limited and the study only investigates one element of decentralization—the association with project outcomes—it does not find an association of task manager decentralization with project performance. At IFC, a number of projects show gaps in quality at entry relative to the institution's credit review guidelines. And for MIGA to deliver on its development mandate and improve project development outcomes, strengthening the quality of underwriting is crucial.

The World Bank Group has strongly raised its participation in international resource flows during the financial crisis. Now ensuring and sustaining the development effectiveness of the response are required to best serve clients.

Vinod Thomas
Director-General, Evaluation

Executive Summary

Over the past year, the response to the global financial crisis has continued to dominate development and the work of international institutions, including the World Bank Group. Challenges of poverty and fragile states, environment, and climate change remain daunting. But the manner in which these are best addressed is shifting.

The World Bank Group, a crucial partner in the solutions to global development, must adapt to these changes for greater development effectiveness. The International Bank for Reconstruction and Development (IBRD), the International Development Association (IDA), the International Finance Corporation (IFC), and the Multilateral Investment Guarantee Agency (MIGA) individually face particular challenges in the increasingly multipolar world. But there are opportunities for coordination across the World Bank Group, whether between public and business activities, among sectors, or across macro and micro concerns.

Emphasizing these synergies, Part I of this joint report discusses recent activities and results of the World Bank Group; Part II focuses on select issues in development effectiveness at each institution. A separate volume of this report contains a detailed review and rating of management response and actions regarding recommendations from the Independent Evaluation Group (IEG) from recent years.

In the past year, the World Bank Group has directed a dramatic increase in financial flows to developing countries, though its institutions have exhibited contrasting responses to the global economic crisis. Following a pattern similar to previous crises, World Bank lending has seen a sharp, countercyclical expansion, and IFC investments as a whole have undergone a procyclical contraction. On a trend basis, the Bank and IFC have shown increased support to IDA countries and to Africa. There are common areas of risk, however: relatively high levels of client and country concentration, high deficits in some borrowing countries, and increased levels of exposure to the financial sector.

IEG ratings of achievement against stated objectives—one important aspect of project performance—show some decline at the World Bank in terms of projects exiting the portfolio in the past three years. However, they remain higher than those of a decade ago. At IFC, project performance measured against market-based benchmarks has been stable in recent years, but a delayed impact of the crisis is emerging, as in past crises. At MIGA, just over half (58 percent) of recently evaluated projects had a satisfactory or better development outcomes rating, based on IEG-MIGA's ex post evaluation methodology, which is endorsed by the Committee on Development Effectiveness of the Board. This is similar to the overall performance level when IEG-MIGA last reported on project performance in fiscal 2006. The performance of infrastructure projects in the MIGA portfolio remains notably better than other sectors when measured against stated goals; outcomes of infrastructure projects during the crisis period will be known later. And a review of the implementation of evaluation recommendations by management points out how the World Bank Group's and IEG's tracking systems must go beyond compliance to accountability and learning.

This review also looks at select issues of current relevance related to development results. Regarding the World Bank, this report considers the importance of decentralization but, based on limited data, does not find any association with project performance. At IFC, a number of projects show gaps in quality at entry—a specific rating—relative to the institution's credit review guidelines. And for MIGA to deliver on its development mandate and improve project development outcomes, strengthening the quality of underwriting is critical.

Current Trends—A Year Dominated by Crisis

Contrasting responses to crisis

Although recent activity at each World Bank Group institution has been dominated by the impact of the global financial crisis, response patterns have been markedly different. New commitments at the World Bank more than doubled in fiscal 2009, a strong countercyclical pattern in public sector support.

In contrast, new investments as a whole at IFC have shown a procyclical pattern: strategic prioritization of portfolio protection over the generation of new business, caused in part by resource constraints. New IFC business activity, which had more than doubled from 2005 to 2008 and had been expected to increase, fell by 18 percent in fiscal 2009. MIGA responded to the crisis by expanding its already significant exposure to the financial sector, issuing more guarantees to financial institutions in Europe and Central Asia. These responses have been similar to those during the Asian crisis of the late 1990s and other episodes. An important question is whether the sharp contraction in activity at the World Bank and the vigorous resumption of growth at IFC that took place after the Asian crisis will occur again in the future.

Regional focus and patterns of concentration

All three institutions have considerable consistency in top borrower/client composition. Over time, there has been some decline in the concentration of activities in the top five borrowing countries at IFC and the World Bank, but recent crisis activity may reverse that trend. MIGA's guarantees, in contrast, are increasingly concentrated in Europe and Central Asia. Similarities in patterns of concentration may suggest the need for closer examination of issues associated with risk at the level of the World Bank Group.

Increased financial sector role and new financing instruments

The share of the financial sector in new commitments has increased sharply with the crisis in all World Bank Group institutions. And IFC has witnessed an increase in financial sector activity over the decade, in part because of the rapid growth in trade guarantees under the Global Trade Finance Program (GTFP), which began in 2006. At MIGA, guarantees in the financial sector have also been increasing for several years.

At the Bank and IFC, the mix of instruments used to promote new lending has changed. At the Bank, shares of development policy loans (DPLs) and financial intermediary loans had remarkable growth. Recent DPL growth reverses a declining trend in the share of policy-based lending. Within DPLs, there was renewed use of the deferred drawdown option in fiscal 2009, demonstrating the value of an instrument that provides contingent credit in a time of crisis. Supplemental financing, intended for cost overruns or for scaling up investment lending, has also increased.

IFC too saw robust growth in the use of its new guarantee products and the GTFP, which mitigates payment risk associated with international and cross-border trade. It also helps foster new relationships among banks operating in challenging markets, thus making it an effective crisis-response tool.

Although the Bank's DPLs have performed generally as well as investment lending, the change in the mix of instruments and the increased exposure to large single-tranche loans and to deferred drawdown options suggest the need for close monitoring. IEG has previously pointed to risks associated with the Bank's financial intermediary loans. Monitoring lines of credit is difficult, as supervision of sub-borrowers is delegated to financial intermediaries. IEG has pointed to similar issues regarding IFC's investments with financial intermediaries and monitoring of environmental, health, and social aspects.

Support to IDA countries, Africa, and fragile states

Increased resource transfers to IDA countries have taken place over the decade at both the World Bank and IFC. Transfers have been sustained during the crisis. At the Bank, IDA commitments increased by a third in fiscal 2009, compared with a 25 percent increase in fiscal 1998–99, relative to the three preceding years. IFC's rapidly growing GFTP is an increasing source of IFC commitments to IDA countries. In addition, IBRD and IFC have made substantial allocations from net earnings to IDA since 2006.

World Bank lending to Africa more than tripled between fiscal 2000 and 2009. In fiscal 2007 and 2008, Africa was the World Bank's largest borrower, with almost 23 percent of the Bank's new commitments. With the onset of the crisis, Africa's share declined, but absolute lending increased by a third. In fragile states, however, lending increases in fiscal 2009 relative to the precrisis period were limited. New IFC commitments to Africa grew fivefold between fiscal 2004 and 2009 and by a third in fiscal 2009.

More social protection lending—concentrated in a few loans

At the World Bank, the biggest increase in activity in the crisis period has been in the social protection sector. However, although many operations have had social protection components, the increase has been concentrated in a few loans, with five loans accounting for more than 70 percent of new commitments under the Social Sector Board in fiscal 2009. In the first half of fiscal 2010, three social protection loans accounted for more than 75 percent of new commitments. Meanwhile, new commitments to education and to health, nutrition, and population, which had declined in fiscal 2008, rose again in fiscal 2009.

Long-term portfolio trends

The Bank's portfolio declined in size from fiscal 2000 until the present crisis. The total portfolio shrank from some $124 billion to $93 billion between 1999 and 2006. IFC's total committed portfolio grew from $13.2 billion in 1999 to $32.2 billion in 2008. The overall portfolio increased to $34.4 billion in 2009, a 7 percent increase compared to an average 13 percent annual growth over the period 2000–08. MIGA's issuance showed signs of growth during fiscal 2005–09, but the average of $1.5 billion in new guarantees a year issued between fiscal 2005 and fiscal 2009 fell short of the targets set in its strategy.

The present crisis response may arrest the trend of decline at the World Bank, though caution on a reversal after the crisis appears warranted. At IFC, if there is a reversion to long-term trends, the lull in activity may be temporary.

Results and Performance at the World Bank Group

Overall outcomes

Overall development results have been affected by the global financial crisis. Together with other international financial institutions, the World Bank Group has sharply boosted financing for developing countries to limit economic contraction and contagion—a goal that appears to have been achieved. Despite deterioration in economic and social results, developing countries have largely maintained access to markets, and many are on a path to recovery—though that upturn remains sluggish and very uneven. Country and thematic reviews bring out a highly variable picture of outcomes.

A first but partial measure of World Bank Group performance is project outcomes. At the World Bank, project performance has declined somewhat over the past year, with 76 percent of closed projects rated moderately satisfactory or higher on achievement of objectives, compared with 78 percent for fiscal 2008 and more than 80 percent in 2005 and 2006. In 2007, 75 percent of ratings were moderately satisfactory or higher. Regression analysis of World Bank evaluative data suggests that recent performance declines are not caused by compositional shifts of the portfolio (which have been broadly positive), but rather by a decline within individual sectors. Current performance has fallen relative to long-term trends in areas such as health, nutrition, and population and even in transport. Project rating declines relative to long-term trends are reflected in both DPLs and investment lending.

During 2007–09, 74 percent of IFC's investment projects that reached maturity achieved satisfactory or higher development outcome ratings when compared with market benchmarks, on a three-year rolling average basis. These results are based on a sample of 214 project evaluations, representing 51 percent of the cohort for this period. This is in line with levels in recent years. Year-on-year development outcome ratings remain stable relative to the preceding year (75 percent in 2008 compared with 74 percent in 2009). Environmental and social effects improved during the evaluation period.

On project performance, at MIGA, 58 percent of recently evaluated projects (underwritten between 2000 and 2006) had satisfactory or better development outcome ratings. Similar development outcome performance ratings were found in an earlier cluster of projects (underwritten between 1997 and 1999). These project-level results are based on IEG-MIGA's database of 33 ex post evaluations of guarantee projects and cannot be extrapolated to the portfolio, as the project sample is too small for statistical inferences about

MIGA's overall portfolio performance. Accordingly, the emphasis is on lessons from common patterns, "success factors" and "weak spots," with less emphasis on project ratings. MIGA projects with better development outcome ratings tend to have sponsors with previous experience in the host country or other developing countries; they also often involve MIGA repeat clients. Significantly, in terms of project performance, poor development outcome ratings and poor quality of underwriting ratings went hand in hand. Projects with lower development outcome ratings had several factors in common, including weak business performance, flawed project design, or inadequate quality of underwriting. Although IEG generally found MIGA's political risk assessment to be good, the quality of underwriting overall had persistent weaknesses, notably in its analysis of project financial viability and assessment of commercial risk.

A second and broader picture of performance and results emerges from country and thematic reviews, which show a variable picture of outcomes across sectors and themes and across countries and regions. Recent IEG reports highlight trends in these aspects, as noted for the financial sector, water, poverty, and gender. Similarly, country evaluations have presented a variable picture of development at the aggregate country level. Recent country evaluations, for example, show solid country program outcomes in the Arab Republic of Egypt and Bangladesh but more problematic outcomes in Ethiopia and Nepal.

Previous work has noted that the share of moderately satisfactory or better outcomes of country programs is lower (about two-thirds) than in the recent past (nearly four-fifths). Clearly, achieving country and sector outcomes requires more than satisfactory project outcomes. Among the issues are the relevance of country strategy; policy leadership and policy dialogue; complementarities among sectors and with analytic and advisory activities (AAA), policy, lending and global initiatives; and exogenous factors such as global shocks.

Financial sector

After a period of declining attention, the financial sector is now the subject of concern and analysis. World Bank project performance in the financial sector has remained steady, but performance of financial projects appears to have declined at IFC. Development outcomes of IFC financial market projects declined from 76 percent to 68 percent on a three-year moving average basis between 2008 and 2009. IFC's European and Central Asian clients that relied heavily on access to capital markets may have suffered declining borrowing capacity in recent years, which could adversely affect their performance ratings. IFC's development outcome ratings for Europe and Central Asia projects have declined from 81 to 70 percent between 2008 and 2009. World Bank projects are evaluated after completion, and project ratings would not yet be affected by recent crisis considerations. At IFC, the rapidly growing guarantee instrument segment is not yet tracked by the monitoring and evaluation Development Outcome Tracking System, and development indicators have not been established.

Photo by Curt Carnemark, courtesy of World Bank Photo Library

Infrastructure and the environment

Recent reviews of the transport and water sectors show considerable progress in infrastructure development. But the area covering environment and natural resources presents a mixed picture and signals challenges in the coming years.

At the World Bank, the overall performance of infrastructure-related sectors remains high, based on projects exiting the portfolio, and the energy and mining sector improved its performance over the past 10 years. A recent IEG review of water-related projects at the World Bank shows that they had higher-than-average project outcome ratings and that performance has improved, especially in Africa. But it will be important for the World Bank to help strengthen groundwater conservation, environmental restoration, coastal zone management, and sanitation, as well as demand management.

Infrastructure has consistently been among IFC's best performing sectors in terms of outcome ratings. IFC's investment in the infrastructure sector declined by almost 40 percent in fiscal 2009. Hence, the decline in the volume of infrastructure activities gives reason for concern.

Environmental and social effects of IFC's projects, reflected in project ratings, have improved, reversing a three-year trend. The improvement largely reflects a reversal in the environmental and social performance of financial sector projects, although this still remains slightly lower than real sector projects. With IFC's movement away from traditional project financing toward financial markets, ensuring compliance of sub-borrowers will become an increasing concern.

IDA countries and Africa

The difficulty in getting results in fragile states was the subject of an IEG review three years ago, and this subject will continue to get attention. World Bank project performance in Africa has consistently been the poorest of all regions. At IFC, although development outcomes in Africa have improved over the decade, they remain lower than in other regions. Recent country program evaluations in Africa, for example, showed generally positive outcomes in Mozambique and Uganda, but less satisfactory outcomes in Ethiopia and Nigeria. This suggests increasing tradeoffs between strategic priorities and outcomes, a situation that needs to be addressed. MIGA projects in IDA-eligible countries performed poorly on development outcomes—only 42 percent were rated satisfactory or better, compared with 58 percent for the portfolio as a whole.

Relative outcomes of projects in fragile states at the World Bank have fallen once more from being close to overall Bank ratings in 2006 to considerably below them in fiscal 2009.

Poverty and gender

IEG has focused attention in the past year on assessing the results of Bank support for poverty and gender. Findings of an evaluation of the Bank's Poverty Reduction Support Credits describe gains in terms of process but difficulties in identification of outcomes. Poverty Reduction Support Credits have made solid contributions toward donor harmonization and country alignments, but more needs to be done to ensure poverty focus and to measure actual results.

Looking beyond income poverty, IEG's recent evaluation of gender finds that gender integration is essential for support to gender equality. It shows that the Bank made notable progress in gender integration compared with fiscal 1990–99, but it needs to renew this commitment, given some slowdown in mainstreaming in recent years.

Advisory services

AAA accounts for a third of the World Bank's outlays in country services, exceeding outlays on lending or supervision. Although AAA as a whole has increased over time, largely in the area of nonlending technical assistance, core economic and sector work has not grown.

A recent IEG evaluation shows that both types of products are of value, and one of that report's recommendations is to reinvigorate the mandate for country teams to maintain a strong knowledge base for countries they support. At IFC, yearly approvals for advisory services have shown some decline (except for the Corporate Advice business line and advisory services to Eastern Europe), although expenditures so far have been sustained because of previous years' approvals. Care must be taken to prevent immediate lending needs from crowding out knowledge work in the face of tight budgets, as this could slowly undermine the World Bank Group's knowledge base—one of its biggest comparative advantages.

At present, the Bank has no comprehensive framework for AAA evaluation, and monitoring of AAA results has been rudimentary. IEG is piloting AAA evaluation to motivate monitoring and self-evaluation by the Bank. Pilot evaluations have been undertaken on growth diagnostics in Africa and on the agriculture sector.

IEG's systematic evaluation of IFC advisory services using project completion reports began in 2008; data are now available for two years. Development effectiveness ratings of advisory services projects evaluated in fiscal 2009 declined in all regions except Sub-Saharan Africa and Latin America and the Caribbean. The one-year decline may be partially explained by the fact that the system is new and ratings, as well as reporting quality, are stabilizing. Only the Access to Finance business line achieved improved development effectiveness ratings.

Follow-Up to Evaluation

Board members have expressed a keen interest in strengthening the follow-up process to IEG recommendations. IEG and management agree that the recommendations are an underutilized instrument, and both are putting reforms in place to make them more useful.

At the World Bank, the majority of IEG recommendations come from thematic evaluations, and corresponding sector boards provide a home for follow-up. However, prioritizing the most important actions to strengthen organizational performance is difficult. Follow-up with IFC is based on an agreement with IEG at the outset on the steps that management will take. At MIGA, the majority of IEG recommendations come from IEG-MIGA's annual reports and from World Bank Group evaluations with MIGA-relevant recommendations. IEG-MIGA has been tracking implementation of the recommendations to MIGA since 2003.

Adoption, implementation, and analysis

At the World Bank, two-thirds of IEG's recommendations from evaluations since 2003 have been substantially adopted after four years. However, the level of adoption of outstanding recommendations in the Management Action Record (the tool that lists recommendations to the Bank and their implementation) in 2010 is lower than in 2009, and the share of recommendations rated high and substantially adopted dropped from 60 percent in 2007 to 36 percent in 2010.

At IFC, the level of adoption of IEG recommendations has increased significantly since 2004 and is now close to 90 percent. IEG recommendations have been consistent with the direction of IFC's evolution and have pointed to specific changes that management later adopted.

Although MIGA has taken up many IEG recommendations with good results—about a third of the outstanding recommendations tracked in the 2009 Management Action Tracking Record were retired in 2010—implementation of recommendations in some key areas still needs to be completed. More systematic and vigorous follow-up is needed on IEG recommendations relating to: business development, quality of underwriting, quality assurance, and strengthening MIGA's ability to cost individual guarantees and business lines.

Comparisons with other multilateral development banks and international development organizations suggest that key elements to an effective follow-up system include the adoption of a set of characteristics and/or a checklist for good recommendations, management ownership of recommendations, quality control during the tracking process, and disclosure and utilization of implementation data. In comparison, IEG reports in detail on the adoption of its recommendations, but not on their utilization or effects on Bank effectiveness. Present practices emphasize compliance with recommendations more than management ownership and learning.

Photo by Trevor Samson, courtesy of the World Bank Photo Library.

Reform of the present system to strengthen it must preserve the independence and accountability of evaluation. Reforms must help harmonize the system across the World Bank, IFC, and MIGA as well as accommodate their inherent differences. The emphasis needs to be on the substantive content of the follow-up. Successful reforms would enhance IEG's effectiveness and credibility and would contribute to the accountability and transparency of the World Bank Group.

Selected Issues in Development Effectiveness

World Bank: Decentralization

Reforms to increase the development effectiveness of the World Bank run from investment lending changes to revamping matrix management. Among these reforms, decentralization of staff has been ongoing for a decade. Enhanced field presence is intended to increase responsiveness to client demand, improve country ownership and partnership, and improve the cost-effectiveness of Bank support. Decentralization is also intended to integrate knowledge, though care must be taken not to lose global expertise. IEG's preliminary and partial review of Bank operations suggests important questions for review prior to an overhaul of the current system. The promised benefits are not automatic, but rather depend on specific factors and circumstances.

This review explores one aspect of decentralization: the association between staff location and project and country outcomes. IEG data show that the location of the task team leader is not significantly associated with project ratings or quality at entry of closed projects. Data from the Bank's Quality Assurance Group show that there is no difference in quality of design, quality of supervision, or quality of partnerships if a task team leader is based in the field as opposed to at headquarters.

An examination of the outcomes of decentralization of country directors into country offices, based on IEG's Country Assistance Strategy Completion Report Reviews, shows that decentralization is associated with improved outcomes in Bank country programs only when the director is located in the country, not in a nearby hub. Bank documents note that the farther a country is from Washington, DC, the stronger the rationale for devolution of work and staff.

IEG analysis shows that differences are only statistically significant in two regions. In South Asia, where decentralization is advanced, outcomes are 21 percentage points better for operations with a team leader based in the field at closing; in Latin America and the Caribbean, where fewer staff are based in the field, outcomes are 21 percentage points better for operations with a team leader based in headquarters at closing. There are no statistically significant differences in other regions. There are undoubtedly many factors besides distance that influence regional patterns of project outcomes, and further work would be required to unbundle them.

Photo by Tran Thi Hoa, courtesy of the World Bank Photo Library.

Qualitative evidence also provides a mixed picture. For recently closed projects for which both IEG evaluations and Quality Assurance Group supervision assessments are available, staff location was specifically mentioned as a material factor directly affecting project outcomes in approximately half.

These findings come with many caveats and represent only one aspect of a range of potential outcomes of decentralization, such as improved policy dialog or swift response. Data that would enable more precise measurement are not readily available. Thus, the lack of evidence for a positive impact of decentralization does not prove that there is none. There are clear avenues for deeper analysis that could reveal a more nuanced understanding of when decentralization helps improve outcomes and when it does not.

IFC: Factors affecting development results

Evaluation results demonstrate that development outcome is affected by country investment climate, and with the global financial crisis, most regions show a decline in investment climate as of the end of 2009, especially Central and Eastern Europe. Partner quality, market conditions, and project risks are further important determinants of development outcomes. Newer projects have had lower sponsor risk but higher risk relating to project type. This reflects a growing trend toward increasing exposure to greenfield or early-stage businesses. Market risk, although recently showing a downward trend, remains high.

IFC exercises a significant degree of control over development outcome ratings through its work quality. Overall work quality has continued its recent upward trend, but with some decline in supervision quality. Changes are taking place simultaneously in several important dimensions that can potentially affect supervision quality. Among these factors are financial crisis and organizational changes that have resulted in the diffusion of portfolio function among cluster managers and the absence of concentrated responsibilities for the portfolio at the vice presidency level.

The need to pay strong attention to work quality and portfolio risk management is particularly acute when the global economy is fragile, and IFC is undergoing profound institutional changes. IEG's review of IFC's Quality at Entry reveals that projects not involving financial intermediaries show some weakness in screening, appraisal, and structuring, whereas most financial intermediary projects have close to full compliance with IFC's Credit Review Guidelines. IEG found that information on sponsor commitment, mandated by the guidelines, is largely available. Comparisons of IFC client companies with others in the industry are often not adequately carried out, especially in real sector projects.

The contrasting routine use of comparators in bank appraisals should be extended to funds and other collective investment vehicles. Information on company accounting systems—essential for benchmarking—is often lacking, and sensitivity analysis, although completed, is rudimentary. Country analysis often has a broadly macro perspective, although IFC's good practice notes suggest that the organization go into political, legal, business, and regulatory risks.

A review of monitorable development impact indicators used during project preparation suggests weak indicators. Some are not incremental and mingle the performance of the project with that of the preproject company. Targets have been inadequate and baseline data often absent.

Regarding IFC advisory services, important drivers of development effectiveness have been client contributions to cost recovery and links with investment operations. Central to the 2007 pricing policy is the principle that IFC does not seek client contributions to maximize revenue, cost recovery, or profits, but rather uses pricing to help strengthen client commitment to implementation and to ensure that any subsidy is justified by the public benefits. In general, advisory services projects that have some level of client contribution tend to achieve higher development effectiveness ratings than those without. On average, management has estimated that clients will contribute an increasing share of total project costs, from 25 percent for fiscal 2008 approvals to 35 percent for fiscal 2009 approvals.

IEG also found that advisory services projects have enhanced development effectiveness when they are linked to investment projects. In fiscal 2009, a quarter of new approvals for advisory services were already linked to investment projects, and a third had expectations of being linked within three years of project approval.

MIGA: Development results and quality of underwriting

There is emerging evidence of linkages between MIGA's quality of underwriting—the quality of MIGA's workmanship at the beginning of the underwriting process, when projects are selected, assessed, and underwritten—and project development outcomes. The quality of underwriting is not a rating of project performance, but of MIGA's own performance in carrying out these upstream tasks.

With respect to project development results, just over half (58 percent) of recently evaluated MIGA projects had development outcome ratings of satisfactory or better. In regard to MIGA's quality of underwriting, this has been good in one aspect—assessing country and political risk.

However, overall, MIGA's quality of underwriting is a significant concern, with more than half (58 percent) of recently evaluated projects rated less than satisfactory. A recurring shortcoming was inadequate analysis of project financial viability, including failure to verify investor representations of project profitability. Other serious shortcomings were failure to monitor Category B projects (projects with potential limited adverse social or environmental impacts) and documentation and record keeping.

Poor quality of underwriting and poor development outcome often went hand in hand. The majority of projects with less-than-satisfactory quality of underwriting ratings were also rated less than satisfactory on development outcome (60 percent). Conversely, the overwhelming majority of projects with good quality of underwriting also had good development outcome ratings (80 percent). Of the projects that performed poorly—that is, with less than satisfactory development outcome ratings—88 percent also had a less-than-satisfactory quality of underwriting rating. IEG found that most of the project weaknesses identified in its ex post evaluations were already evident in the underwriting documents, and that with a better quality of underwriting these shortcomings would have been identified and brought to the attention of MIGA's decision process.

The association between poor quality of underwriting and low development outcomes is striking, even if it is not possible to establish causality with available data. MIGA's quality of underwriting has been a persistent weakness for many years—and one that is fully under MIGA's control. Although IEG issued recommendations to address these shortcomings in 2004, 2007, and 2009, follow-up is needed from MIGA management. To deliver on MIGA's development mandate and to improve project development outcomes, strengthening the quality of underwriting is critical.

Management Response

I. Introduction

Management welcomes the opportunity to comment on the Independent Evaluation Group's (IEG) first World Bank Group Results and Performance Report (RAP). We appreciate the contribution of this report and the underlying work of IEG to strengthen the World Bank Group's accountability for results and enhance the learning from evaluations undertaken over the past years.

Organization of the comments

This note first provides comments on IEG's findings on the World Bank Group's overall performance in Part I. It then responds to what IEG puts forward with regard to Bank management follow-up of IEG recommendations. Lastly, in Part II, it discusses the three divergent topics covered by IEG in the second section of the RAP: Bank decentralization, factors affecting International Finance Corporation (IFC) performance, and Multilateral Investment Guarantee Agency (MIGA) development outcomes and underwriting.

II. Results and Performance

Management welcomes the World Bank Group approach in the report. We believe, however, that the report should better delineate which findings apply—and to what extent—for which of the institutions. Management comments on the report's review of the results and performance of the World Bank Group are presented below. However, management has a general comment about the period covered by the report and the data used for analysis.

The period covered by the report. For the Bank, the report is mainly based on projects that exited the portfolio in fiscal 2009 or earlier; even for fiscal 2009 exits, this means on average these projects in question entered the portfolio in fiscal 2003 or 2004. Some of the supplemental performance information is based on IEG sectoral or thematic evaluations from as early as 2001, without citing progress in the interim. The information on lines of credit comes from a 2006 evaluation (covering operations through 2003), and the report would have benefitted from an analysis of the major actions taken by management in response to the findings of the evaluation and their impact on performance. For the IFC, the report is based largely on evaluations of five- to seven-year old projects (fiscal 2002–04). For MIGA, the project sample comprises 33 ex post evaluations of MIGA guarantee projects, all of which were underwritten between fiscal 1996 and 2006, and the majority of which (70 percent) date back to fiscal 2000 or before. It is therefore important to bear in mind that whatever findings may have been derived from the MIGA project evaluations, they refer to a past version of the Agency, which has undergone many substantial changes in virtually every aspect of the business, including organizational structure, project selection criteria, development impact assessment methodology, underwriting procedures, and staffing.

A. World Bank results and performance

Because of its commitment to results, management monitors IEG project outcome findings virtually on a daily basis. Recent operational results as reported by IEG as projects exit the portfolio are shown below in Table MR.1. Management has set a target of 80 percent or higher satisfactory ratings for projects it supports in IBRD countries and 75 percent or better in International Development Association (IDA) countries. Results to date on projects evaluated since fiscal 2007 are on average close to those targets (a little under for International Bank for Reconstruction and Development [IBRD] and almost exactly on target for IDA). (The data weighted by lending volume, not reported below, show a higher share of satisfactory outcomes.)

Further improvement in development outcomes is the aim of Bank investment lending reform. Of course, there is no reason for complacency, and management has under way a set of actions aimed at increasing its focus on results. The whole thrust of investment lending reform, now in full swing, is around operational results—to better contribute to the achievement of the client's project development outcome goals. In particular, the new investment lending risk framework (risk specifically to the achievement of development outcomes) and the greater emphasis on implementation support went into full operation starting on July 1, 2010.

Financial intermediary loans. The report's observations on financial intermediary loans need to be nuanced, as IBRD saw growth in these loans but IDA did not. Overall IBRD lending increased dramatically, meaning that financial intermediary loans remained a relatively small share.

Analytic and Advisory Activities (AAA). In a recent evaluation, IEG found AAA to be of generally high quality and appreciated by clients (IEG 2008c). The RAP discusses the issue of AAA evaluation by management. There is a system in place. Each AAA product is subject to self-evaluation at completion. As it should be, that self-evaluation is simple and straightforward, and, in recent years, centralized review has enhanced the implementation of these evaluations. However, evaluating individual pieces of AAA at completion, except for quality, is of limited benefit. (It is much different from evaluating projects at completion, after five or more years of implementation on average.) AAA impact normally occurs with a lag and as a component of an overall integrated program of support. Therefore, as part of Country Assistance Strategy (CAS) completion reporting, country teams self-evaluate AAA programs. The CAS Completion Reports are then independently evaluated by IEG. That said, more can be done, and as part of the Knowledge Reform Agenda, management is working on a broader approach to AAA monitoring and evaluation, looking across Regional and country programs.

Country programs. Management notes that there remain important issues in independent ratings of country programs. As reported by management over several years, in contrast to projects, IEG and management lack a common understanding on a standard methodology for country program evaluations. A good example is Ethiopia, where management and the client saw strong objective evidence of a satisfactory outcome of Bank support during the period evaluated by IEG. (The RAP also highlights the 2008 Nigeria Country Assistance Evaluation; IEG rated that program as satisfactory for the second half of the period covered by the evaluation.) Also, as IEG notes but does not highlight, the outcomes of country programs are at a higher level and, therefore, the impact of other factors, such as exogenous events, are more likely to affect the achievement of program objectives.

B. IFC results and performance

IFC thanks the IEG team for its work in the assessment of development results and rating of the implementation of IEG recommendations over the last few years. IFC continues to strengthen performance on its strategic priorities, deliver greater development impact, and scale up its crisis response through special initiatives. As we continue to maximize our impact in IDA and Africa, we have launched the IFC Asset Management Company LLC, and we are actively increasing mobilization and partnerships.

The report confirms IFC's strong development results and the continuous upward trend in overall work quality. Despite the crisis, during 2007–09, 74 percent of IFC's projects achieved high development outcomes, the portfolio showed increases in most areas of development reach, and the advisory program continued to grow. Importantly, the environmental and social effects of IFC's projects have significantly improved and IFC has a solid record in implementing IEG's recommendations (now close to 90 percent).

We strongly welcome the IEG emphasis on portfolio work, and we have taken several steps to further strengthen the supervision process. The monitoring and evaluation systems at IFC continue to be strong, and the Development Outcome

TABLE MR.1 IEG Ratings of IBRD- and IDA-Supported Operations at Exit

	Exit Fiscal Year								
	2007			2008			2009		
	No. of Projects Closed	Percent Reviewed	Percent Satisfactory	No. of Projects Closed	Percent Reviewed	Percent Satisfactory	No. of Projects Closed	Percent Reviewed	Percent Satisfactory
IBRD	110	90	79	101	75	76	119	50	80
IDA	142	89	71	125	84	78	122	48	75

Source: World Bank internal database.
Note: IBRD = International Bank for Reconstruction and Development; IDA = International Development Association.

Tracking System (DOTS2) is being implemented throughout the project cycle. While the IFC 2013 initiative is under implementation, IFC is scaling up efforts to define a set of high-level ex ante development goals to guide strategy development, with measurable progress indicators.

Presented below are management comments on several important issues, findings, and conclusions included in the report.

IFC being procyclical? We welcome the elaboration in the report on the World Bank Group role and the challenges it faces in helping countries and the private sector cope with the aftermath of the global economic crisis. *Management disagrees, however, with the report's statement* that "IFC's procyclical pattern is caused by strategic prioritization of resource allocation toward existing clients, instead of the generation of new business."

Comments

- Regarding past crises, IEG's *Independent Evaluation of IFC's Development Results 2008* (IEG 2008b, p. 67) shows that, unlike other investors, IFC's typical response was to increase its investments in the years following a crisis. In the 17 crises identified by IEG between 1994 and 2001, IFC increased its exposure in 12 cases (over 70 percent) and maintained it in 4 (only in Argentina did IFC contract), whereas private sector investments often displayed the opposite pattern. It is also important to point out that IFC had in the past achieved poor development results when investing during a crisis year, thus investing quite selectively is appropriate in this situation.
- Regarding the current crisis, IFC executed its countercyclical role in a number of ways, many of which are acknowledged in the IEG report and also highlighted in the recent IFC Roadmap. At the onset of the crisis IFC's capital position provided the opportunity for steady to modest growth in commitments. Within this context IFC focused on a number of concurrent areas. It worked with existing clients to support their business and maintain viability in difficult times. For new business, while many pipeline projects were postponed or cancelled as the market situation changed dramatically, IFC kept its focus on IDA countries and Africa, and expanded trade finance to meet the growth in liquidity needs in the marketplace. In addition, IFC launched a broad range of crisis initiatives to mobilize capital from many organizations and address critical global needs in liquidity, banking and finance, infrastructure, and agribusiness.
- The results of this effort are apparent in many dimensions, including a continued strong portfolio, strong development outcome (DOTS) results, expanded operations in IDA, Africa and trade finance, and expanded advisory operations. Fiscal 2010 results have exceeded 2009 levels for both IFC own account and mobilization, and growth is expected to continue in fiscal 2011—all this in an environment where global commercial finance, especially banking finance, remains quite constrained. IFC crisis initiatives have helped mobilize over $10 billion from partners, and participation in regional initiatives, such as the Joint Action Program for Europe, have been instrumental in marshalling and coordinating action to address the crisis from a wide range of players, well beyond what is accounted for in IFC's own financial accounts.
- With respect to other international financial institutions, we have worked in concert with many of these institutions and coordinated activities are growing. Individual institution results reflect their different regional roles in the overall financial architecture. For example, in 2009 the European Bank for Reconstruction and Development greatly increased funding to the Baltics and the more advanced countries in Central Europe like Hungary, while IFC, within the Joint Action Plan for Europe, continued to focus its scarce resources on the more difficult countries to the east and on equity products, areas which have considerable potential for development impact even though volumes could be lower.

Performance in Africa and fragile states. We strongly welcome the report's attention on World Bank Group's role and activity in Africa. While noting the improvement in development outcomes in Africa, the report points out that "they remain lower than in other regions."

Comments

- IFC's involvement in Africa over the decade has grown significantly, with commitments reaching over $1.8 billion in fiscal 2009 compared to only $140 million in fiscal 2003 and $699 million in 2006. As this growth occurred, the improvement in development outcome performance in Africa outpaced that for IFC overall. Importantly, based on a rolling three-year average, environmental and social success rates results for 2009 in Africa are now at par with IFC overall.
- DOTS data also show a long-term improvement in development impact, which we expect will also show continued improvement in Expanded Project Supervision Report (XPSR) ratings in the future as well. When weighted

by project size, results in Africa have been better than the IFC average.

- IFC has increased its investment and advisory operations in fragile states. IFC's analysis suggests that while overall investment portfolios in these countries perform below IFC averages, including on XPSR results, the performance for recent investments made in these countries is comparable to the overall IFC average.

IFC in infrastructure. Infrastructure remains among the key strategic priorities of IFC's business. The report states that "infrastructure has been consistently among IFC's best performing sectors in terms of outcome ratings. Hence, the decline in the volume of infrastructure activities gives reason for concern."

Comments

- Commitments in the infrastructure cluster remain strong, $3.3 billion in fiscal 2010, which is significantly higher than the IFC's commitments in this cluster in 2007 ($2.4 billion). IFC has successfully completed a larger number of smaller-volume projects. Furthermore, IFC commitments in the infrastructure cluster in IDA countries have increased to $1.4 billion in fiscal 2010 from $1.2 billion in 2009.

Global Trade Finance Program (GTFP). The report points out that GTFP investments are "not tracked" by DOTS and there is "no systematic method of defining and assessing development outcome or impact." *Management disagrees* with this statement.

Comments

- While GTFP transactions are not tracked in DOTS, we have already commented previously that, in our view, DOTS is not the appropriate system to track the much shorter-term trade finance activities. However, there is systematic tracking of specific trade finance indicators both at the project and program level, which is supplemented by evaluations at the program level. It is important to point out that IEG has also found in the past that some activities are better evaluated at the program, rather than at the project level (for example, Africa Enterprise Fund investments). However, we would welcome IEG's suggestions on what else could and should be tracked—at the project and at the program level.

Overall advisory services program directions. The report draws certain inferences about growth and direction of Advisory Services business based on recent project approval data. For example, "At IFC, yearly new approvals for [Advisory Services] have shown some decline (except for the corporate advice business line and advisory services to Eastern Europe). . . ." The report includes also a margin highlight, stating: "[Advisory Services] is a growing business line for IFC, especially in Europe and Central Asia."

Clarifications/Corrections

- Unlike similar data for investment projects, project approval data are not an easy source from which to infer program trends or directions. This is because Advisory Services projects are lumpy and multiyear, and the level of new approvals is usually closely tied to the multiyear funding cycle of regional facilities. This means a region going through a renewal will show a significant uptick in approvals in that year, while a region that is midcycle (including those with much larger programs) may show very few new project approvals.

C. MIGA results and performance

MIGA's management thanks IEG for the report, and would especially like to underscore the conclusions IEG has drawn concerning the effect of recent external trends, including most significantly the global financial crisis, which has had a very substantial impact on MIGA's core business of providing political risk insurance.

MIGA management would like to comment on several points raised that specifically address MIGA's capacity and performance, expressly in the areas of Quality of Underwriting and Development Outcome (see below in Part II on special topics covered by IEG). Before doing so, however, management needs to draw close attention to two factors relating to the sample of evaluated projects from which the report's conclusions on MIGA are drawn.

First, as noted above, the project sample comprises 33 ex post evaluations of MIGA guarantee projects, all of which were underwritten between fiscal 1996 and fiscal 2006, and the majority of which (70 percent) date back to fiscal 2000 or before. Also as noted above, it is therefore important to bear in mind that whatever findings may have been derived from the project evaluations, they refer to a past version of MIGA, and the Agency has gone through unprecedented changes in the past two years.

Second, it is also important to keep in mind that the sample size of evaluations is too small to either be statistically robust (that is to say, a change in just one or two underlying project subratings has a significant effect on the overall "score") or to be able to draw statistical inference with respect to MIGA's overall portfolio. Thus, assertions that are made in this report do *not* convey to MIGA's overall portfolio of business, either today or previously.

Both these factors are acknowledged in the report; however, management believes it is important to highlight these constraints so that the report's findings are understood in proper context.

D. The Bank's Management Action Record

As noted above, Bank management values independent evaluation and takes it seriously. As a result, it takes seriously the recommendations that come out of IEG evaluations. All draft management responses to major IEG evaluations are discussed by Executive Directors (normally at the Board's Committee on Development Effectiveness—CODE). These responses include an initial Management Action Record (MAR) that sets out what management commits to do as a result of the IEG recommendations. Given the importance of these commitments, which often have resource implications, they are carefully vetted and cleared by senior management. Management then reviews these commitments in the light of the CODE discussion and revises them as needed. Management monitors and reports annually to IEG and Executive Directors on progress against its commitments in the annual overall MAR. While this system is valuable and necessary as an accountability tool, management agrees with IEG that it is time for a reevaluation.

MAR methodology issues. The RAP presents data on the rate of adoption of IEG recommendations (as recorded in the overall MAR). However, Bank management notes the importance of the difference between how IFC and IEG produce and monitor the Management Action Tracking Record (MATR), compared to how the Bank and IEG do the MAR. In the MATR, IFC management reports against its original commitments and agreed indicators in response to IEG recommendations; then IEG validates IFC actions against those commitments, using the indicators. That is not the case in the Bank. In providing its self-ratings, Bank management reports against what it originally committed to do. By contrast with the MATR, for the Bank, IEG reports against its original recommendations in the MAR. The differences between these approaches are significant and provide a guide for reform of the MAR process.

Reforming the MAR. Management agrees with IEG on the need to reform the MAR process. As IEG notes, there is currently no way to know whether a high rating of adoption is important or not, as there is no prioritization of recommendations nor any assessment of the development impact of undertaking the actions in question. Another key issue is the sheer number of recommendations and subrecommendations. The current MAR contains 55 separate recommendations, often with a significant number of subrecommendations under each recommendation. (In addition to IEG, management commits to take action in response to the findings of other entities, including the Inspection Panel, the Internal Audit Department, and the Integrity Vice Presidency.) Management stands ready to work with IEG on a system that reduces and prioritizes IEG recommendations and monitors progress directly against management commitments.

Other uses of IEG findings. The MAR should not be taken as the only measure of IEG effectiveness. Bank management and staff take IEG recommendations very seriously in their daily work. For example, past evaluations of projects and sectoral reviews are used as input into sector strategies and project concept reviews and decision meeting discussions. They are also used in portfolio review discussions with governments (for example, in Country Portfolio Performance Reviews). CASs also reflect IEG findings relevant to the country programs and Bank activities.

III. Special Topics

The RAP examines one special topic for each of the three institutions: decentralization at the World Bank, key factors affecting performance at the IFC, and development outcome and quality of underwriting at MIGA.

A. World Bank decentralization

Analyzing the costs and benefits of decentralization is complex. If IEG had developed a more comprehensive evaluation framework for assessing decentralization, using, for example, the tools of impact analysis, by constructing a "with" and "without" structure, the lessons that emerged would have been more useful. Moreover, management also has some concerns about the methodology of the analysis that was undertaken. Therefore, the IEG analysis is less useful than it could have been for decision making.

Factors in determining the benefits of decentralization. Looking at the outcome of operations supported by the Bank is a very narrow measure of the benefits. A few additional benefits that may arise from decentralization but that are not analyzed in this report include: a higher quality of country dialogue; increased understanding of what country ownership means, based on the daily interaction with a wide variety of stakeholders in the country; the impact of programmatic AAA and just-in-time policy notes that are facilitated by decentralization; a stronger country program and project pipeline more aligned with country poverty reduction priorities; improved partnerships with the donor community; faster response, especially in crises and after natural disasters; and fewer missed opportunities for timely and effective support.

Explanatory variable. Another issue with the IEG analysis is that the location of the task team leader (TTL) is a questionable explanatory variable for the benefits of decentralization, as the Bank works in teams to support country preparation of operations. Irrespective of the location of the TTL, teams include staff with global knowledge, from the country office, from Washington, or other country offices, and staff, often from the country office, who have local knowledge. Having key team members in the country office may make the difference even if the TTL is in Washington. Therefore, the location of the TTL omits a number of relevant contributors to the success of our operations. A related second point is that the data do not seem to take into account team composition and experience. Third, because the Bank carries out quality assurance in the same manner for projects with TTLs in Washington as for projects with TTLs in country offices, it is not surprising that the results are relatively consistent across the location of TTL. Fourth, costs and cost-effectiveness are not addressed. These same issues apply to the analysis by location of country director.

B. IFC—Key factors affecting performance

Quality at entry. Quality at entry is one of the most essential elements in designing and developing every investment and advisory operation at IFC. In this context, we strongly welcome the elaboration and the importance given to this issue in the report. Management wishes to reiterate that it is committed to continue strengthening the adoption of a comprehensive screening process and intensive credit review procedures.

Management appreciates the review undertaken by IEG and the findings that there were no serious contraventions against the high standards of the credit review guidelines. However, the report states, "At IFC a number of projects show gaps in quality at entry relative to the institution's credit review guidelines." *Management disagrees* and has a significantly different view from IEG on this.

Comments

- The Credit Notes (guidelines) themselves make clear they are simply guidelines on how to think about and carry out a due diligence process. They are not compliance checklists, and as such, it is incorrect to treat them as a checklist where some things are done and everything else is "missing" or "not in compliance."
- A comprehensive analysis, including country issues, risks assessed, evaluations, sensitivity, and projections is done for every project based on the nature and specifics of the project while following the IFC's credit review guidelines. Such analysis, therefore, can and should vary substantially from project to project.
- After thoroughly reviewing with the investment teams the sample (and in particular 24 projects where IEG has found shortages in quality at entry), management found that:
    - All the projects had a clear assessment of risks and followed the credit review guidelines in completing the due diligence.
    - In two cases the team completed the scenario analysis but had not filed and documented the discussion in iDesk. In one of these cases the team filed only the scenario with 15 percent drop in yield, leaving out the scenario completed for the 25 percent drop in yield. In another project, the sensitivity analysis was thoroughly completed and the attached PDS-IR was filed in iDesk under the parent project. As IEG has pointed out, misfiling is not an acceptable excuse for lack of documentation, and management agrees with this and will reemphasize to staff the importance of accurately filed documents.
    - A number of cases counted as "shortfalls and gaps" by IEG related to the specifics and nature of the project. For example, breakeven analysis and debt service coverage analysis are not used and may not be necessary for projects with financial institutions.
    - Similarly, other concerns raised by IEG relate to repeat clients, where IFC had sufficient information from ongoing supervision.
    - On many other issues, such as the sale prices, margins, foreign exchange volatility, tariffs, and custom protection, after reviewing the projects management found that the investment teams adequately analyzed and documented the issues during the due diligence process.

Supervision quality. Management welcomes the IEG's emphasis on the importance of further strengthening supervision quality. The report states that "IFC's overall work quality has continued a two-year gradual upward trend but there has been a recent decline in IFC's supervision quality" and "The need to pay strong attention to work quality and portfolio risk management is particularly acute under the current circumstances when the global economy is fragile and IFC is undergoing profound institutional change."

Comments

- In order to improve its supervision processes, IFC has taken or is implementing several steps, including: (i) strengthening its risk management system and adapting it to a decentralized operating environment; (ii) improving

IFC portfolio and risk management capabilities under the IFC 2013 initiative; (iii) deploying more industry/ portfolio management, senior credit officers, and environmental/social expertise to the field, enabling the convergence of IFC's global expertise with local knowledge; and (iv) adopting the portfolio review concept with portfolio quality regularly discussed in Quarterly Regional Portfolio Reviews.

- We also believe that IEG's findings should be put in context. The highlighted reduction in supervision success rates between 2008 and 2009 follows a more or less continuous improvement in supervision ratings every year since evaluation year 2000.
- The report gives the impression that all of the shortfalls identified relate to recent events, when in reality many of them occurred as far back as 2005. Linking them to the IFC 2013 initiative, which started much later, is thus spurious.

Some of the apparent shortfalls relate to obtaining adequate reporting, rather than actual performance shortfalls. We do not agree that supervision should be downgraded where IFC repeatedly tried—but failed—to obtain adequate reporting.

Advisory services. *Client Contributions, Client Commitment, and Development Results*: The report states that "IEG findings show that, in general, advisory services projects that have some level of client contribution tend to achieve higher development effectiveness ratings" (IEG-IFC 2009).

Comments

- More generally, the level of project contribution needs to be considered in the context of the overall project design. If an Advisory Services project delivered solely private benefits, fully captured by the client, a contribution of 100 percent would be required under our pricing policy. If, as is more commonly the case, an Advisory Services project involved a mix of public and private goods, the client would be expected to contribute only to the extent of the private good component, which may be 50 percent or less of total project costs. Care needs to be taken in assuming that the first project will offer stronger development results than the second project because the client contribution as measured by share of total project costs is higher. Indeed, other things being equal, we would expect the second project to offer stronger development impact because of the public good component.

Progress in implementing the pricing policy. The report states that "On average, management has estimated that client contribution will amount to 25 percent of total project costs from its fiscal 2008 approvals and 35 percent from fiscal 2009 approvals. Based on estimates made at project approval, there are expectations that levels of client contributions from the Latin America and the Caribbean Region will rise. Other regions such as South Asia and the Middle East and North Africa have declining estimates. This may be a reflection of the strategic focus or design of advisory services projects in the particular Region (that is, public versus private sector focus)."

Comments

- On the 25 percent versus 35 percent number, it is important to emphasize (as the source material did) that these are the estimates that were made at time of project approval. We have been careful to explain that experience in collections may be driven by multiple factors, and that we are monitoring experience closely.
- The region-specific discussion raises a few issues. First, the samples are too small to draw any credible inferences. More importantly, as drafted, it might be thought that regions were free to determine how much emphasis to place on client contributions. It should be clear that all regions are subject to the identical pricing policy. Differences in strategy relate to the choice and design of individual projects to meet local strategic priorities, which has implications for pricing based on the balance of public and private benefits involved in each project.

Additionality. *IFC's Additionality and Development Impact:* We welcome the elaboration on additionality and development impact throughout the report. The report states that "IFC's upfront review process is mature and sophisticated. However, weaknesses exist in key areas related to assessing client commitments, understanding political and regulatory risks at the country level, *and fully integrating and mainstreaming additionality and development impact considerations into the project cycle*" (emphasis added).

Comments

- Additionality and development impact are now fully integrated in the project cycle at IFC. They are tracked in iDesk, and are assessed at each project stage, including (i) as a criterion for project screening and risk-management tiering (PDS-Concept), (ii) as part of IFC's public disclosure; (iii) as a criterion for management and Board decision (Board Approval Paper); and (iv) management reporting on additionality achievement (PSR, MOR, quarterly reporting to the Board and management team).
- As part of the additionality database in the new online system, 699 projects were reviewed. Of these projects, 99 percent had risk mitigation additionality identified, 49 percent had standard setting or policy work, and

46 percent had knowledge and innovation identified as an additionality. Less than 10 of the projects reviewed lacked sufficient justification for the additionality identified and required additional follow-up with the team.

- In December 2008, the Board Paper Guidelines were revised to further improve the articulation of IFC's role and additionality. We are again revising the guidelines to increase the focus on IFC's strategic context, expected additionality, and development impact.

C. MIGA—Development outcomes and quality of underwriting

The report makes a number of conclusions with respect to the overall quality of MIGA's underwriting. It is noted that that MIGA has been strong in areas of country and political risk assessment. This is a core function of the Agency and one of MIGA's comparative advantages, and it is obviously important that the Agency perform this analysis well. At the same time, the report notes that other aspects of underwriting quality have been weak, especially with respect to the ex ante assessment of the evaluated projects' development outcomes, and that overall, MIGA's quality of underwriting is weak. From this, the report notes that poor quality of underwriting and poor development outcome often went hand in hand. On this point, management would note that the underwriting quality may drive a decision about whether or not MIGA will offer a guarantee to a project, but it is not a critical factor in whether or not the project subsequently performs well. MIGA has limited leverage in modifying project design; its strength is in providing comfort for private investors to make the investment. The project and its impact therefore occur essentially independently of the underwriting.

Nevertheless, management does recognize that both (i) quality of underwriting and (ii) identifying projects which will yield strong development impact are extremely important and are areas where MIGA wishes to excel. Management would point to important steps that have been taken in recent years, such as the introduction of the self-evaluation program, and the planned introduction in fiscal 2011 of Key Development Performance Indicators, both of which are intended to help MIGA improve in these areas.

Concerning quality of underwriting, the report notes that the most recurrent shortcoming here was inadequate analysis of the project's financial viability. Management agrees that this is a crucial component of the underwriting process and shares IEG's firm underlying assertion that good financial performance is a necessary condition for a project to make a positive developmental contribution. Management would note that important steps have been taken within MIGA to strengthen internal capacity in this area, including the introduction of a standardized training program for staff and the hiring of new staff with strong backgrounds in performing project due diligence and financial analysis in particular. At the same time, management would also like to underscore its commitment to further improving MIGA's capabilities in this area.

The report notes that poor documentation and record-keeping is another fundamental issue regarding quality of underwriting. This is a procedural element, and an important aspect of underwriting. Here too, MIGA management would note that the report's assessment may have been characteristic of the evaluated projects which date from fiscal 2006 or earlier; however, it believes that the situation in MIGA today has evolved in a positive direction. In particular, management would point to the major investment that has been made in developing MIGA's new Guarantees Database. In fiscal 2006, MIGA embarked on a major systems renewal process to replace MIGA's legacy database system with an updated system that would fully support the Agency's complete range of business needs. The SAP-based new system, which took several years to design, build, and test, has been launched and operationalized in fiscal 2010. It sits within the World Bank's secure information technology environment and ensures that different functional areas within MIGA (for example, underwriting and accounting) are linked electronically so that all parts of MIGA's business are properly integrated. Going forward, it allows for a more efficient and reliable database functionality to manage all key guarantees data, and enables the entire underwriting process to be done online. As well as being more efficient, the system strengthens quality control and is helping to significantly improve MIGA's record-keeping capabilities.

Finally, the report finds that MIGA's implementation of environmental and social performance standards has been weak, particularly because MIGA has devoted inadequate resources in this regard. Here, MIGA management would again reference the timing of the projects upon which this finding is based. Past performance in this area may have left room for improvement, but the situation today is considerably different. MIGA has taken a number of important steps that squarely address this issue, including the strengthening of MIGA's Environmental and Social team, which has increased by 300 percent in terms of staff size since fiscal 2006, and the introduction of new safeguard and disclosure policies. In addition, MIGA created the chief economist position at the end of fiscal 2004 to strengthen development impact analysis and oversee MIGA's adherence to Performance Standards. Here, MIGA would also note that IEG's findings in the recent report titled *Safeguards and Sustainability Policies in a Changing World: An Independent Evaluation of World Bank Group Experience* noted that fully 100 percent of MIGA's projects underwritten since 2007 (for which the new environmental and social Performance Standards apply) that have been evaluated have received a satisfactory rating on environmental and social due diligence.

IV. Conclusions

The World Bank Group management appreciates that submitting the Bank to the learning and accountability discipline of independent evaluation is a strength that sets it apart from many other development institutions. It is confident that the benefits are worth the costs of being held to this high standard.

Chairman's Summary: Committee on Development Effectiveness (CODE)

The Committee on Development Effectiveness (CODE) met to consider the report *IEG Annual Report 2010: Results and Performance of the World Bank Group*, prepared by the Independent Evaluation Group (IEG) and the draft management comments. A second volume of the IEG report containing the records of IEG recommendations to management and management responses for each World Bank Group institution and the tracking of these recommendations and responses is available online.

The Committee commended IEG for its first consolidated single report which described the current trends in the World Bank Group activities and presented a review of the performance and support of investment, lending, guarantees, and analytical and advisory activities. IEG noted that it consolidated three separate annual reports by IEG-World Bank, IEG-International Finance Corporation and IEG-Multilateral Investment Guarantee Agency. The Chairman added that this was the first of a series of CODE discussions focusing on quality of portfolio followed by subsequent meetings on, for example, impact evaluation and cost-benefit analysis, as well as management's approach to corporate results reporting. Members' interventions focused on how the IEG report could be improved going forward; how to achieve a balance between portfolio analysis and thematic issues; and what the main messages are for improving portfolio quality and follow-up of IEG recommendations.

Members underscored the benefits of considering a comprehensive report across the World Bank Group and highlighting and assessing common issues as well as opportunities for better coordination. However, they also noted the challenges ahead of adopting a more analytical approach to assessing the quality of the World Bank Group assistance. Members also made general observations regarding the appropriateness of the title of the report, given that the data presented generally cover a time period prior to 2010. Further dialogue between IEG and management was encouraged to strengthen understandings on the follow-up of IEG recommendations through the Management Action Record/Management Action Tracking Record. In addition, members welcomed IEG's attempt to quantify the impact of decentralization on outcomes. They also shared IEG's views that more systematic analysis and quantitative assessment could deepen the understanding of the cost and benefits of decentralization, noting that its analysis was limited in scope.

During the discussion, members commented on the need to separate the analysis and monitoring of trends associated with the response to the global crisis (for example, increase use of Development Policy Lending) from before-crisis portfolio performance and asked what will happen to the World Bank Group activity beyond the current global crisis and whether there will be a contraction of Bank support as in the case of the post-Asian crisis. They also stressed the need to focus not only on the International Development Association but also on middle-income countries, and to continue to rethink quality-at-entry of the Bank's portfolio. In this regard, IEG and management were encouraged to work together on quality measurement issues including assessment of risk. Questions were raised on what the current changes and new approaches (for example, investment lending and knowledge reform) mean for measurement of portfolio quality, quality at entry, performance, and outcome of Bank support, including advisory services.

Part I ACTIVITIES AND RESULTS

Chapter 1

Photo by Thomas Sennett, courtesy of the World Bank Photo Library.

EVALUATION HIGHLIGHTS

- World Bank Group members have had contrasting responses to the global economic crisis that has dominated the past year.
- Response at the World Bank has been strongly countercyclical; International Finance Corporation investments have been procyclical.
- Lending for projects that fall in the financial sector has increased, as has the use of new financial instruments.
- Concentration patterns have shown some increase.
- Volumes of support to International Development Association countries and Africa have been maintained; social protection lending has increased but has been concentrated in a few operations.
- Development outcome ratings at the World Bank suggest a decline in project outcomes; IFC, meanwhile, has maintained its position, but with possible delayed crisis impact.
- Development outcomes in infrastructure and environment have improved at the Bank and IFC, but the share of activity in these sectors has declined.
- Development outcomes in Africa remain challenging.

Results and Performance

The external environment in which the World Bank Group operates has been dominated over the past year by the global financial crisis. Challenges of poverty and fragile states, environment, and climate change remain daunting. But the manner in which these are to be addressed is shifting, and the Bank Group must adapt to shifting circumstances.[1]

Unprecedented Change at the World Bank Group

Within the World Bank Group, these events have had a striking impact on the volumes and nature of lending, investment, and guarantee activity. The World Bank, comprising the International Bank for Reconstruction and Development (IBRD) and the International Development Association (IDA), is charting internal reforms and new postcrisis directions with an enhanced voice for developing and transition countries. These changes have contributed to recent capital increases at the IBRD and at the International Finance Corporation (IFC). And the Multilateral Investment Guarantee Agency (MIGA) is modifying its Convention to expand its range of services.

Rationale for a Review of the Whole World Bank Group

This new annual document from the Independent Evaluation Group (IEG) proposes to address, in a single report, the evaluation of performance and institutional effectiveness previously addressed by the *Annual Review of Development Effectiveness* of the World Bank, the *Independent Evaluation of IFC's Development Results,* and the *Independent Evaluation of MIGA's Development Effectiveness.* This joint presentation permits the identification of common messages cutting across the three institutions of the World Bank Group, as well as areas of potential difference.

This report first reviews patterns of activity across the Bank Group and development outcomes and discusses present arrangements for learning and accountability. In Part II, the report examines select issues of institutional effectiveness relevant to the historic shifts in direction, decentralization at the World Bank, risk mitigation through better quality at entry at IFC, and quality of underwriting at MIGA.

> This report examines the performance and institutional effectiveness of the World Bank, IFC, and MIGA, with a particular focus on results.

Although the World Bank has primarily a public sector focus and IFC and MIGA have a primary focus on the private sector, the World Bank does support private sector development and public-private partnerships through analytical and advisory work as well as through lending. IFC invests with government agencies, provides advisory services to government entities, and assists local governments by providing partial credit guarantees and syndication assistance. MIGA supports private investors in public sector projects and is also prepared to support state-owned enterprises that operate under commercial conditions.

In fiscal 2009, the World Bank Group's $59 billion in commitments was dominated by IBRD's new commitments of $33 billion and IDA commitments of $13.5 billion.[2] IFC investment operations in guarantees, loans, and equity investments amounted to $10.5 billion. MIGA issued $1.37 billion (gross exposure) in new guarantees.

> The report considers the complementary and overlapping support the Bank Group institutions provide.

Bank and IFC programs are complementary and can overlap. The potential opportunities for synergies from operations and for coordination of interventions across the Bank Group have not always been exploited, although increased efforts have been evident in recent years. An example of such lost opportunities is offered by *The World Bank Group Guarantee Instruments 1990–2007* (IEG 2009b), which identifies inconsistent pricing, unclear boundaries across risk mitigation products, and limited staff awareness of the various products. The report highlights overlapping mandates for risk mitigation products, engendering competition among staff and confusing clients.

Managements of the Bank, IFC, and MIGA have taken several steps to address these issues, with significant progress in some areas. Conversely, IEG's 2009 Project Performance Assessment Report for the Chad-Cameroon Petroleum Development and Pipeline Construction Program showed that the project demonstrated exemplary cooperation between IFC and the World Bank, based on a division of labor at all stages that played to each institution's mandates and strengths. Furthermore, after the Bank exited from Chad's oil sector, IFC continued to monitor the environmental and social aspects of the project.

Despite its shortcomings from an outcomes perspective, the project shows how World Bank–IFC cooperation can ideally work in complex projects with multiple stakeholders and how the institutions can complement each other. At the country level, six joint IDA-IFC Country Assistance Strategies (CASs) have been piloted in the past year, which will help determine the modalities for IFC interventions in the CAS cycle.

> The comparison of development outcomes is limited by differences in the evaluation processes and in coverage of project-level evaluations at each World Bank Group institution.

The comparison of development outcomes is limited not only by differences in the nature of the evaluative process at each institution but also by differences in the coverage of project-level evaluations across institutions (appendix A). At MIGA, the absence of mainstreamed self-evaluation has led to a database of project evaluations that is too small for ratings to be representative at the portfolio level. The World Bank, in contrast, self-evaluates 100 percent of its projects, although a system for evaluation of its analytic and advisory activities is still lacking. IFC evaluates a representative sample of investment services and initiated systematic evaluation of its advisory services in 2006. Furthermore, World Bank and IFC projects are evaluated at different stages in the project cycle—at project completion and at project maturity, respectively. The most striking missing area of evaluation at IFC is for its Global Trade Finance Facility, a growing business segment that—so far—lacks a systematic method of defining and assessing development outcomes and impacts.

Current Trends—A Year Dominated by Crisis

Recent activity at each World Bank Group institution, influenced by the impact of the global financial crisis and the changed external environment, raises questions about the impact on the internal operating environment and longer-term results. Recent trends in operations are discussed below and a perspective on overall development results is offered in the following section.

> New commitments for all three institutions have been affected by the ongoing financial crisis, but the patterns of the institutions' responses differ.

New commitments of all three institutions have been considerably affected by the ongoing financial crisis, but their patterns of response are markedly different (figure 1.1). New World Bank commitments in fiscal 2009 increased more than twofold compared to the year before, and the escalation has continued in fiscal 2010. Strong demand from middle-income countries and, on the supply side, historically low pricing and capital headroom contributed to the growth in Bank lending. This growth is consistent with the Bank's response to the fiscal 1998–99 crisis, when lending also increased sharply. Such consistency suggests a strong countercyclical pattern in Bank lending of providing public sector support.

Comparing country-specific crisis responses, the contrast between the Bank and IFC is even clearer. New IFC commitments to a range of crisis countries and regions contracted during crises but increased in times of economic recovery. In contrast, new World Bank commitments increased relative to the precrisis periods and declined after the crisis (figure 1.2). In the regions, World Bank new lending in fiscal 2009 increased the most for Latin America and the Caribbean, where lending tripled, and in Eastern Europe

FIGURE 1.1 **New Commitments, Investments, and Guarantees at the World Bank, IFC, and MIGA—Present and Past Crises, Fiscal 1990–2009 ($ millions)**

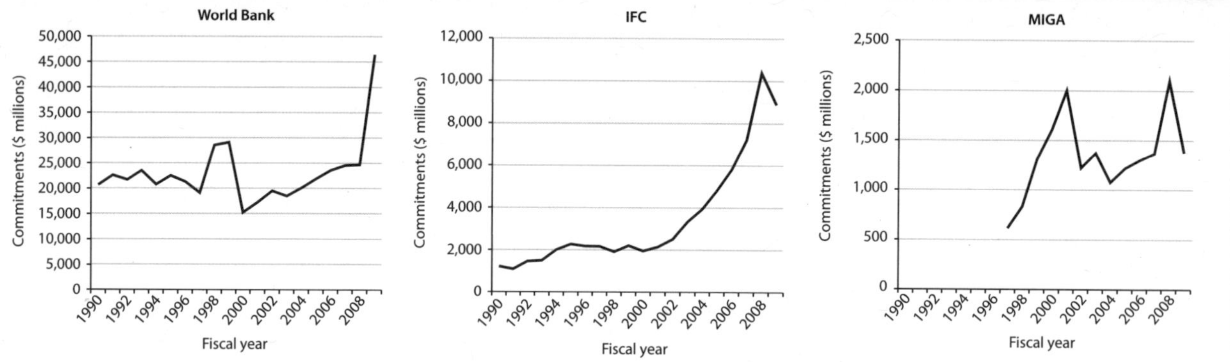

Sources: World Bank internal database; IFC management information systems data; IEG-MIGA.
Note: World Bank data include IBRD/IDA new loans and new supplemental loans.

and Central Asia, where it more than doubled. New IFC commitments to these regions declined by a fifth in Latin America and the Caribbean and by more than half in Europe and Central Asia.

Relevant to the present crisis, a background analysis of 72 previous World Bank crisis operations in nine countries from 1990 to 2004 finds that development outcomes of crisis lending are not generally lower than of noncrisis lending (box 1.1). Outcomes tend to follow patterns that borrowers have in noncrisis periods, with relatively good crisis lending outcomes in countries that are better performers and poorer outcomes in countries that perform less well.

New IFC business, which had more than doubled from 2005 to 2008, fell by 18 percent in fiscal 2009. IFC's procyclical investment pattern is caused by the strategic prioritization of resource allocation toward existing clients, instead of the generation of new business. For the first time, IFC departments were rated and rewarded for portfolio management quality. Targets for new business generation were suspended. The gap between targets and results seems to stem from constraints on the supply side, not only demand—this is based on IFC's estimate of demand for private financing; data from IEG country visits; and the growth during the crisis in the private business of the European Bank for Reconstruction

FIGURE 1.2 **World Bank and IFC: Precrisis, Crisis, and Postcrisis New Commitments ($ millions)**

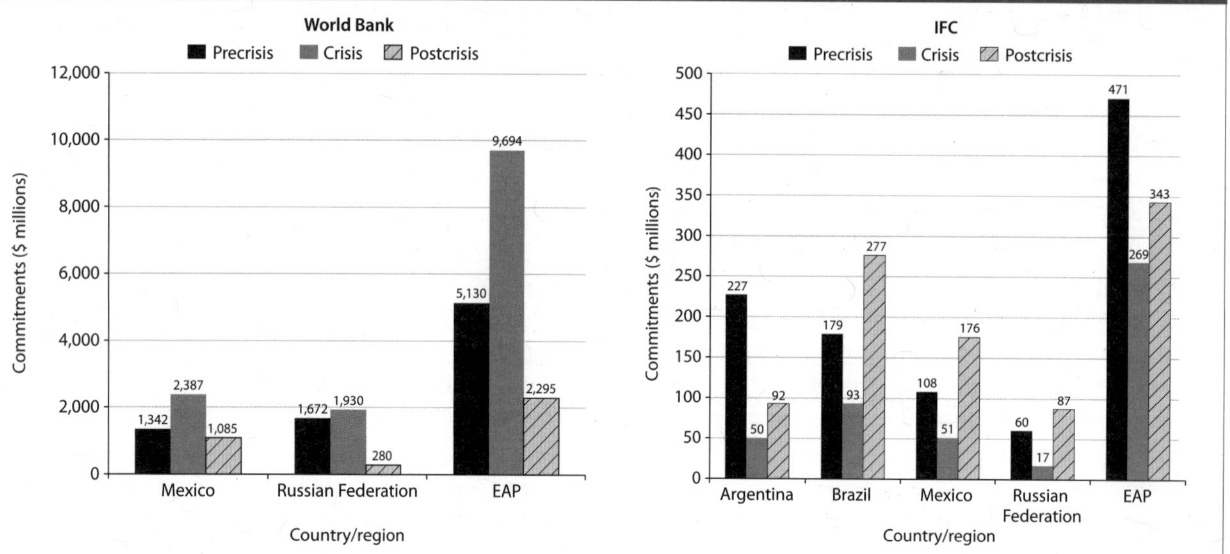

Sources: World Bank internal database and IFC management information systems data.
Note: Precrisis refers to the average of the two fiscal years preceding the crisis; postcrisis refers to the average of the three years succeeding the crisis. Crisis periods referred to are Mexico (fiscal 1995), East Asia and Pacific (fiscal 1998–99), the Russian Federation (fiscal 1999), Argentina (fiscal 2001–02), and Brazil (fiscal 2000). World Bank data include IBRD/IDA new loans and new supplemental loans. EAP = East Asia and Pacific Region.

BOX 1.1 How Well Have Previous Crisis-Related Loans Performed?

By measuring outcomes by approval year instead of exit year, IEG explored the relationship between the quality of outcomes of Bank projects undertaken during periods of crisis.

First, comparing the average outcomes of all projects Bank-wide that were approved during the Asian crisis years—fiscal 1998 and fiscal 1999—with those approved in the three years before and after the crisis, there was no notable difference in performance between crisis years and noncrisis years. Seventy-five percent of all projects were satisfactory in the three precrisis years (fiscal 1995–97), compared with 77 percent during the peak of the crisis (fiscal 1998–99) and 79 percent in fiscal 2000 to 2002.

Second, analyzing loans to the East Asia and Pacific Region specifically, IEG found that 80, 85, and 75 percent of projects rated satisfactory during these same three periods, respectively, achieving average scores of 4.3, 4.4, and 4.1 on a 6-point scale. Regional results for crisis years, such as aggregate results, are similar to those of noncrisis years.

Third, IEG expanded the analysis to other countries that had undergone crises during fiscal 1990–2004, as the large majority of all loans in these years have been closed and evaluated. Countries in the East Asia and Pacific Region were not the only crisis borrowers during the period. Other countries also experienced crisis borrowing. Seventy-two crisis operations were identified for nine countries during this period. Evaluation outcomes of the crisis operations in each country were compared to the average of evaluative outcomes for noncrisis projects in the same country.

Results suggest that those countries that perform better during normal times are generally also good performers during crisis periods. Thus, in the Republic of Korea, noncrisis loans all achieved a rating of satisfactory or higher; on a 6-point scale Korea received an average rating of 5.1. Korea's rating for crisis loans was similar, at 5.

Argentina, Brazil, Malaysia, Mexico, Thailand, and Turkey achieved ratings averaging between 4 and 5 for noncrisis borrowing (79–95 percent of projects satisfactory), and all except Thailand achieved a rating at least as high or higher for crisis borrowing. Indonesia and the Russian Federation, in contrast, had lower average project outcomes for noncrisis borrowing (3.9 on a 6-point scale and 67–68 percent satisfactory projects). Their results on crisis loans were also poorer (3.3).

The overall finding is that outcomes for crisis lending depend on underlying borrower performance on a long-term basis, and not noticeably on the crisis-related nature of a specific operation.

Source: IEG analysis of Bank data.

and Development, the European Investment Bank, and the African Development Bank.

In light of these constraints, IFC has launched several strategic initiatives covering trade, bank capitalization, infrastructure, microfinance, and advisory services. They are targeted, temporary, based on partnerships, and include knowledge services, and they were structured relatively quickly. However, implementation is far behind schedule. As of March 31, 2010, of the $9.2 billion approved for these initiatives (half of which came from partners), only $2.5 billion had actually been committed and $1.2 billion disbursed (20 percent of expected deployment at this stage; see table E.3 in appendix E).

IFC's selective approach to new investments may have resulted in missed opportunities. Past experiences indicate a potential for greater development impact from investments made after a crisis and suggest the importance of adequate financial capacity for a robust countercyclical response.

The current global financial crisis has only heightened attention to MIGA's financial sector guarantees. Beyond its already significant buildup of exposure to the financial sector, MIGA adopted the financial sector initiative in March 2009, a MIGA-specific crisis response effort focused on supporting financial institutions in Europe and Central Asia; it is part of the internationally coordinated Joint International Financial Institution Action Plan agreed to by the European Bank for Reconstruction and Development, the European Investment Bank, and the World Bank Group. The aim was to provide extended support to financial institutions needing political risk insurance on cross-border investments to recapitalize or provide liquidity support to their banking subsidiaries. Initially geared toward the Europe and Central Asia Region, its reach is potentially broader.

MIGA's total net exposure (that is, after reinsurance) under the initiative was targeted to not exceed $1 billion in the region and is expected to support, with reinsurance, capital flows of \$2–\$3 billion in gross terms.[3] This highlights MIGA's potential to contribute countercyclically with financial sector guarantees, albeit in limited amounts. It also points to a continued deep engagement by MIGA in the financial sector.

Another interesting contrast is offered by the sharp historic contraction in activity after the previous crisis at the World Bank and the slow recovery compared with the vigorous resumption of growth at IFC. New World Bank commitments declined to an all-time low in fiscal 2000—some \$15 billion—and did not recover to precrisis levels (\$21 billion on average between fiscal 1995 and 1997) until fiscal 2005. By fiscal 2002, new IFC commitments, in contrast, expanded to above their precrisis levels and continued to increase until fiscal 2008.[4]

Differential responses to the current crisis among the three institutions are embedded in each institution's structures. In crises, the Bank prioritizes support to governments facing macroeconomic and fiscal imbalances. IFC must protect its existing client portfolio, may face capital constraints because of a decline in profitability of its investments, and is constrained in attracting new investors. The Bank Group as a whole could position itself to benefit from these complementary patterns.

> The differential responses to the crisis are rooted in each institution's structure.

At the World Bank, these patterns echo findings observed with the financial crisis of 1997–98. They suggest trends that could be noted for the future. However, some important differences are also relevant to the current response, which may enhance risk.

First, volumes of lending in response to the present crisis are unprecedented. New commitments in fiscal 2009 increased some 90 percent, relative to the average of the three precrisis years, and continued to rise steeply in the first two quarters of fiscal 2010. In contrast, during the Asian financial crisis, lending increased by barely a third, to some \$29 billion, compared with precrisis levels of \$21 billion. The surge in lending for the current crisis is proportionally much greater.

Second, there has been a steeper increase in the average loan size, which almost doubled in the present crisis (fiscal 2009 versus the average of fiscal 2006–08), compared with just a 20 percent escalation from fiscal 1995–97 to 1998–99.[5] Third, total numbers of operations in the present period have remained virtually unchanged, compared with an increase in numbers by nearly a fifth (from 257 operations to 300) at the height of the Asian crisis. These differences emphasize the increase in loan size with the present crisis. Could these factors suggest that the World Bank has assumed new dimensions of risk?

Finally, in both crises, there has been an increase in lending concentration. In fiscal 2009, the five largest loans accounted for 18 percent of new lending, compared with a lower share of some 11–14 percent in the precrisis years. Similarly, in fiscal 1998 and 1999, the top five valued approvals accounted for 26–27 percent of new commitments, compared with a precrisis concentration that was similar to the present period.

> In both the current and previous crises, the concentration of World Bank lending has increased.

Mitigating factors of the present crisis are the smaller increase in concentration and greater diffusion in Bank borrowing countries, as well as new entrants. New lending increased substantially for all regions in fiscal 2009. On a trend basis, large proportions of World Bank lending (a quarter on average over the past 10 years) have been consistently directed toward just three countries—China, India, and Brazil—that remain big borrowers today and enjoy above-average development outcome ratings on past borrowing.

Regional focus. MIGA guarantee issuance is increasingly regionally concentrated—57 percent of all guarantees issued were for projects in Europe and Central Asia in fiscal 2005–09, up from 34 percent in 2000–04. Regional concentration was even more pronounced in fiscal 2009, when 88 percent of all guarantees were for projects in Europe and Central Asia.

Since fiscal 2007, Europe and Central Asia has consistently been IFC's second highest region for new commitments, after Latin America and the Caribbean (Europe and Central Asia dominated in fiscal 2003–06), accounting for about a fifth of the commitments over the past four years. New commitments for the World Bank appear more diversified. Africa, Latin America and the Caribbean, and South Asia have hovered around the top position between fiscal 2005 and 2008.

> Despite apparent regional concentrations, at the country level, the borrower or client concentration has been very consistent in all three institutions.

At the country level, there is considerable consistency in top borrower or client composition. At the Bank, Brazil, China, Colombia, India, Mexico, Turkey, and Vietnam have been among the top 10 borrowers in at least 8 of the past 10 years. At IFC, a similar set of countries—Brazil, China, India, Mexico, and Turkey—have been among the top 10 client countries in at least 6 of the past 10 years. In terms of volume, in fiscal 2009, 35 percent of new Bank commitments went to its largest five borrowers, which closely parallels IFC's 33 percent.

Between fiscal 2008 and 2009, there has been some decline in the concentration of the top five client countries at both IFC and the World Bank, from 49 percent to 38 percent for IFC and from 45 percent to 33 percent for the Bank. Recent crisis activity may reverse this trend.

MIGA's guarantees have also become increasingly concentrated in terms of clients or guarantee holders, that is, those purchasing the guarantee coverage. The top 10 clients accounted for 68 percent of guarantees issued during fiscal 2005–09, whereas the top 5 clients accounted for 57 percent of guarantees issued and the top 2 clients for 36 percent. Client concentration increased significantly in fiscal 2009—the top 2 clients alone accounted for 79 percent of guarantees issued. Finally, MIGA guarantees have been highly concentrated with respect to investor countries. One-third of all MIGA guarantees were provided to investors from one country, Austria, in fiscal 2005–09. The top 10 investor countries together accounted for 82 percent of guarantees issued in the same period.

MIGA guarantees have increasingly been concentrated in terms of client companies and investor countries.

Similarities in patterns of concentration suggest the need for a closer examination of issues associated with risk at the level of the Bank Group as a whole. However, it must be noted that Bank clients are country governments, and thus concentration at the country level is the relevant measure. In contrast, at IFC and MIGA, there are multiple clients, and relevant measures of concentration must also include sectoral and company dimensions.

Support to IDA countries and to Africa. The focus on IDA countries has increased over the last decade at the World Bank and IFC, and that focus was not lost during the crisis (figure 1.3). In dollar terms, this represented an eightfold increase at IFC from fiscal 2002, to $2.8 billion in 2008. There was a further 25 percent rise in 2009, supporting one of IFC's five strategic pillars of "strengthening the focus on frontier markets (IDA countries, fragile and conflict-affected situations, and frontier regions in middle-income countries)." IFC's rapidly growing trade finance facility is an increasing source of IFC commitments to IDA countries. In addition, since 2006, IFC has contributed $1.5 billion to IDA.

FIGURE 1.3 New World Bank and IFC Commitments and MIGA Guarantees to IDA Countries and Africa

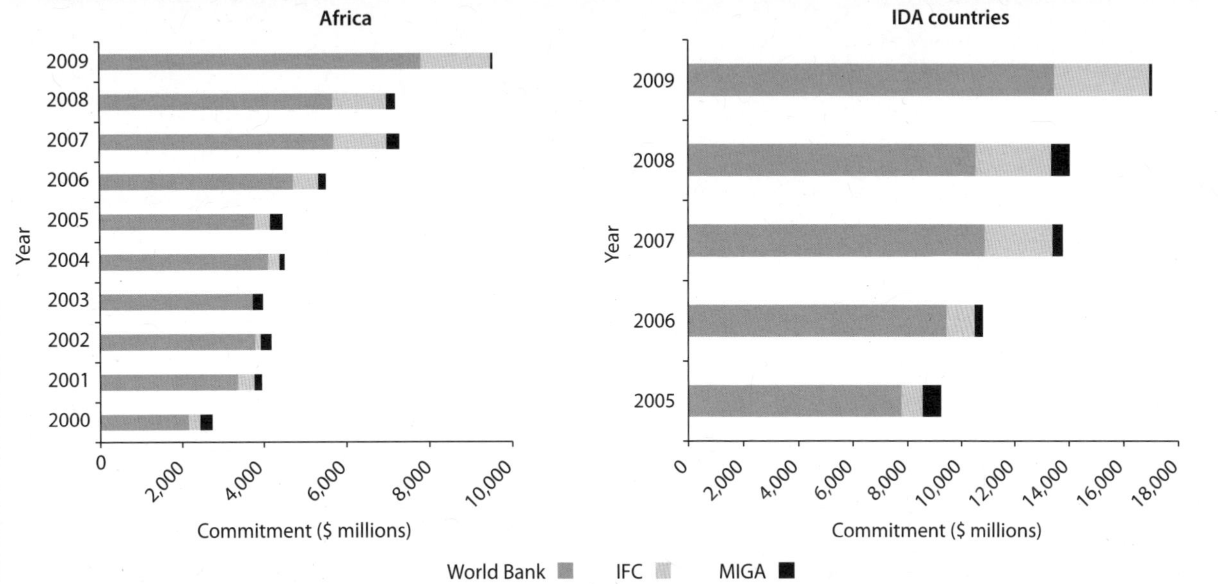

Source: World Bank Business Warehouse database, IFC management information systems database, MIGA, and IEG-MIGA.

IDA countries' shares in Bank lending, which have steadily increased over the past decade, inevitably decline in periods of crisis. This partially reflects differences in IBRD and IDA funding modalities and the relative ease with which IBRD lending levels can be scaled up. It also reflects the greater vulnerability of middle-income countries to contagion through capital movements at a time of crisis. Yet in dollar terms, commitments to IDA countries have increased by a third in fiscal 2009 alone, compared with the precrisis years 2006–08; that is more than the 25 percent increase of IDA lending following the previous crisis.[6] This suggests that the Bank has not lost sight of its poorest clients.

Though IDA's share of Bank lending has declined during the crisis, commitments to IDA countries have increased.

As with IFC, new World Bank lending to Africa has risen steadily, more than tripling between fiscal 2000 and 2009. In fiscal 2007 and 2008, Africa was the World Bank's largest borrower, with a share of almost 23 percent of new commitments. With the onset of the crisis, the share of African borrowing declined in 2009 to 17 percent, but absolute lending levels still increased by a third. In fragile states, however, lending increases in fiscal 2009 relative to the precrisis period were limited.[7]

World Bank lending to Africa has increased steadily since fiscal 2000, and lending to fragile states has kept pace with the rise in new commitments.

New IFC commitments to Africa have been on the increase since fiscal 2004; in fact, they grew fivefold between 2004 and 2009, more than doubling their share in IFC's new commitments.[8] Even with the onset of the current crisis, new investments in Africa grew by a third in fiscal 2009, relative to the previous year. The share of MIGA's new guarantees issued in Africa remained fairly steady over the past 10 years at 14 percent of guarantees issued between fiscal 2000 and 2004 and 15 percent between fiscal 2005 and 2009.

Increased financial sector role

In all World Bank Group institutions, the share of new commitments in the financial sector has increased sharply with the crisis. In IFC in fiscal 2009, commitments to financial markets reached almost 50 percent of new volume. Financial sector guarantees are now MIGA's most important business segment in terms of volume of newly issued guarantees. The share of new guarantees rose to 53 percent between fiscal 2005 and 2009, compared with only 30 percent in fiscal 2000–04. In fiscal 2009, they accounted for 89 percent of MIGA's new guarantee volume; that figure is a result of MIGA's support for Austrian banks' investments in their subsidiaries in the Europe and Central Asia Region, in response to the global crisis. Absolute levels of lending to the financial sector have more than doubled at the World Bank, compared with the precrisis period.[9]

The share of new commitments in the financial sector has increased for all Bank Group institutions.

Perhaps more significant is the fact that IFC has witnessed an increase in financial sector activity over the decade, partly because of the rapid growth in trade guarantees under the Global Trade Finance Program (GTFP), which began 2006. The share of total IFC investments in the financial sector increased from 17 percent in fiscal 2000 to 70 percent in the first half of fiscal 2010. Traditional project finance has lost significance as corporate finance has increased. The GFTP saw strong crisis-related increases in demand and also a robustly supported private sector trade in IDA-eligible Sub-Saharan African countries.

In contrast, at the Bank, precrisis lending to the financial sector had declined from fiscal 2002 to 2008 (from 21 percent to 7.6 percent)—a trend that was reversed with the recent increase. Thus, the Bank has a more significant role in the financial sector during times of crisis. However, there are differences in the nature of services offered by each institution, and these activities are not substitutable.

IFC has more than doubled the volume of its financial sector activity over the decade, in part because of rapid growth in trade guarantees.

New financing instruments

With the onset of the financial crisis, at both the Bank and IFC there has been a change in the mix of instruments used to promote new lending. At the Bank, shares of development policy loans (DPLs) and financial intermediary loans had remarkable growth. Recent DPL growth—from $2.2 billion in fiscal 2008 to $8.2 billion in the first half of 2010—reverses a trend of decline in the share of policy-based lending, from half of all lending in fiscal 2002 to barely a quarter in 2008.

By the first half of fiscal 2010, DPLs accounted for more than half of all Bank lending. This spike in policy-based lending is similar to the last crisis. Meanwhile, financial intermediary loans have increased from $0.4 billion in fiscal 2008 to $1.8 billion in the first two quarters of 2010 (figure 1.4).

The mix of instruments has shifted since the onset of the financial crisis.

Within DPLs, fiscal 2009 saw a new spurt in popularity for the deferred drawdown option, demonstrating the value of an instrument that provides contingent credit at a time of crisis. Thirteen deferred drawdown option DPLs made up more than a quarter of new commitments for policy-based lending operations in fiscal 2009.[10]

Special DPLs, introduced in 2005 as an instrument for countries approaching crisis with structural and social dimensions, were used after the revision to the special DPL policy approved in September 2009. The Latvia Social Safety Net DPL was approved by the Board as a Special DPL, and two financial sector DPLs—in Hungary and Latvia—were also extended on special DPL terms. And supplemental and additional financing, for cost overruns or scale-ups in investment lending, have also increased sharply, from 4 percent of new lending in fiscal 2006 to 10 percent in 2009.[11]

Policy-based lending has increased and, with it, the popularity of the deferred drawdown option.

Although the Bank's DPLs have generally performed at least as well as investment lending, according to present criteria, the change in the mix of the Bank's instruments and increased exposure to single-tranche large loans and to deferred drawdown options suggests the need for close monitoring. IEG previously pointed to risks associated with the Bank's financial intermediary loans (IEG 2006f). Monitoring of lines of credit is difficult, as supervision of sub-borrowers is delegated to the financial intermediary.[12]

IEG has pointed to similar issues regarding IFC's lines of credit and the monitoring of associated environmental, health, and social aspects. A tracking and evaluation system for the rapidly growing IFC guarantee instrument segment is still to be devised.

The Bank's increased exposure to large DPLs and deferred drawdown options needs close monitoring.

IFC also saw robust growth in the use of its new guarantee products and the GTFP (figure 1.5).[13] GTFP works by mitigating the payment risk associated with international and cross-border trade and helps foster new relationships among banks operating in challenging and risky markets, thus making it an effective crisis response tool (box 1.2).

IFC has seen robust growth in its new guarantee products and the GTFP.

MIGA's Operational Regulations were amended in 2009 to allow MIGA to provide coverage for nonhonoring of Sovereign Guarantees in the absence of an arbitral award

FIGURE 1.4 World Bank Policy-Based Lending, Investment, and Financial Intermediary Lending ($ billions)

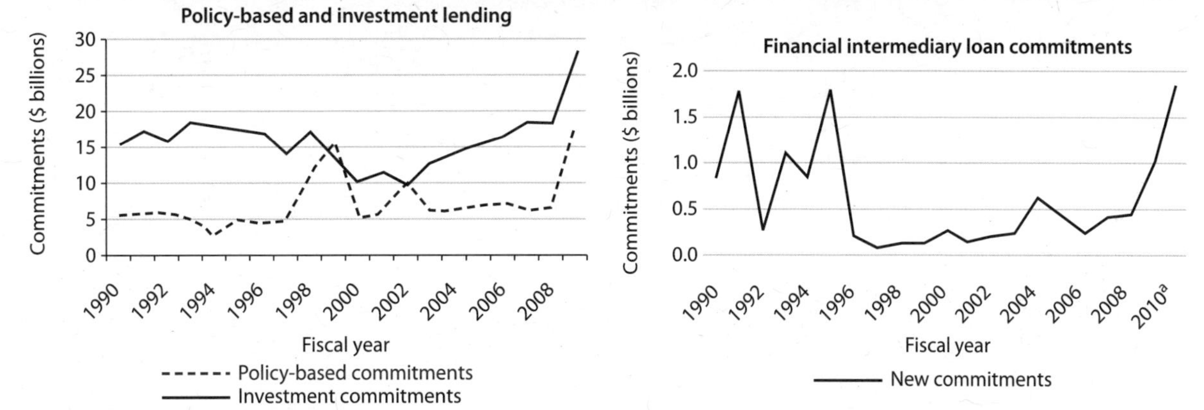

Source: World Bank internal database.

a. Refers to first two quarters.

FIGURE 1.5 IFC Net Commitments by Instrument, 2000–09 ($ millions)

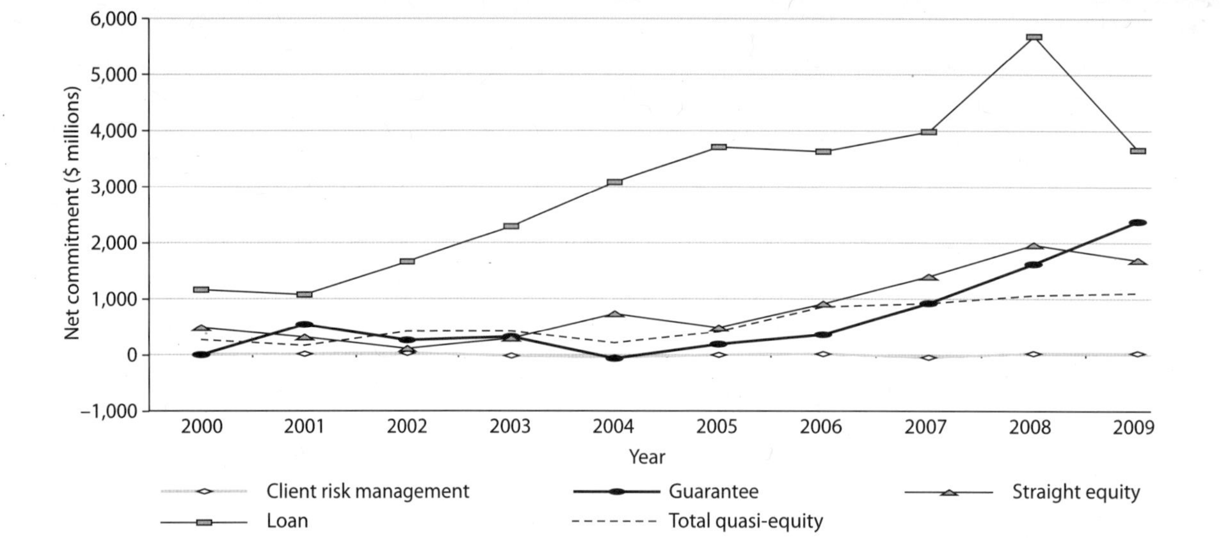

Source: IFC management information system database.

and risk of temporary business interruption. Transactions are under way, although none has yet been finalized.

MIGA has also proposed changes to its Convention, which, if approved, would remove the most important external constraint on its business. If the changes are approved, MIGA would be able to provide coverage for stand-alone debt, investments in existing assets and acquisitions, and specific additional noncommercial risks approved by the Board, without joint application of the investor and host country. These changes would allow MIGA to pursue more effectively its development mandate and position itself as a full-service provider of political risk insurance capable of encouraging investment into the least served parts of the market.

Social protection and human development

At the World Bank, the biggest increase in activity in the crisis period (fiscal 2009 and the first half of fiscal 2010) has been in the social protection sector (500 percent), followed by environment (433 percent), economic policy (220 percent), and finance and private sector development (180

BOX 1.2 IFC's Global Trade Finance Program

The GTFP, approved in fiscal 2005 and operational in fiscal 2006, was established to facilitate trade activities in developing countries—activites that would otherwise not have occurred, given the countries' nascent financial systems and the local financial institutions' limited or untested creditworthiness. The facility has become an increasingly large portion of IFC's annual net commitments.

In 2007, the GTFP accounted for a quarter of the Global Financial Market's total net commitments and more than 10 percent of total IFC net commitments. By 2009, these shares grew to 60 percent and 28 percent, respectively. In response to increased demand, IFC doubled GTFP's authorized ceiling in 2009 to $3 billion. Since 2006, around a third of all guarantees (by volume) issued under the GTFP have supported South-South trade; this portion has remained stable during the crisis.

Measuring the development impact of the GTFP poses some difficulties. The program's transactions are not tracked by the Development Outcome Tracking System, and there is no systematic method of defining or assessing development outcome and impact. Transactions under the GTFP are booked as off-balance-sheet contingent liabilities, making risk management more challenging. IFC correctly recognizes that programs such as the GTFP, which are self-liquidating in nature, will not provide long-term capital growth for IFC as global markets recover.

Source: IFC.

percent).[14] However, increased social protection lending has been concentrated in a handful of loans, with five loans accounting for more than 70 percent of new commitments under the social protection sector board in fiscal 2009. Similarly, in the first half of fiscal 2010, three social protection loans accounted for more than 75 percent of new commitments under this sector board.[15]

> The Bank has emphasized social protection and other human development sectors, although lending in these areas shows signs of increasing concentration.

Meanwhile, new commitments to education and to health, nutrition, and population, which had declined in fiscal 2008, rose again in fiscal 2009.[16] Lending concentration in these sectors also showed some increase from fiscal 2008.[17]

Long-term portfolio trends

A notable feature of the Bank's overall portfolio has been its underlying decline in size from fiscal 2000 until the present crisis. Numbers of projects declined, from some 1,540 to around 1,340 over the postcrisis decade, and pre-Asian crisis levels have still not been regained. In value terms, the total portfolio shrank between 1999 and 2006 from some $124 billion to $93 billion. And in constant dollar terms, the aggregate portfolio, which had remained broadly constant through the early 1990s at around $110 million, shrank to $67.5 million over 2004–08. The present crisis may afford an opportunity for arresting the trend of decline at the World Bank, though caution on reversal after crisis appears warranted, based on past experience.

MIGA issuance showed signs of growth during fiscal 2005–09, but the average of $1.5 billion in new guarantees issued per year between fiscal 2005 and 2009 fell short of the targets set in its strategy. MIGA's business volume has been affected by the global crisis, which has reduced capital flows, especially for foreign direct investment, as projects were delayed because of the difficulty of arranging project finance.

The overall portfolio increased to $34.4 billion in 2009, a 7 percent increase, compared with an average 13 percent annual growth over the period 2000–08. The growth in IFC's future commitment volumes depends in part on the increase in the institution's capital base, including through its retained earnings.

Results and Performance

Even though lags between project implementation and IEG evaluations do not yet allow full accounting of the impact of the most recent global economic developments, overall development results have undoubtedly been affected by the crisis. Together with other international financial institutions, the World Bank Group has sharply boosted financing for developing countries to limit economic contraction and contagion—a goal that appears to have been achieved. Despite deterioration in economic and social results, developing countries have largely maintained access to markets, and many are on a path to recovery—though that upturn remains sluggish and uneven.

Both project evaluations and country and thematic reviews bring out a variable picture of outcomes across sectors and themes and across countries and regions. Recent IEG evaluations—such as those on environment; water; health, nutrition, and population; and gender—highlight trends in various dimensions of outcome that in the end tell a story of development results beyond what project performance can indicate.

> The financial crisis has had a negative effect on development results, but developing countries have maintained access to markets and are on a recovery path.

Similarly, country evaluations have presented a variable picture of developments at the aggregate country level. Recent IEG country evaluations, for example, show solid country program outcomes in the Arab Republic of Egypt, Bangladesh, and Uganda but more problematic outcomes in Ethiopia, Nepal, and Nigeria. Previous work has noted the lower share of country program outcomes rated moderately satisfactory or above (about two-thirds) than of projects (nearly four-fifths) in the recent past.

Clearly, achieving country and sector outcomes requires more than satisfactory project outcomes. Country program results are also affected heavily by exogenous factors. Among the issues are the relevance of country strategy; policy leadership and policy dialogue; complementarities among sectors and with analytic and advisory activities (AAA), policy, lending and global initiatives; and exogenous factors such as global shocks.

Portfolio outcomes

Project ratings across the Bank Group are not comparable, as they refer to distinct frameworks and methods. The World Bank uses an objectives-based system. IFC and MIGA's project rating systems are based on quantitative and qualitative benchmarks rather than on achievement of specific development objectives. The Bank and IFC use a six-point scale; MIGA uses a four-point scale. Importantly, MIGA project performance cannot be extrapolated to the portfolio level—findings apply only to the project sample and inferences cannot be drawn beyond.

So elements of the aggregate rating system differ across IEG (appendix A). Yet trends are useful to look at, and they indicate some decline in moderately satisfactory and better outcomes at the World Bank, reasonably sustained performance at IFC (but with an emerging lagged impact of the crisis on outcomes), and little change at MIGA (figure 1.6).[18]

Measured in terms of three-year moving averages, at the Bank, the share of projects rated as satisfactory—that is, moderately satisfactory or better—declined somewhat to 76 percent in fiscal 2009 (from 79 percent in 2008 and 80 percent in fiscal 2007 and 2006).[19] Looking at year-on-year changes, the decline is sharper, from 83 percent to 76 percent over the same period.[20]

At IFC, project performance during 2007–09 shows that 74 percent of projects by number achieved mostly successful or higher development outcomes, on a three-year rolling average basis. Year-on-year figures suggest stable development outcomes relative to the previous year (75 percent in fiscal 2008, compared with 74 percent in 2009).

At MIGA, just over half (58 percent) of recently evaluated projects had satisfactory or better development outcomes, that is, were rated excellent or satisfactory. Similar development outcome performance was found in the cluster of projects evaluated in fiscal 2006.

Overall development results have declined for the World Bank, have been reasonably sustained for IFC, and are unchanged for MIGA.

Drivers of development outcome ratings at IFC. Project outcomes for IFC are assessed in four major dimensions: business success, economic sustainability, environmental and social effects, and private sector development impacts. IFC's recent good performance has been reflected on most of these fronts: sustained financial and economic performance; upward trends in environment; social indicators, especially in financial markets projects; and stable contributions to the development of the private sector.

IFC project development outcome ratings hinge significantly on two groups of factors: first, those that are external to IFC, such as risks from changes in the business climate, the capacity of the sponsor, and the competitiveness of the product and the market in which it operates; and second, those that are internal, such as work quality at appraisal and restructuring and the quality of supervision. These factors are discussed in greater detail in appendix F.

IFC separately tracks investment outcome, which measures IFC's own financial performance. Eighty percent of projects (by number) achieved or exceeded performance criteria. When analyzed by commitment amount, the investment out-

FIGURE 1.6 Performance Ratings across the World Bank, IFC, and MIGA

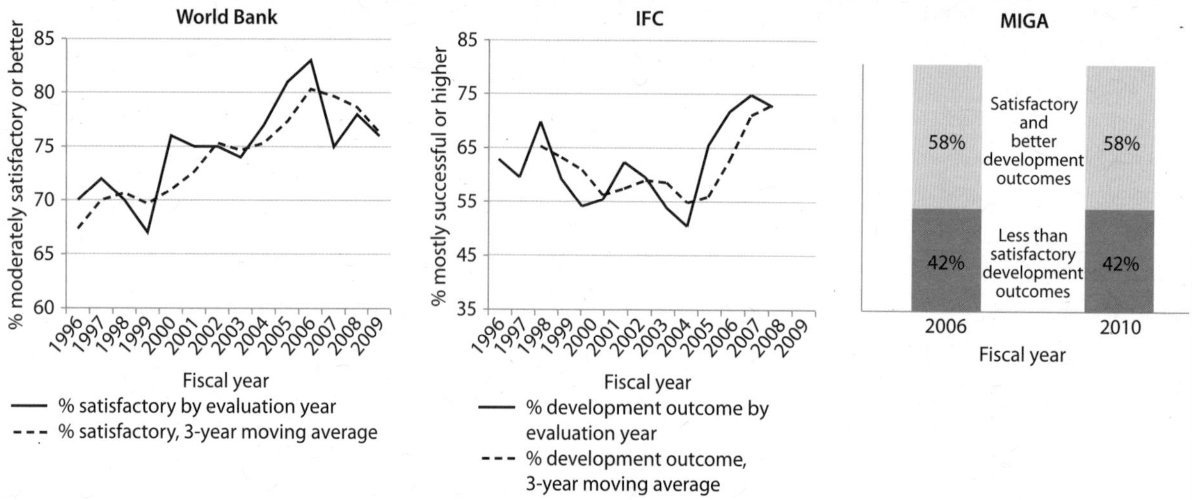

Sources: World Bank internal database, IFC Expanded Project Supervision Report ratings database, and IEG-MIGA.
Note: MIGA ratings refer to evaluated projects only, not to MIGA's entire guarantee portfolio performance.

come at IFC appears stable on a three-year rolling average and shows a slight year-on-year decline (declining just from 88 percent to 87 percent and from 91 percent to 86 percent, respectively). Disaggregating loan and equity investment outcomes, it is clear that any downward pressure is a result of the decline in equity performance. Year-on-year, equity investment outcomes declined from a high of 57 percent in 2007 to 50 percent for 2009 (see figure 1.7). This likely reflects the effects of the financial crisis on the equity markets.

> IFC's investment outcomes ratings have remained largely stable, but there has been some decline in equity performance.

It is unlikely that IFC's high positive investment outcome ratings will be sustained once the effects of the global financial crisis are fully realized. In addition to the effect of business climate deterioration, projects under implementation—most affected by the crisis—will enter the evaluation sample as they reach maturity over the next two to three years.

Projects at IFC with good investment outcome ratings tend to be associated with good development outcome ratings. Over 2007–09, two-thirds of IFC projects with high development outcome ratings also had high investment outcome ratings; at the same time, 13 percent of projects (8 percent by volume) achieved low investment outcomes and low development outcomes (figure 1.8).

Dimensions of development outcome at MIGA. At MIGA, just over half (58 percent) of recently evaluated projects had satisfactory or better development outcomes.

Looking at the four dimensions that make up the development outcome synthesis rating, MIGA projects performed best with regard to their contribution to private sector development—83 percent of recently evaluated projects were rated satisfactory or better on contribution to private sector development. A large proportion of recently evaluated projects (67 percent) also performed well in terms of their economic sustainability. Performance was not as good on business performance, where only 58 percent of recently evaluated projects were rated satisfactory or better. In contrast, performance on environmental and social effects was generally weak: only a third of recently evaluated projects performed well—that is, were rated satisfactory or better. Similar patterns were found in the earlier fiscal 2006 cluster of evaluated projects.

> MIGA projects performed best with regard to their contribution to private sector development.

Projects with better development outcome ratings had several things in common. Of the 17 recently evaluated projects that were rated satisfactory or better on development outcome, a striking 94 percent also had strong business performance; that is, they did well financially. This highlights the importance

FIGURE 1.7 IFC Investment Outcomes

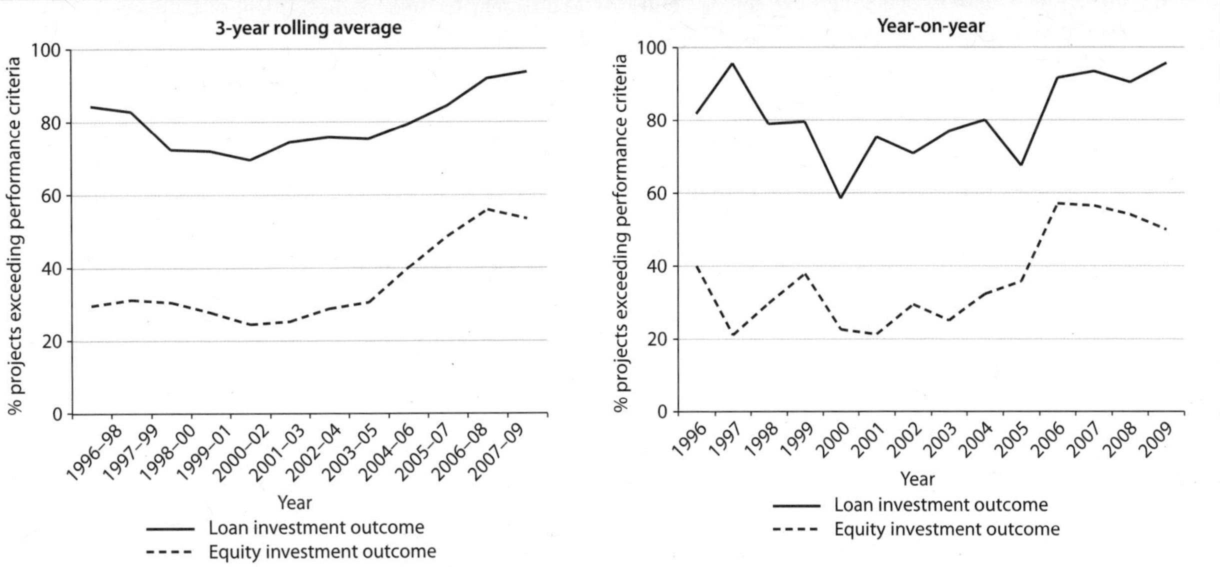

Source: IEG-IFC.

Note: Three-year moving averages.

FIGURE 1.8 Development Outcomes and IFC Investment Outcomes Correlated (2007–09)

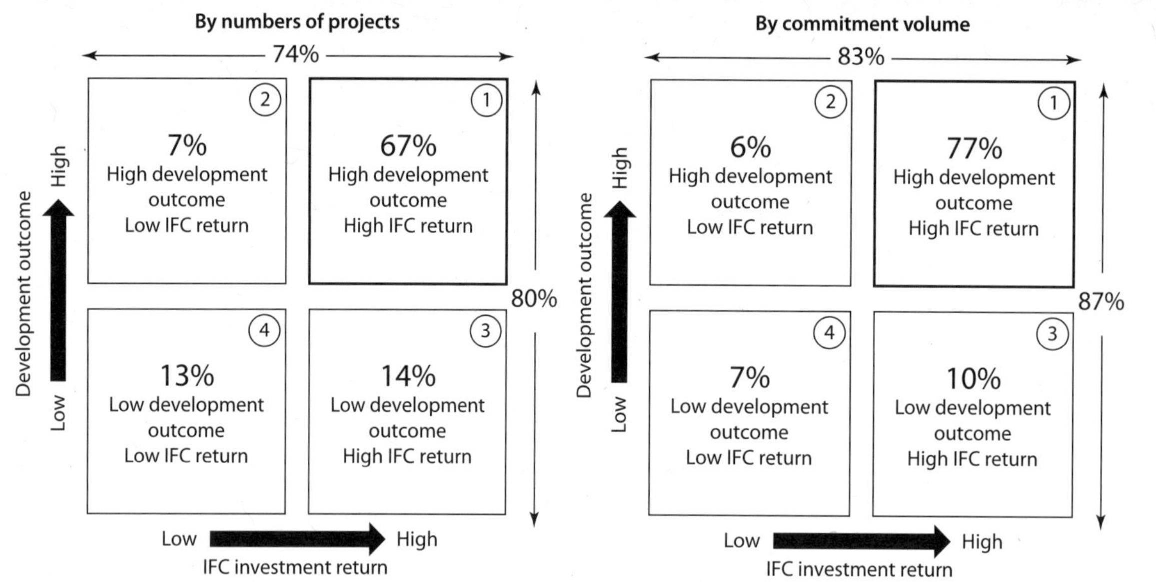

Source: IEG, based on 2007–09 Expanded Project Supervision Report evaluations.
Note: Volume refers to IFC investment size.

of good financial performance—a project cannot be a commercial failure and have a satisfactory development outcome rating.

Better development outcome ratings were also linked with experienced investors and MIGA repeat clients. Almost all projects with higher ratings on development outcomes had sponsors or project management with previous experience operating in the host country or another developing country—for example, an investor who tested the new products in the local context before expanding the product lines or an investor who structured part of the concession revenue to flow offshore to protect it from government rent seeking. Seventy percent of projects sponsored by repeat clients had better development outcome ratings.[21]

Projects with better-rated development outcome ratings tended to have sound business models.

Projects with better development outcome ratings (82 percent) tended to have sound business models, such as in-depth knowledge of customers, solid marketing plans, use of appropriate technology for the country, and not being highly leveraged. Such projects tended to cope better with riskier business environments and other exogenous factors such as sector adjustments, market restructuring, and/or macroeconomic shocks.

MIGA's quality of underwriting was less than satisfactory in more than half of recently evaluated projects; that is, 58 percent were rated partly unsatisfactory or unsatisfactory. A similar pattern was found in an earlier fiscal 2006 set of evaluated projects.

MIGA's quality of underwriting has been good in the area of country and political risk assessment. IEG found that in most of the evaluated projects, assessment of country risk had been thorough, and many of the identified risks have been borne out by subsequent events. MIGA's analysis of project-level risk mitigants has also generally been good.

MIGA's quality of underwriting was less than satisfactory in more than half of recently evaluated projects.

Poor development outcome and poor quality of underwriting went hand in hand. Projects with low rated development outcomes were likely to also have quality of underwriting rated less than satisfactory. Of the 16 recently evaluated projects with low development outcome ratings, 88 percent also had poor quality of underwriting ratings.

Evaluating the outcomes of lending operations at the World Bank. The World Bank does not have a specific set of benchmarks on which the overall development outcome rating is based. Outcomes are compared to project objectives. A review of the percentage of satisfactory projects in the most recent exit year, fiscal 2009, suggests a possible decline in project performance for the last year, with 76 percent of projects rated as moderately satisfactory or above, compared with 78 percent in 2008.[22] There is also a decline in terms of average project ratings per year, on the IEG 6-point scale, from 4.2 to an average score of 4.0—a level last achieved in 2003.[23] A three-year moving average displays the same result (figure 1.9).

> World Bank project performance suggests a decline in the past year, though it may be due to normal fluctuations.

Regression analysis suggests that the recent performance is not due to compositional shifts of the portfolio (which have been broadly positive) but rather to a declining overall trend, compared with the previous decade, within individual sectors.[24] Current performance has fallen relative to long-term trends in most sectors, particularly health, nutrition, and population; education; social protection; and transport, which in 2008 had the highest average trend performances. Economic policy and financial and private sector development performed somewhat better in 2009 than expected compared with long-term trends (table B.1 in appendix B). Project rating declines are reflected in both DPLs and investment lending (figure 1.10).

> The decline in performance is evident in both investment and policy-based lending.

IEG's evaluative framework includes a parameter that assesses the contribution of the Bank versus its borrowers to project performance (figure 1.11). Results suggest that for projects with ratings of moderately satisfactory or better, Bank and borrower performance closely mirror each other. For projects with ratings of less than satisfactory, Bank performance tends to be rated slightly above borrower performance. Some examples of satisfactory and unsatisfactory performance are described in box 1.3.

> Ratings on Bank and borrower performance indicate that when Bank performance is less than satisfactory, borrower performance is also typically low.

FIGURE 1.9 World Bank Project Performance (1993–2009)

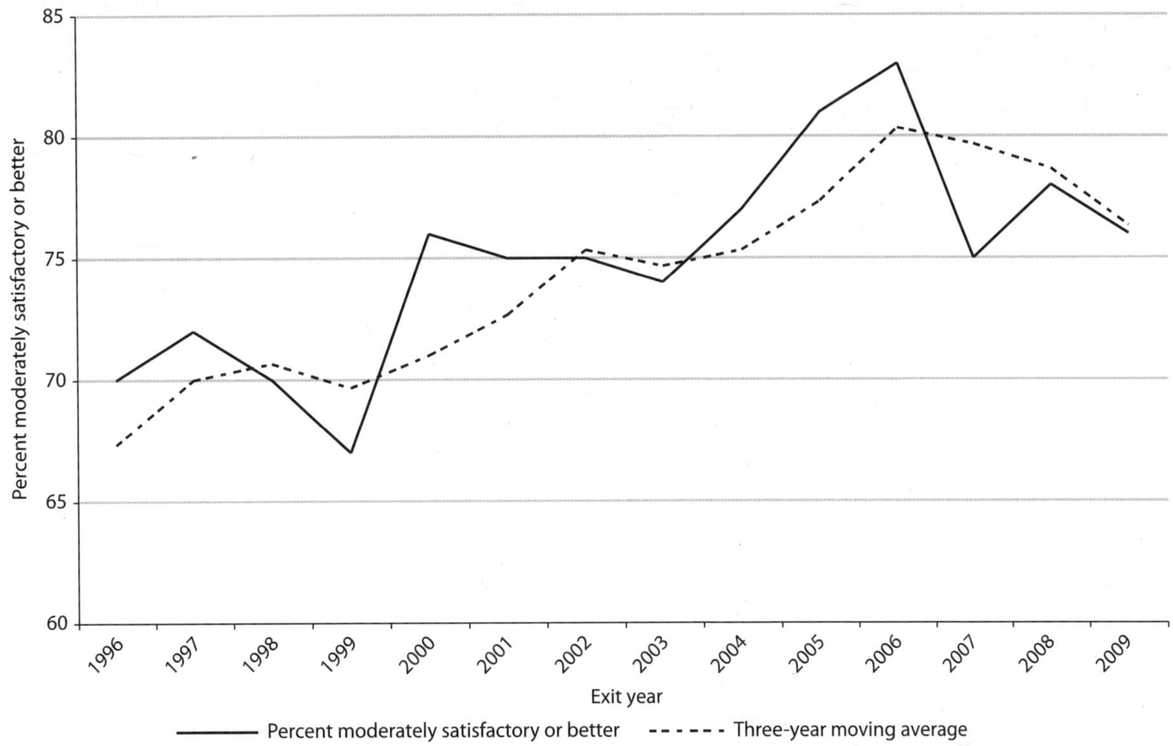

Source: World Bank internal database.

Note: Three-year moving average.

FIGURE 1.10 World Bank DPLs and Investment Lending Outcomes (Fiscal 1993–2009)

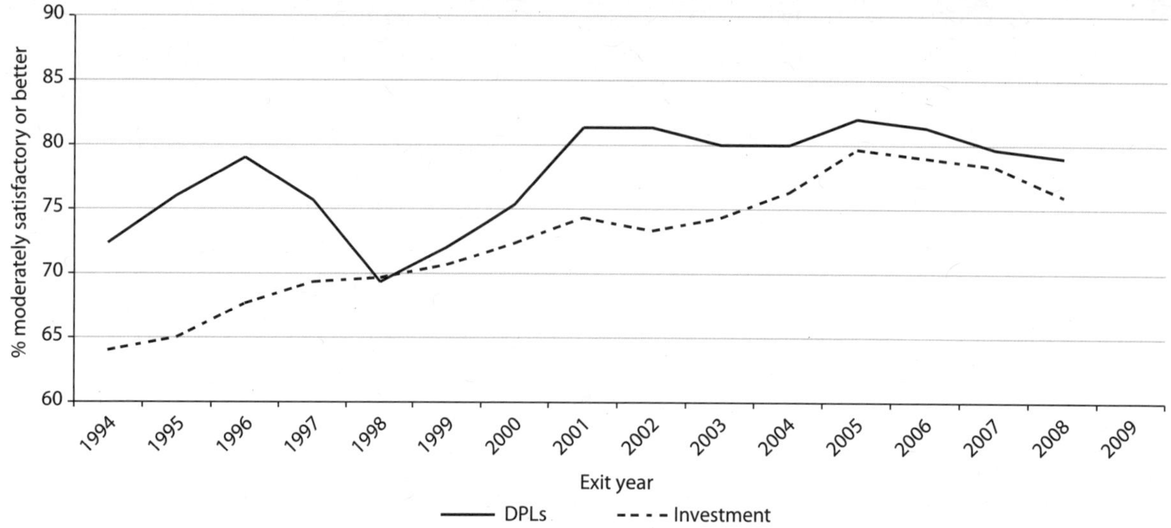

Source: World Bank internal database.

Note: DPL = Development Policy Loan.

FIGURE 1.11 World Bank versus Borrower Performance (1990–2009)

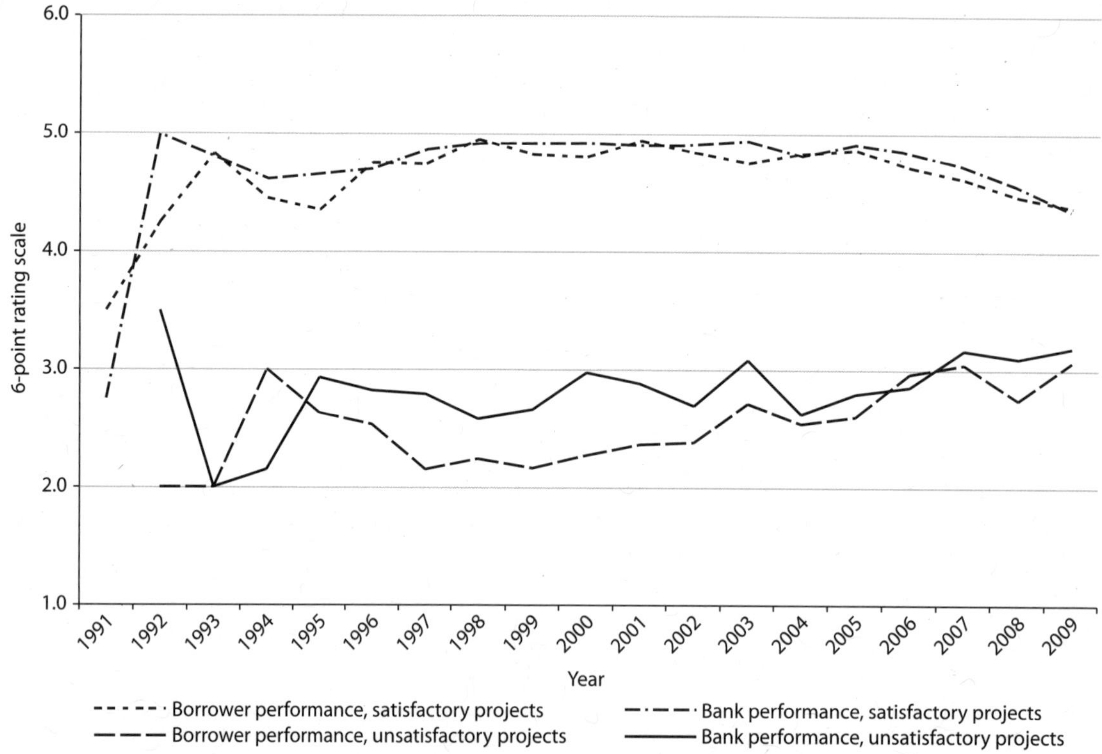

Source: World Bank internal database.

Note: Satisfactory refers to moderately satisfactory or better ratings; unsatisfactory refers to moderately unsatisfactory or poorer ratings.

BOX 1.3 Satisfactory and Unsatisfactory Projects

The Private Irrigation Pilot Project in **Niger,** funded by the Bank for $38 million, closed in fiscal 2009 with a **highly satisfactory** rating. The project sought to increase the production and profitability of high-value, irrigated crops by private, smallholder farmers with simple, low-cost technologies.

The evaluation found the project's objectives and design to be highly relevant to both the borrower and the Bank's strategies, making good use of the lessons from the previous phase of the project. Moreover, the project substantially exceeded its targets: crop yields for four main crops increased by 57 percent to 85 percent over baseline over a period of seven years, and profitability increased by 200–2,000 percent in constant terms (far beyond the appraisal target of 35 percent). The scale of the project was also substantial, increasing the irrigated area in Niger by 7 percent and consolidating some 14 percent of the existing area. Finally, the monitoring and evaluation (M&E) framework was well designed, remarkably well implemented (especially given the general data problems in Niger)—including good use of baseline data, well-chosen indicators, and well-designed surveys—and M&E information was used for effective supervision by the task teams.

A **satisfactory** loan to **China's Tri-Provincial Highway Project,** which closed in 2008, was completed on schedule and under budget and exceeded its goals of increasing the efficiency and safety of traffic. It facilitated improved access to poor counties and improved highway sector institutional capacity. Environmental and other safeguard policies were implemented beyond mere compliance, and design and implementation of monitoring and evaluation were strong.

Challenges in the project concept, identification, and preparation were compensated for by exceptionally good Bank supervision. There was also effective cooperation between the borrower and the Bank throughout and strong local government support. Land acquisition and resettlement issues were addressed and carried out satisfactorily and without delay.

The Bank provided $35 million for **Lithuania**'s Klaipeda Port project, which closed in fiscal 2009 with a **moderately satisfactory** rating. The project's main aim was to strengthen the competitiveness of the port and improve environmental conditions. The project was extended twice because of delays relating to the construction of the disposal facility caused by changing site selections, related property rights, approval needs from several government agencies, and delayed technical decisions.

However, project objectives were largely met: the port can now receive and serve bigger ships, thus achieving economies of scale with increased traffic and volume; conditions are safer; and the number of days of port closure has been reduced to zero. Environmental conditions have also improved modestly since the waste monitoring and reception facilities were improved, but disposal facilities for contaminated material have not yet been built.

In contrast, in **Brazil,** the Bank signed a $30 million loan for a Rural Poverty Reduction Project in the state of Maranhao in an effort to raise its Human Development Index from 0.647 to 0.700. The project, which closed in 2009, was rated **unsatisfactory.** Its implementation was delayed for nearly two years, and federal support was undermined because of state-level political tension and the slow processing of subprojects by the implementation agency, which failed to sufficiently train community members in the project's range of operating procedures.

Although the project was considered relevant to the needs of the state, it failed to consider in its design the lessons of similar projects and underestimated institutional capacity prerequisites. In the end, there was little progress with institutional strengthening, evidence of Human Development Index improvements was lacking, and the state government's commitment to the results-based management and performance components was "uneven." There was no impact evaluation or baseline or follow-up surveys conducted as planned. The project closed without any extension (partly because of a declaration of misprocurement) in late 2008 with $10.8 million still undisbursed.

Sources: IEG Project Performance Assessment Reports on the Kazan Municipal Development Loan and the Forest Concession Management and Control Project.

Financial sector projects. Given the increased share of financial sector projects in current Bank Group lending, how have financial sector projects performed in terms of project performance? World Bank and IFC development outcomes for the financial sector wavered over much of the decade, between 61 percent and 82 percent satisfactory at each institution.

Prior IEG findings have pointed to risks associated with the Bank's financial intermediary loans. Preliminary findings suggest that World Bank project performance in the financial sector improved somewhat for projects exiting in fiscal year 2009, although IFC findings based on its Expanded Project Supervision Report sample suggest some decline. From 2008 to 2009, development outcome ratings of IFC financial market projects declined from 74 to 69 percent and from 75 to 72 percent on a year-on-year and three-year moving average basis, respectively. Financial sector outcomes at the World Bank have been more stable, with a year-on-year increase over the same period, from 77 to 80 percent satisfactory, and a modest change on a three-year moving average basis, from 73 to 72 percent.

The modest increase in ratings of Bank financial sector projects as compared with the modest decline for IFC should be interpreted in the context of the evaluation approaches of the two institutions. IFC evaluates projects when they reach operating maturity, taking into account their resilience to market shocks. Especially in Europe and Central Asia, clients that relied heavily on access to capital markets may have suffered a declining borrowing capacity in recent years, which could adversely affect their performance ratings. Ratings of World Bank projects, which are evaluated after completion, would still be largely unaffected by the crisis.

The limited number of MIGA financial sector guarantees evaluated to date prevents conclusions at this stage; however, based on a purposive sample of guarantees in this sector, an evaluation of MIGA's financial sector guarantees is planned for next year.

Infrastructure and the environment

Infrastructure lending, although slow disbursing, saw a large increase in the follow-up to the financial crisis—55 percent on an annualized basis in fiscal 2009–10, compared with the precrisis period.[25] Overall performance of infrastructure-related sectors remains high at the World Bank, based on projects that have exited the portfolio. The performance of recent projects will be known later. Although IEG estimates show that the transport sector performed somewhat below trend expectations in 2009, it performed better than other sectors (box 1.4 and appendix B). Looking at two subperiods within the last 10 years (fiscal 2000–04 and 2005–09), there has been no significant change in the urban and water sectors from the first period to the second. The energy and mining sector improved its performance.

Recent evaluations indicate that infrastructure has performed better than other sectors in the World Bank.

Infrastructure has been consistently among IFC's best performing sectors in terms of development outcome ratings.[26] Thus the decline in the volume of infrastructure activities is some cause for concern. IFC's investment in the

BOX 1.4 Evaluating the Performance of World Bank Water-Related Projects

Over the decade 1997–2007, the Bank approved or completed 1,864 projects and grants that included a water-related activity. Water projects thus represented 31 percent of all Bank projects approved and 28 percent of Bank funding commitments.

Of the 857 completed projects, 77 percent had an aggregate IEG outcome rating of moderately satisfactory or higher when measured against stated objectives; that is just above the Bank-wide average of 75 percent for this period. Performance for almost all types of water projects improved during the second half of the period. Performance in water projects in Africa improved by 23 percentage points.

The 2003 Water Resources Sector Strategy developed a series of strategic objectives. A recent IEG evaluation (IEG 2010c) found evidence that achievements have been made under each of those objectives. For example, more attention is being given to wetlands, and the Bank has been more cautious about financing irrigation projects that rely on failing underground aquifers. Its approach to dams has become more balanced and more environmentally and socially sensitive, as has its commitment to "new" hydropower. First steps with watershed management and water resources management are in the right direction. It will be important for the Bank to strengthen attention to groundwater conservation, environmental restoration, coastal zone management, and sanitation and to make demand management a central theme of its water assistance.

Source: IEG 2010c.

FIGURE 1.12 IFC Environmental and Social Results

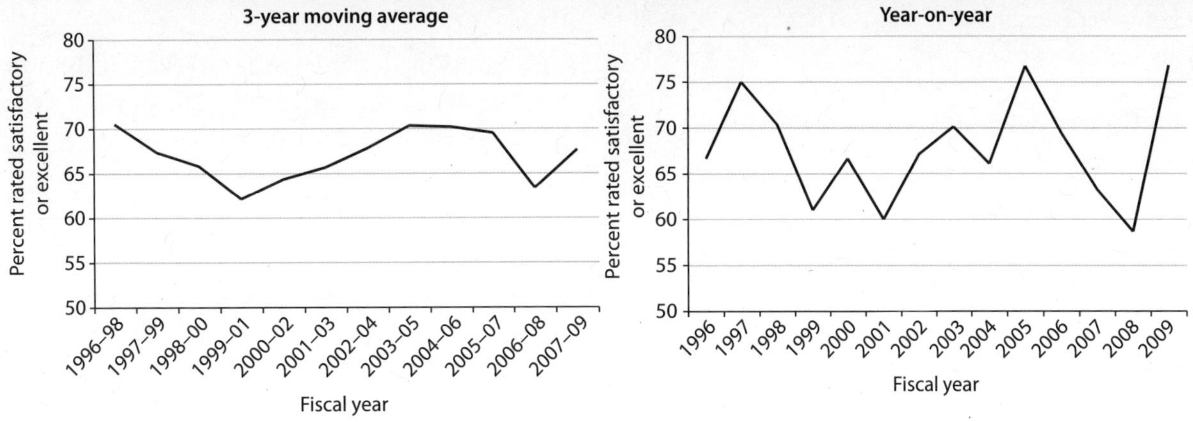

Source: IEG-IFC.

Note: Reflects ratings of satisfactory or excellent on a four-point scale.

> Infrastructure is the best performing sector in IFC.

infrastructure sector declined by almost 40 percent in fiscal 2009 and by another 20 percent in the first two quarters of 2010. Since 2005, IFC's net commitments in infrastructure have more than tripled, to around $2,500 million in 2008, but they dropped by a third in 2009. As a percentage of total net commitments, the infrastructure sector accounts for 18 percent in 2009, compared with its peak of 27 percent in 2000.

Environmental and social (E&S) effects at IFC are reflected in development outcome indicators. Despite pressure on clients from the effects of the crisis, this indicator has improved, reversing a three-year downward trend, albeit from a low level (figure 1.12). IFC increased the number of E&S specialists in the Environmental & Social Development Department from one to five between 2005 and 2009 to supervise and build capacity of financial institution sector clients. When the E&S effects ratings at the real sector remained at about the same 65–75 percent level, improvement in the financial institution sector had enhanced overall E&S ratings (see box 1.5 for some

BOX 1.5 IFC Environmental and Social Performance Case Studies: Client Commitment Is Key to Success

Favorable E & S Effects

In 2003, IFC invested in a small- and medium-sized enterprise fund in Eastern Europe. The fund had developed an adequate social and environmental management system with procedures for E&S appraisal, screening, and due diligence and had hired an experienced consultant to conduct E&S audits. Only after the fund concluded that a prospective client was in compliance would it prepare an investment agreement that included E&S covenants.

IEG found that the project complied with all IFC requirements. Overall, environmental policy implementation was excellent. IEG field visits to two subprojects found them in compliance with local environmental, health, and safety regulations and IFC guidelines.

Unfavorable E&S Effects

In 2004, IFC financed a process industry company in South Asia so that the efficiency, cost competitiveness, and environmental performance of the company's two mills could be improved. The project focused on replacement of the old mill's highly polluting production processes.

After conducting a field review, IFC's Environmental and Social Development Department found that the old mill's pollution control and health and safety management were weak and that the mill dumped toxic effluents into a lagoon that IFC required to be reclaimed. IFC provided a grant for the client to commission a detailed cleaner production and energy audit. However, the client did not implement any of the recommendations until IFC pressured it to do so. A change in the company's senior management early in the project contributed to the noncompliance issues.

Sources: IEG and IFC Environment and Social Development Department.

successful and unsuccessful examples). As IFC's investment activities become more concentrated in finance, ensuring and verifying the compliance of sub-borrowers will increasingly become important.

> Despite the effects of the crisis, IFC E&S effects have improved.

IDA countries, Africa, and other priority areas

Both the Bank and IFC have had an increase in the share of lending to IDA countries overall, and to Africa in particular. Results in the Sub-Saharan Africa Region have consistently been the poorest of all regions in the Bank Group over the past decade, partly reflecting acute challenges of capacity and fragile political situations.[27] Although development outcomes ratings on IFC projects in Africa have improved to 58 percent rated moderately satisfactory or higher, from a low of 40 percent over the decade, they still remain lower than in all other regions (figure 1.13).

> Outcomes in the Sub-Saharan Africa Region have been consistently low in both the Bank and IFC.

In addition, relative outcomes of projects in fragile states at the World Bank have deteriorated. The difference in Bank outcome ratings in fragile states compared with overall Bank ratings has widened, from being almost the same in 2006 (80 percent, compared with 83 percent for all Bank projects closing that year) to being well below the overall average in 2008 and 2009 (73 percent, compared with 78 percent Bank-wide in 2008, and 57 percent compared with 76 percent in 2009).

FIGURE 1.13 IFC Development Outcome Ratings

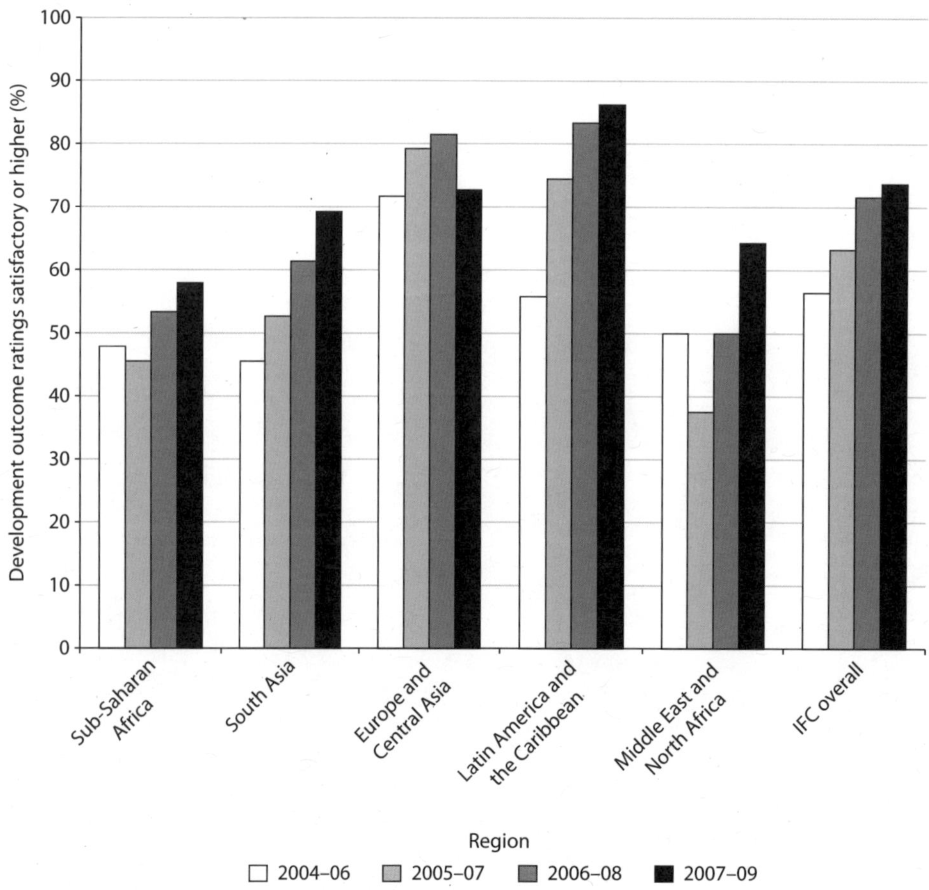

Source: IEG-IFC project evaluation database.

MIGA priority areas

The number of projects supported in MIGA's priority areas remained substantial. These comprise projects in IDA countries, especially Africa, conflict-affected environments, complex infrastructure projects, and South-South investments.[28] About three-quarters (77 percent) of the projects supported by MIGA fell into at least one of these four priority areas in fiscal 2005–09, the same proportion as during the fiscal 2002–04 prestrategy period (74 percent).

However, as a share of MIGA's overall guarantee volume, projects in priority areas have declined in recent years. The share of guarantees issued that fell into at least one priority area averaged 51 percent over fiscal 2005–09. The decline in share started in fiscal 2007 and dropped to 16 percent in fiscal 2009, largely as a result of a growing volume of financial sector guarantees.

> The number of projects in MIGA priority areas remained substantial, but more than half of those rated performed poorly.

In terms of development outcome ratings, many evaluated projects in MIGA priority areas (56 percent) performed poorly, that is, were rated partly unsatisfactory or unsatisfactory on development outcome. Within the four priority areas, MIGA projects in IDA countries had the same poor performance on development outcome (58 percent were less than satisfactory).[29] This stands in sharp contrast to the better development outcome ratings of projects outside MIGA's priority areas, only a quarter of which (25 percent) were rated partly unsatisfactory or unsatisfactory.

PRSCs and support for gender at the World Bank

IEG has focused attention in the past year on evaluating Bank performance and results in the important areas of poverty and gender. One of the Bank's key tools in supporting IDA countries over the past decade has been the Poverty Reduction Support Credit (PRSC). PRSCs were introduced in 2001 amid global changes in aid architecture calling for greater country ownership, predictability of resource flows, government commitment to reform, and a focus on poverty reduction. They provided broad-based programmatic budget support to IDA countries to underpin their poverty reduction strategies and to accelerate pro-poor growth.

A recent IEG evaluation of PRSCs (IEG 2010b) found that, in terms of process, PRSCs were largely successful in meeting their objectives and served as a prototype for later DPLs—providing greater country ownership, eased conditionality, more predictable resource flows, and greater emphasis on public sector management and pro-poor service delivery. PRSCs also improved the dialogue between sectors and central ministries, raising the accountability of sector ministries and complementing sector lending in budget or cross-cutting issues. In some countries, PRSCs also improved donor harmonization by serving as a donor focal point.

> PRSCs were found successful in meeting their objectives and serving as a prototype for later development policy lending.

In terms of development outcomes, however, results of PRSCs were more mixed. Despite an increase in resources to poverty reduction and service delivery, many PRSC objectives in health, education, and water supply and sanitation lacked a pro-poor focus. Furthermore, although PRSC countries achieved substantial progress in terms of poverty reduction, attribution of these results to the PRSC instrument is difficult to establish. Much of this progress occurred before the introduction of the PRSC, and other well-performing IDA countries saw similar improvements.

> The development outcome ratings of PRSCs have been mixed.

Looking beyond income poverty, IEG's most recent evaluation of gender finds that gender integration is essential for support to gender equality (IEG 2010a). IEG's evaluation of Bank support for gender and development, covering fiscal 2002–08, finds that the Bank made notable progress in gender integration compared with fiscal 1990–99, though with some loss of momentum in the latter part of the review period (box 1.6).

Although there is scope for improvement, gender integration into the design and implementation of Bank support increased in quantity and in scope. The evaluation finds that good gender analysis, effective consultation with men and women in project design and implementation, integrating gender activities where necessary, and monitoring progress in a gender-aware manner help enhance development effectiveness and lead to benefits for both men and women.

Gender integration into the design and implementation of Bank support increased in quality and scope, but there is room for improvement.

BOX 1.6 Attention to Gender Issues Enhances Development Effectiveness

An assessment of Peru's Rural Roads Project demonstrated how engagement of women as decision makers led to the construction of footpaths, because footpaths are the easiest and safest way for women to take their animals to pasture and to collect firewood and water. At the same time, the Implementation Completion and Results Report for a gender-blind water project in Kyrgyzstan concluded that the lack of women's participation resulted in decreased development effectiveness.

In Ghana, participation of women in a community water and sanitation project succeeded because of strategic gender-aware decision making at the local level and effective gender-aware capacity building of both men and women for operation and maintenance. In the Philippines, the issuance of a Department Administrative Order removing a long-standing gender bias in land titling facilitated registration of land in women's names.

A program of conditional cash transfers in Turkey provided opportunities to empower women through engagement with institutions such as banks. In the Republic of Yemen, microfinance was provided to women, even if the first loan met the needs of male family members. With this start, men became more comfortable with women borrowing money for their own income-generating purposes. In more conservative regions, however, sociocultural biases against schooling for girls can be more powerful than cash incentives, and complementary approaches are needed to overcome these constraints.

Source: IEG 2010a.

Trends and results in advisory services

At IFC, although expenditures on advisory services trended upward over the decade, the yearly volume of new approvals declined in fiscal 2009 to less than half the 2007 level of $250 million (figure 1.14) across all regions (except Europe and Central Asia) and all business lines (except Corporate Advice). However, approvals through the first half of 2010 suggest that advisory services volumes will likely recover and exceed those of 2009.

IFC's sustained approvals of advisory services to Europe and Central Asia have been the main growth area over the past year. They suggest countercyclical provision of corporate advice during the crisis.

Advisory services is a growing business line for IFC, especially in Europe and Central Asia.

In contrast, at the Bank, technical assistance to that region declined from $17 million in fiscal 2008 to $10 million the following year. In crisis-affected countries such as Hungary, Latvia, and Ukraine, nonlending technical assistance (NLTA) outlays declined to a fraction of former levels. And aggregate outlays on AAA—comprising economic and sector work (ESW) and NLTA, which had risen to $37 million in fiscal 2007—declined to $25 million in fiscal 2009.

FIGURE 1.14 World Bank and IFC: Expenditures on Advisory Services, Fiscal 2000–09

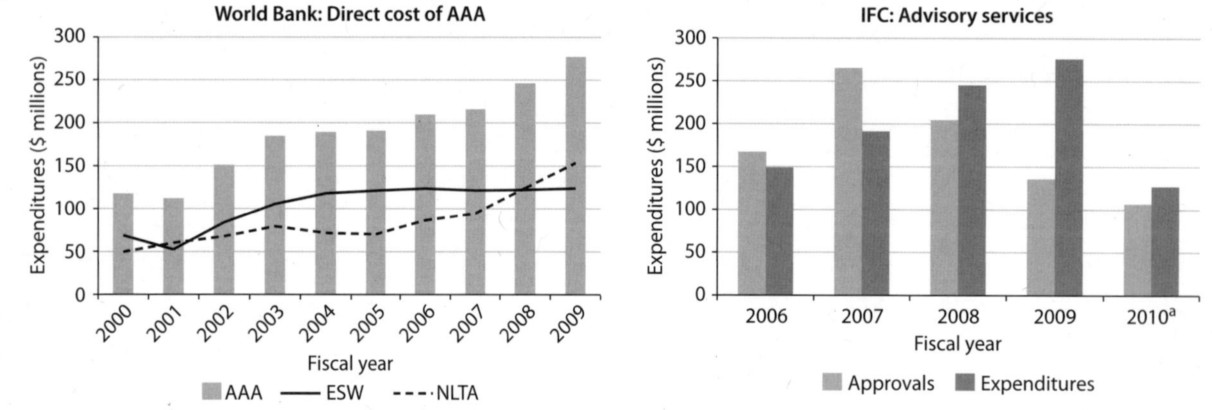

Sources: World Bank internal database and IFC Donor-Funded Operations quarterly advisory services financial reports.

Note: AAA = analytic and advisory activities; ESW = economic and sector work; NLTA = nonlending technical assistance.

a. First two quarters.

The pricing of IFC advisory services and linkages between advisory and investment services remain priority areas for establishing sustainability and maximizing development impact.

AAA accounts for a third of the Bank's outlays on country services and has been increasing.

At the Bank, AAA accounts for a third of the Bank's outlays on country services, exceeding outlays on lending or supervision.[30] Over the past decade, Bank outlays on AAA as a part of total country services increased in dollar terms, from some $118 million in fiscal 2000 to $277 million in fiscal 2009.

There was a parallel increase in the share of AAA in country services, most notably in NLTA, which rose from 8 percent in fiscal 2000 to 17 percent in fiscal 2009 (compared with 11–14 percent for ESW over this period). Most of the increase in ESW outlays occurred in the first half of the decade, whereas NLTA rose rapidly later in the decade (from $86 million in fiscal 2006 to $153 million in fiscal 2009).[31]

ESW increased from some 370 deliveries per year at the beginning of the decade to more than 730 in 2004; ESW numbers later declined to around 430 per year in 2009. In contrast, NLTA numbers show an increase from around 130 deliveries in 2000 to 545 in 2009.

Knowledge products under AAA differ, with ESW typically focusing on analysis of policy issues and NLTA providing more hands-on guidance to clients. Core ESW report types show marked declines since 2005–06, with the number of Country Economic Memoranda and fiduciary reports each halving in annual numbers.[32] There has been a notable decline in AAA in the Europe and Central Asia, Latin America, and East Asia Regions, including declines in many large borrowers: Brazil, India, Mexico, and Indonesia. In contrast, expenditures on AAA delivered in the Sub-Saharan Africa Region have grown steadily, increasing fourfold, from $16 million in fiscal 2000 to $62 million in fiscal 2009.

The findings and recommendations of a recent IEG evaluation of Bank ESW and NLTA (IEG 2008b) are especially relevant at this time of global crisis and difficult tradeoffs in World Bank Group budgets. The evaluation concluded that both types of products are of high value to the Bank and to its clients. One of the evaluation's recommendations was to reinvigorate the mandate for country teams to maintain a strong knowledge base in countries and sectors where the Bank is providing, or planning to provide, funds. Care must be taken to avoid the crowding out of analytic work by immediate lending needs in the face of tight budgets; this could slowly undermine the Bank's knowledge base—one of its biggest comparative advantages.

World Bank: Getting results in AAA. At present, the Bank is not able to measure the outcomes of its AAA, as it has no comprehensive framework for AAA evaluation. Bank monitoring of AAA has been rudimentary, especially in the area of cost information, and slippages in delivery times have increased over the last decade, especially in the Africa region (box 1.7).

BOX 1.7 Monitoring AAA Resources

Entry of basic information, especially on costs, is of variable quality. An IEG analysis shows that around 5.5 percent of AAA (fiscal 2000–09) has negative, zero, or implausibly low recorded delivery costs. At the other end of the distribution and after excluding all global/regional studies, there are 68 remaining country-specific AAAs costing more than $1 million. Nineteen were in Indonesia, which alone accounts for a third of AAA tasks of that size. Data on planned costs are even less reliable: more than 10 percent of AAA had negative, zero, or implausibly low planned costs, and 10 had planned costs greater than $3 million. IEG's analysis is based on data submitted by task team leaders. The Bank's Operational Policy and Core Services Unit is making efforts to prepare a cleaned-up database.

There are also wide divergences between planned and actual costs. In Africa, where average costs of AAA delivered grew most rapidly over the past decade (and at more than $260,000 on average, are now the highest Bank-wide), there is also the greatest divergence between planned ESW costs (at the time of activity initiation) and actual costs. Overruns were twice as high in fiscal 2009 as in 2005 ($64,000 versus $138,000). In contrast, average costs in Europe and Central Asia were the lowest (around $138,000 in fiscal 2009), as were differentials between planned and actual costs—around $27,000 per output.

Slippages in delivery times (planned versus actual) have also increased over the past decade Bank-wide, from an average of around two months to around seven months, especially for ESW outputs. Regionally, rates of slippage in fiscal 2009 were the highest for South Asia (10 months) and Africa (9.2 months), compared with around half that in Europe and Central Asia (5.1 months) and Latin America and the Caribbean (5.8 months).

Source: World Bank internal database.

The Bank currently does not measure the outcomes of its analytic activities.

The only instrument currently available for self-reporting on AAA outcomes is the Activity Completion Summary (ACS), which is due within six months of client delivery. However, this is mainly an administrative exercise and lacks agreed-on evaluative criteria.[33] Moreover, ACS reports are far from universally completed, and completion has been declining somewhat in recent years. AAA with a completed ACS declined after fiscal 2005, from 89 percent to 84 percent in 2008. Regionally, rates vary from as low as 70 percent in Africa and East Asia and Pacific to a high of around 95 percent in Latin America and the Caribbean and Europe and Central Asia. Recognizing some of these issues, the Africa region is piloting a system for improved AAA monitoring and has implemented new guidelines to address problems of slippages.

The Bank's Quality Assurance Group (QAG) has prepared periodic accountability assessments of country AAA, but these were discontinued in February 2008. QAG undertook a quality enhancement review of NLTA in 2010; that review found that NLTA is performing well, with 86 percent of fiscal 2009 tasks (above $30,000) rated moderately satisfactory or better. However, corroboration of IEG findings, reporting, and documentation of NLTA tasks remains inadequate, and there is no basis for evaluation.

IEG is piloting a set of evaluations of the Bank's analytic and advisory activities.

IEG is piloting a set of AAA evaluations to motivate the Bank's monitoring and self-evaluation of AAA. The pilots are based on a standardized design template that draws on the findings of past IEG work on knowledge products, including the recent evaluations on AAA and middle-income countries, as well as the well-established QAG methodology. The evaluation methodology is cast in the context of existing practices in the Bank: no self-evaluation for AAA, which precludes the process of IEG validation and the lack of a results framework for AAA—that is, no uniform expectation that AAA contains a statement of objectives with measurable indicators.

IFC: Getting results in advisory services. In 2006, IFC introduced a new monitoring and evaluation (M&E) system for advisory services, including standardized project approval, supervision, and completion reports. At completion, the advisory service team provides a self-assessment of performance in a Project Completion Report, followed by independent review and validation by IEG. The Project Completion Report and independent evaluation note are completed following project closure, in contrast to early operating maturity as with investment operations, which tend to have longer project lifecycles. These reports are completed for all advisory services projects, unless they were dropped

FIGURE 1.15 Development Effectiveness of IFC Advisory Services

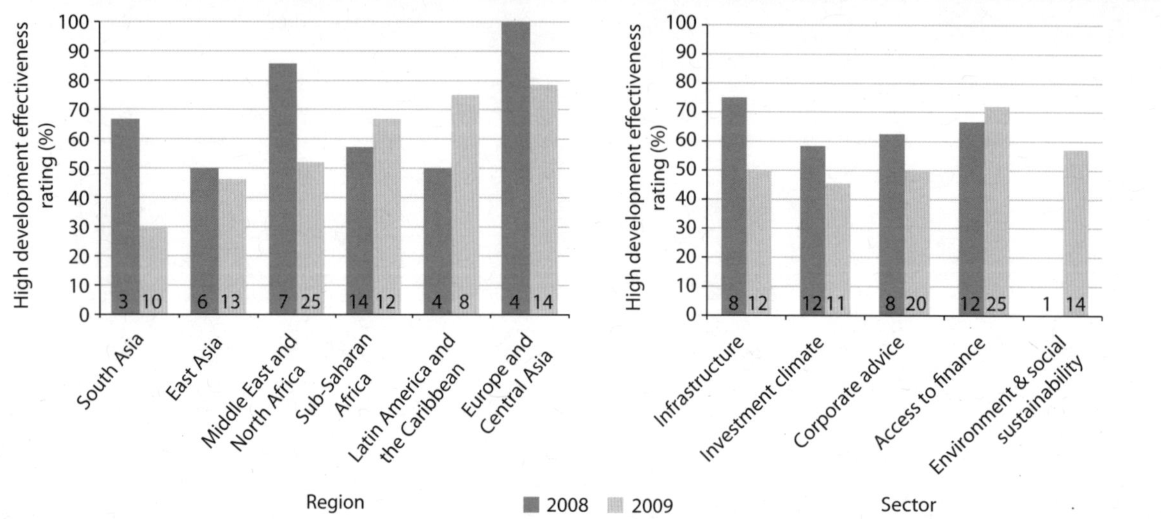

Source: IEG-IFC.
Note: High development effectiveness ratings refer to projects rated mostly successful or higher, on a six-point scale. Numbers in bars refer to numbers of projects.

or terminated (which may be a lost opportunity for learning and bias results).

IFC introduced its M&E system for advisory services in 2006.

Development effectiveness ratings of advisory services projects evaluated in fiscal 2009 declined in all regions except Sub-Saharan Africa and Latin America and the Caribbean. IEG's systematic evaluation of advisory services Project Completion Reports began in 2008, and data are now available for two years: 2008 and 2009. The Access to Finance business line alone achieved improved development effectiveness ratings (figure 1.15). The decline may be partially explained by the fact that the system is new and ratings are stabilizing. IEG's country evaluation of Nigeria found that unless advisory services directly affect a company's bottom line, clients tend not to be deeply committed. IFC's advisory service pricing policy is intended to increase the level of client commitment; it is discussed in greater detail in chapter 4.

Ratings for IFC advisory services declined in all regions except Africa and Latin America and the Caribbean in fiscal 2009.

The next chapter of the report reviews the role of IEG's recommendations in influencing institutional effectiveness. It traces the process of follow-up to IEG recommendations by the managements and Boards of the World Bank, IFC, and MIGA, comparing the processes across the three and offering insights from other institutions.

Chapter 2

Photo by Dominic Sansoni, courtesy of the World Bank Photo Library.

EVALUATION HIGHLIGHTS

- IEG makes recommendations to improve World Bank Group development effectiveness and validates the implementation of its recommendations by management.
- IEG and the managements of the Bank Group institutions agree that the existing processes for tracking implementation could benefit from reform.
- The degree of adoption of IEG recommendations increases with time, but there are outstanding issues regarding implementation and process.
- Good practices can be drawn from the different approaches and experiences within the World Bank Group and from those of relevant comparators.

Management Follow-Up to IEG Recommendations

Through evaluations, the World Bank Group generates information to account for the results of operations in which its resources were used. IEG contributes to the achievement of development results by making recommendations to improve Bank Group development effectiveness and then monitors the implementation of those recommendations, promoting accountability and generating knowledge that can be used as a source for learning and improving organizational effectiveness.

IEG recommendations are "designed to help improve the development effectiveness of the World Bank Group's programs and activities, and their responsiveness to member countries' needs and concerns."[1] IEG is also mandated to report "periodically to the Boards on actions taken by the World Bank Group in response to evaluation findings."[2] This follow-up and reporting serve an accountability function in which the Board and the general public are informed about management's actions in response to evaluation findings. It also serves a learning function by showing what has worked and what has not and by making specific recommendations to improve future performance.

This chapter analyzes IEG's follow-up to its evaluation recommendations through the tools known as the Management Action Record at the World Bank, or the Management Action Tracking Record at IFC and MIGA. It consists of an overview of the processes for follow-up across IEG-World Bank, IEG-IFC, and IEG-MIGA and incorporates international practices in other multilateral and national development agencies. IEG's recommendations over recent years are reviewed to establish the thrust of IEG's recommendations and their possible effect on the World Bank Group's development effectiveness.

> The managements of the World Bank, IFC, MIGA, and IEG agree that existing processes for tracking the response to recommendations would benefit from reform.

The managements of the World Bank, IFC, MIGA, and IEG agree that the existing process offers potential win-win reforms that would turn this into a system that contributes to the development effectiveness of the World Bank Group. The Board of Executive Directors has asked IEG to make follow-up to evaluations a stronger feature in its work program, with a view to enhancing the Board's ability to exercise its oversight function. This section therefore aims to draw from past experience and concludes by identifying areas where reforms could be made to enhance the impact and value of IEG's evaluations.

The World Bank Management Action Record and Implementation Report and the IFC and MIGA Management Action Tracking Record for 2010 constitute Volume II of this report. All three are available online at http://ieg.worldbank.org/rap2010/volume2.html.

Overview of the IEG Follow-Up Processes/Systems

The recommendations contained in IEG's evaluations are the outcome of a large amount of information and analysis, often covering decades of World Bank Group activities. This richness is a source of value to the organization, yet also a potential obstacle to effective follow-up. IEG has been tracking management's actions in response to its recommendations since the late 1990s in the case of IEG-World Bank. Because of differences across the Bank Group institutions, each IEG unit has developed different approaches to developing recommendations and tracking follow-up actions (see table 2.1 for a detailed comparison).

These differences offer a broad set of considerations that can lead to meaningful reform when combined with the experience from other development agencies. At the same time, the differences also mean it is impossible to make comparative statements about the effectiveness of the follow-up to IEG recommendations across the Bank Group. With the rising emphasis on joint evaluations, reforming the system so it is more aligned across the Bank, IFC, and MIGA—which can only be done in full collaboration with management—becomes essential.

Although far from perfect, the most detailed follow-up process to individual recommendations arguably takes place at the World Bank. With the majority of IEG recommendations coming from sector and thematic evaluations, the Bank's matrix structure means that evaluations often apply to the work of a sector board. This provides a clear home for follow-up action. At the same time, with each evaluation taking a partial view of the World Bank (or the World Bank Group's) business, it is difficult to take a composite view or prioritize the most important actions to strengthen organization performance.

In contrast, recommendations related to MIGA primarily emerge from IEG-MIGA's annual report. This virtually ensures consistency across the range of recommendations and

TABLE 2.1 Comparison of IEG Management Action Tracking Systems

Issue	IEG-World Bank	IEG-IFC	IEG-MIGA
Which reports are being tracked?	Corporate Sector Thematic	Corporate Sector Thematic Country	Corporate Sector Thematic
What is being tracked?	Implementation by Bank management	Implementation by IFC management, based on negotiated indicators	Implementation by MIGA management
How many recommendations are currently being tracked?	55 recommendations from evaluations issued 2007–10	65 recommendations in 2010	16 outstanding recommendations in 2010
What rating system is used for tracking?	***Status of adoption*** (high, substantial, medium, low) ***Status of implementation*** (active, complete, incomplete, overtaken by events, difference of opinion) ***Written assessment*** of management response	***Status of adoption*** (high, substantial, medium, low) ***Status of implementation*** (active, inactive) ***Written assessment*** of management response	***Status of adoption*** (completed, medium, low) ***Written assessment*** of management response
What is management's role?	Self-ratings Written self-assessment Coordinated by OPCS	Self-ratings Written self-assessment Coordinated by IFC strategy unit	Written self-assessment Coordinated by MIGA management
When are recommendations retired?	Retired after four years through the Implementation Report to the Board unless rated active by IEG	When "implemented," "superseded," or "no longer relevant"	"Completed" recommendations retired every year, retired when "implemented," "superseded," or "no longer relevant"
How frequently does IEG update?	Annually	Biannually	Annually
Who can access it?	***Internal:*** Final MAR report accessible as e-MAR, Implementation Report submitted to CODE ***External:*** Summary including a table of management and IEG ratings of level of adoption published in annex to annual report (ARDE until 2009)	***Internal:*** Implementation indicators, management and IEG comments accessible to management and IEG ***External:*** Recommendation, management response, level of adoption, and status in BROE (2008)	***Internal:*** MATR is annexed to IEG-MIGA annual report, includes recommendations, management comment, and IEG implementation rating; accessible on MIGAnet and E-Board ***External:*** Redacted version of MATR annexed to IEG-MIGA annual report posted on MIGAnet or E-Board

Source: IEG.

Note: As of December 2009. ARDE = ***Annual Report on Development Effectiveness;*** BROE = ***Biennial Report on Operations Evaluation;*** CODE = Committee on Development Effectiveness; MAR = Management Action Record; MATR = Management Action Tracking Record; OPCS = World Bank Operations Policy and Country Services.

close alignment with institutional effectiveness considerations. Therefore, the report tracks what is most important, relevant, and actionable for MIGA. This is reflected in a much smaller number of recommendations to track for MIGA than for the Bank and IFC.

Although the managements of the World Bank, IFC, and MIGA address each IEG recommendation as part of the management response submitted to the Board's Committee on Development Effectiveness and disclosed as part of the IEG report, determining what to track in the follow-up is often difficult.

> Management Action Records have been underutilized to date.

A useful intermediate step is part of IEG's follow-up with respect to IFC. IEG-IFC reaches an agreement at the outset on the steps that management will take. IEG-IFC and IFC negotiate indicators for implementation of recommendations, which are suggested by IFC and validated by IEG.[3] This practice can help increase the level of clarity on the follow-up at the beginning of the process.

These action records have been underutilized to date. The focus has been primarily on accountability, with limited attention to organizational learning. Management response to IEG recommendations has only been partly disclosed and has not played a prominent role at Board discussions to date, even though the Board has expressed its interest in the issue recently (IEG 2009a, p. xxv). Overall, there has not been sufficient focus from IEG, management, and the Board on IEG recommendations and management actions, and the use of follow-up information could be enhanced.

Adoption, Implementation, and Historic Analysis

This section reviews the adoption and implementation of each IEG unit's recommendations to understand the challenges of analyzing follow-up and utilization. Given the differences in the number of recommendations that have been followed up in the Management Action Records over time, and in the retirement rules (table 2.1), each analysis tries to develop its own angle on making sense of IEG's ratings and response data.

It should also be noted that the degree of confidence in the ratings is not as high as it could be. As with other evaluative work, IEG's ratings reflect the validation of self-assessments made by management. Both the quality of the self-assessment and the resources IEG uses to appropriately assess and validate actions against the recommendations need improvement.

World Bank

The management responses and IEG assessment of those responses in the Management Action Records and Implementation Reports were analyzed to (i) review the implementation of IEG evaluation recommendations and (ii) discern the effect or impact of the recommendations on Bank effectiveness. Only the Bank's corporate and sectoral evaluations are included in the Management Action Record and analyzed.[4]

A total of 155 recommendations from 43 reports were analyzed using 2003–10 Management Action Records and Implementation Reports.[5] The review included evaluations produced after 2003 to provide a longer view. That year was chosen as the cut-off point because evaluations produced after 2003 were subject to new procedures that were introduced in 2007. For reports produced after 2007, responses are available only for the number of years they were included in the Management Action Record. In addition, the follow-up to selected evaluations was reviewed to understand the reasoning underlying these ratings.[6]

> IEG analyzed 155 recommendations from 43 evaluation reports over 2003–10.

IEG evaluations covered a wide range of topics considered important to the Bank's development effectiveness. They ranged from specific Bank procedures (for example, Operational Directive 4.20 on Indigenous Peoples), to new approaches and programs (such as the Poverty Reduction Strategy Initiative), to sectors and themes, to global programs. About half the evaluations were on sectors/themes (such as transportation, trade, decentralization, natural disaster management, and the environment) and about half on programs/instruments (such as the Financial Sector Assessment Program, country financial and procurement assessments, Doing Business indicators, guarantees, and ESW). In addition, a few evaluations of country grouping (for example, middle-income countries) were done.

The majority of the recommendations focused on improving the Bank's operational performance, with the remainder focusing on strategic directions and operational learning. Approximately two-thirds of the recommendations were on improving the Bank's performance through greater client engagement, better internal coordination, or specific actions that the Bank could take (such as develop guidance, increase analytical work, and the like). About a quarter of recommendations called for the formulation of a strategy or for focusing or refocusing Bank priorities at both the institutional and country levels. Finally, just over 10 percent promoted greater operational learning, including better M&E.

The majority of recommendations were on improving the Bank's operational performance.

Some recommendations applied primarily to the relevant sector or thematic group, whereas others cut across sectors, themes, programs, and instruments. Recommendations on strategic directions and elaboration of actions to be taken focused primarily on the topic being evaluated, such as "systematically promote the removal of energy subsidies" or "increase Bank support for regional partnerships." However, recommendations to improve operational learning and M&E, increase client involvement and commitment, build client capacity, and improve groupwide or sectoral coordination cut across multiple sectors and themes and were also included in program and instrument evaluations.

Some recommendations recur and reflect institutional challenges that remain to be addressed. Such recommendations include improving internal coordination to better exploit the Bank's comparative advantage as a global, multisectoral institution, improving learning and M&E, and focusing more on results.

The overall level of adoption of outstanding recommendations declined between 2009 and 2010.

The overall level of adoption of outstanding recommendations in the 2010 Management Action Record declined from 2009. The share of recommendations rated high and substantial for adoption has been decreasing, dropping from 60 percent in the 2007 record to 36 percent in 2010 (figure 2.1).[7] Recommendations rated high for adoption dropped from 15 percent to 7 percent during this period.

In contrast, recommendations rated medium have doubled from 25 percent in 2007 to 58 percent in 2010. This reflects a similar drop in management's own assessment, which also fell from 88 percent rated high and substantial in 2007 to 54 percent in 2009. However, in 2010, management's

FIGURE 2.1 IEG-World Bank Ratings since 2007

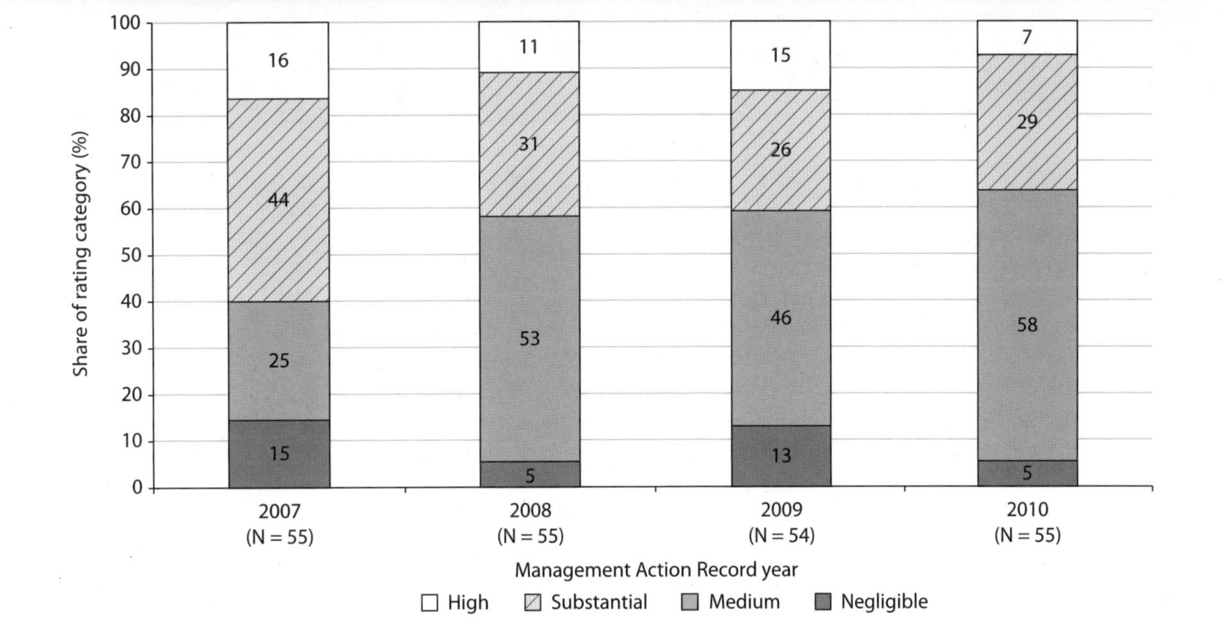

Source: IEG-World Bank Management Action Record.

FIGURE 2.2 IEG Average Level of Adoption Ratings over Time (2003–10)

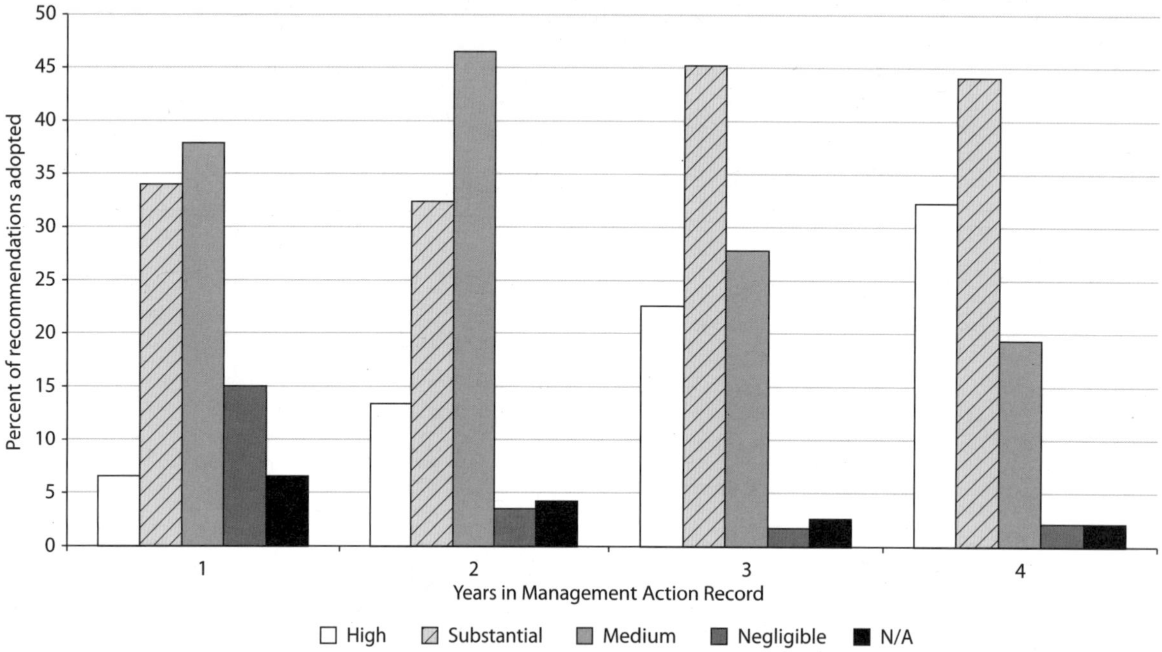

Source: IEG-World Bank Management Action Record.

own ratings increased to 73 percent based on 91 percent of first-year recommendations being rated high or substantial for adoption.[8] IEG downgraded many of these ratings because of lack of evidence of adoption.

With time, most IEG recommendations are eventually adopted. A review of the 155 recommendations over four years showed that, on average, 41 percent were rated high or substantial by IEG in the first year of implementation.[9] This improved to 76 percent in the fourth year of implementation (figure 2.2).

However, this does not necessarily imply that the issues raised in the evaluations, which led to the recommendations, were resolved. Full adoption of the recommendation may be a necessary but not sufficient condition to address those issues. In any event, only 32 percent of the recommendations were considered fully adopted in year four—put another way, 68 percent of the recommendations were not fully incorporated into policy, strategy, or operations.

The degree of adoption increases over time.

There are recognized weaknesses in the follow-up system that need to be addressed. Management generally reports on the actions it took that fell within the scope of the recommendation (usually during the past year). IEG can only validate management's self-assessment and has no independent basis for assessing the impact of the actions taken by management. Therefore, IEG bases its rating on management's response and IEG staff knowledge of developments in the area.[10]

Clarity about what constitutes adoption would improve the rating system.

Most of the recommendations rated medium or negligible for adoption by IEG reflected differences on what constituted adoption. For example, management listed actions it had taken institution-wide to strengthen capacity, but IEG was looking at actions specific to Africa, as stated in management's original response to the evaluation of capacity building in Africa.

An estimate of the effects of the proposed follow-up actions would also strengthen the usefulness of the Management Action Record.

In addition to clarity on adoption, an assessment of the effects of follow-up actions will eventually be needed to determine their contribution to overall development effectiveness. Management does not report on the effects of the actions taken, which may only materialize after a significant amount of time. Generally, identifiable follow-up focuses on

BOX 2.1 Opportunities for Assessing Effectiveness of Recommendation Follow-Up

World Bank Support for Primary Education

This IEG evaluation (IEG 2006d) recommended that the Bank invest more in improving learning outcomes, particularly among the poor and disadvantaged. In its initial response, management reported that the Education Sector Strategy Update had incorporated these findings of the evaluation and included the strategy update as part of its proposed follow-up.

But the strategy was not mentioned in subsequent management responses. Management initially reported on new projects that had incorporated learning outcome improvements in response to a recommendation to make learning outcomes a core objective. However, management discontinued the practice, making it difficult for IEG to assess the extent to which the Bank's primary education portfolio was shifting toward learning outcomes.

World Bank Support for Low-Income Countries Under Stress

The Bank was also looking into issues for low-income countries under stress and conducting its own review. Management did address the human resource constraints to working on these countries that were raised in IEG's evaluation (IEG 2007) and that were the basis for one of IEG's recommendations. It may have been possible to assess the extent to which the human resources reforms responded to recommendations if there had been some performance indicators established when the evaluation was completed (for example, changes in number of GG or GH level staff working on low-income countries under stress).

World Bank Assistance for Natural Disasters

All recommendations for this evaluation (IEG 2006e) were rated high for adoption and were completed within two years of the evaluation. A key action was Operational Procedure 8.0, Rapid Response to Crises and Emergencies. Follow-up stopped with the issuance of the Operational Procedure. The evaluation stressed the need to come up with country-level approaches to better manage disaster risk. Operational Procedure 8.0 also emphasizes the need to integrate risk reduction and crisis prevention into country strategies. It may have been useful to monitor the CASs of vulnerable countries to establish to what extent risk management was incorporated.

Source: IEG World Bank Management Action Record.

actions at the institution or network anchor level, not necessarily at the country level, where results are produced. Opportunities for assessing effectiveness do exist (see box 2.1).

IFC

IEG has tracked the implementation of recommendations in IFC since 2004. IFC's Management Action Tracking Record was established through a joint effort by IEG and IFC management to identify how best to monitor the implementation of IEG's recommendations. The tracking system employs an iterative approach and relies on two-way feedback between IEG and IFC management.

> IFC's tracking system has two stages and employs an indicator approach.

The Management Action Tracking Record was designed as a two-stage system. In the first stage, IEG and IFC agree on indicators by which to assess each recommendation's level of adoption. In the second stage, IEG and IFC independently rate implementation progress.

When the Management Action Tracking Record system was established, it was decided that recommendations from IEG reports starting January 1, 2000, would be included. At that time, 37 recommendations were active and 127 were considered to have been implemented or were no longer relevant. As of April 2010, the system contained 256 recommendations. Of those, 58 were rated active by IFC and 65 by IEG.[11] The average age of the currently active recommendations is 2.7 years.

The level of adoption of IEG recommendations has improved significantly since 2004, when 70 percent were rated high or substantial, compared with 89 percent in fiscal 2010 (figure 2.3).

> IFC's level of adoption of IEG recommendations has improved significantly since 2004.

There has been an average of eight recommendations per report in the 2000–04 period and five recommendations in the 2005–09 periods. The fall in this average may be caused by the introduction of the Management Action Tracking Record and by the difficulty of monitoring a multitude of recommendations.[12] Approximately 39 percent of IEG's 256 recommendations have come from its two flagship reports: the annual

FIGURE 2.3 Management Action Tracking Record Ratings since 2004

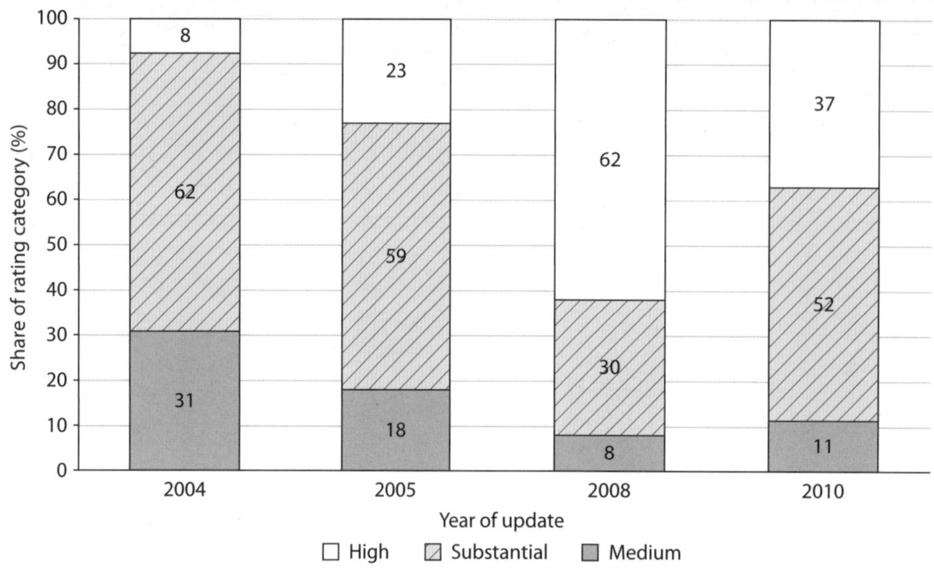

Source: IEG-IFC Management Action Tracking Record.

Independent Evaluation of IFC's Development Results[13] and the *Biennial Report on Operations Evaluation.*[14]

These two reports have accounted for 12 of 40 IEG recommendations since January 1, 2006. Most active recommendations from these process reports have been related to work quality (29 percent) and measurement and reporting (28 percent). In reports focusing on process, IEG frequently repeated recommendations to "remind" management and the Committee on Development Effectiveness of their importance. The introduction of the Management Action Tracking Record has eliminated the need to repeat recommendations. Examples of recommendations from process reports are in box 2.2.

BOX 2.2 IEG Recommendations Consistent with the Direction of IFC's Evolution

It is not possible to separate IEG's influence from the many other factors that have combined to shape IFC's evolution. However, IEG recommendations have been consistent with the direction of IFC's evolution and, in cases, have pointed to specific changes that management later adopted.

Highlights of IEG's recommendations are project and corporate scorecards in a format similar to IFC's Development and Outcome Tracking System; public accountability for development results, which has been incorporated in IFC annual reports since 2007; improved learning from evaluation findings; systematic staff training in core skills; better environmental supervision; and embedded evaluation within the operational departments and expanding to advisory services.

Source: IEG.

The Management Action Tracking Record has been generally effective in tracking the implementation progress of recommendations; and there is evidence that management ensures both the appropriateness of the indicators and the implementation of the recommendations. However, the Management Action Tracking Record is still underutilized by IFC staff and management, as well as by IEG, and improvements could be made in a number of areas (box 2.3).

> The average number of recommendations being tracked in IFC has declined.

IEG-IFC groups recommendations according to 10 themes. Small and medium enterprises, investment climate, environment and social, and advisory services are the most prevalent (33 percent). Twenty-seven percent of the recommendations deal with measurement and reporting and administration issues. Strategic recommendations account for 17 percent, and work quality and incentive-themed recommendations account for 14 percent.

Recommendations from IEG's five country evaluations have mostly focused on strategy (33 percent), whereas IEG's sector and thematic evaluations have been more likely to focus on environment and social (30 percent) and investment climate (24 percent), respectively. Compared by report category, the ratings for recommendations from country evaluations were lowest in the 2010 Management Action Tracking Record (figure 2.4).

BOX 2.3 Lessons from IEG-IFC's Management Action Tracking Record

- **Results:** The Management Action Tracking Record usually is updated in the period leading up to the completion of an IEG report. This approach, in contrast to an ongoing, scheduled update cycle, may reduce opportunities for action and for achieving better adoption levels and results.
- **Learning:** The turnaround times required in the current update process may diminish the Record's potential as a learning tool and as a management tool for achieving better results, because interactions with staff in IEG and IFC are rushed and stress reporting, with minimal time for action.
- **Focus:** Recommendations are rated only on two dimensions—status and level of adoption—and are not prioritized or flagged with respect to their urgency or importance. Therefore, even with high adoption levels, more important recommendations—or parts of recommendations—can be ignored or remain unimplemented.
- **Accessibility and utility:** The Management Action Tracking Record is a reasonably well-designed electronic platform, but it was not built to process many updates in a short time. In the latest round of updates, IEG and IFC opted to work outside the system to expedite the process, thereby limiting staff familiarity of and access to the system.
- **Usefulness:** Before this, only updated ratings from the Record were disclosed, and only once and without narrative. The disclosure of narrative updates may help increase the use of the Record as a practical development tool.
- **Best practice and methodology:** IEG has not yet developed best practice guidelines for writing recommendations. Thus, recommendations can lack specificity, be multilayered, or be overly prescriptive. Also, IEG found that IFC's failure to address parts of recommendations in its Management Response was often deemed a rejection by IFC. Absent best practice guidelines for writing recommendations and agreeing on indicators, the full potential of the Management Action Tracking Record may be unrealized.
- **Cross-institutional constraints:** Recommendations directed at the World Bank Group in evaluations of IFC work are not tracked in any Management Action Record. Such recommendations are therefore untracked and possibly unimplemented. To date, fewer than five recommendations from IEG reports on IFC work have been directed at the Bank Group.
- **Online access:** The ability of the Management Action Tracking Record to enable online queries by the Board, World Bank Group staff, and the public has not been developed, inhibiting access and transparency.
- **Outputs versus outcomes or results:** IEG and IFC have agreed to base indicators on outputs that are within the control of IFC. It is not clear if achieving the desired outputs improves the institution's development effectiveness. Such an evaluation is beyond the scope of this report.

Source: IEG.

The Management Action Tracking Record has been generally effective in tracking implementation of recommendations but is still underutilized.

MIGA

IEG-MIGA's annual flagship reports include recommendations for MIGA management, as do some IEG joint thematic reports.[15] IEG-MIGA has been tracking MIGA's implementation of these recommendations since 2003. The Management Action Tracking Record is updated annually to record new recommendations and to "retire" those that MIGA has implemented or that are deemed no longer relevant. IEG assesses the implementation status of each recommendation that remains outstanding, based on information provided by MIGA management, and records this assessment in the Management Action Tracking Record.[16]

IEG-MIGA's recommendations target what is relevant, important, and actionable by MIGA for improving its institutional performance.

IEG-MIGA's recommendations target what is relevant, important, and actionable by MIGA for improving its institutional performance. IEG-MIGA's recommendations have focused on actions that, if implemented, will make a real difference to MIGA's institutional performance (box 2.4).

FIGURE 2.4 Management Action Tracking Record Ratings for Country Evaluations in 2010

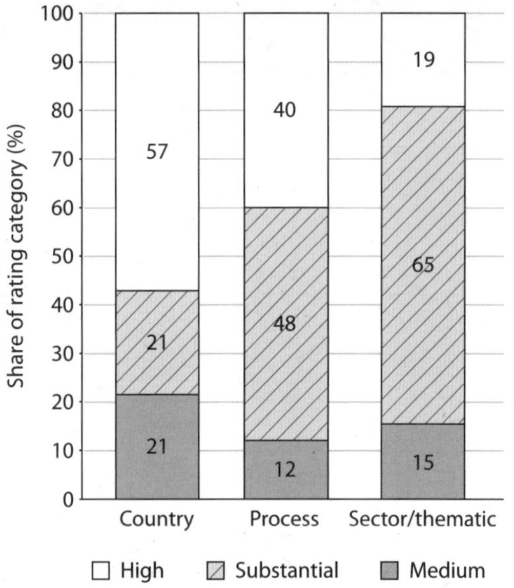

Source: IEG-IFC Management Action Tracking Record.

Each is based on a solid "results framework" that lays out intended outcomes and how IEG's recommended actions link to achieving the outcomes.[17]

Given this selectivity and the annual winnowing process, the Management Action Tracking Record tracks what is most important for improving MIGA's performance. The outstanding recommendations in the record are thus priorities for MIGA attention and early action.

> MIGA has made little progress on implementing some important recommendations.

MIGA has made less progress on recommendations that are important for development effectiveness. Recommendations that have not had effective follow-up relate to (i) business development and client responsiveness; (ii) ensuring that projects have positive development impacts and are sustainable; (iii) addressing weaknesses in MIGA's quality of underwriting, and more generally, in quality assurance, including for back-office systems; (iv) improving business processes; and (v) strengthening MIGA's ability to set a price for or cost its guarantees and business lines (box 2.5). These issues have been long-standing concerns for IEG, and are again highlighted in the Management Action Tracking Record (see Volume II—http://ieg.worldbank.org/rap2010/volume2.html) and elsewhere in this report.

Overall, MIGA's record on implementation is mixed. Of the outstanding recommendations tracked in the 2009 Management Action Tracking Record, MIGA's implementation was rated medium on a third. On the rest, MIGA's implementation was rated low.

BOX 2.4 Many IEG Recommendations Have Been Taken Up by MIGA

Many IEG recommendations have been taken up by MIGA over the years. This has led to—

- Greater alignment of MIGA guarantees with country strategies
- More MIGA resources and staff devoted to assessing projects' environment and social aspects
- Creation of MIGA's Environment and Social Unit
- Introduction of performance standards to replace environment and social safeguards
- Increased MIGA collaboration with other World Bank Group entities, including joint projects
- Amendment of MIGA's Operational Regulations and Policies
- A proposal to amend MIGA's Convention
- Transfer of MIGA's technical assistance function to the Foreign Investment Advisory Service
- Better controls over administrative costs, so that the ratio of administrative cost to net premium income is no longer rising
- Introduction of key performance indicators to track MIGA's performance
- Piloting the self-evaluation of MIGA guarantees.

Source: IEG-MIGA Management Action Tracking Records.

BOX 2.5 Key IEG Recommendations to Strengthen MIGA's Effectiveness

Several IEG reports since 2006 have addressed institutional effectiveness issues, and several recurring themes have emerged. To deliver effectively on its development mandate and strengthen its position as a full-service political risk insurance provider, able to encourage investment into the least-served parts of the market, MIGA needs to address these recurring issues more vigorously than in the past.

Improving project development outcomes has been an ongoing challenge for MIGA. IEG reports have stressed the need for MIGA to make significant progress in implementing initiatives related to assessment and monitoring, with recommendations aimed at strengthening development outcome performance. MIGA has taken some steps, but implementation has been partial with respect to IEG's recommendations that the Agency—

- Make significant progress in implementing initiatives related to development impact assessment.
- Consistently undertake development impact analysis for underwriting guarantees to ensure that the projects it supports are sound and have positive and sustainable development impact.
- Adopt practical tools to assist underwriting teams in undertaking development impact analysis (for example, clear guidelines, sector-specific checklists, templates).
- Improve the quality of development impact analysis for Small Investment Program projects and improve documentation of the analysis that underpins MIGA's support for Small Investment Program projects.

Quality of underwriting has also been flagged by IEG as an ongoing issue. Implementation has also been partial for IEG-MIGA's recommendations that MIGA—

- Strengthen its upstream quality assurance of project decision documents before they are finalized to ascertain that analysis of project impacts is consistent with MIGA guidelines and that project impacts are well documented and adequately reflected in the decision documents.
- Assess the quality of underwriting for a few recently underwritten guarantees to enhance institutional learning.
- Develop rules of engagement for projects involving concession agreements.
- Strengthen its systems and standards for underwriting and introduce a robust quality assurance system for its operations as a key element of enhancing its overall institutional effectiveness.

There are also challenges relating to MIGA's **"client friendliness"**—for example, IEG has recommended that MIGA—

- Develop its business development function and improve its client management.
- Increase efficiency of its business processes and decision making for underwriting.

Finally, IEG has recommended that MIGA capture costs associated with underwriting processing and monitoring guarantees so that it can cost its business lines.

Source: IEG-MIGA Management Action Tracking Record.

> Recommendations on projects' development impact, quality of MIGA's underwriting, and quality assurance show little progress.

Recommendations on projects' development impact, MIGA's quality of underwriting, and quality assurance show little progress, despite their importance for MIGA's effectiveness. "Aging analysis" shows an average "age" of recommendations of 2.7 years. However, recommendations relating to strengthening development outcomes of MIGA projects, quality of underwriting, and quality assurance have been in the Management Action Tracking Record for four years on average, indicating that MIGA has yet to come to grips with these core institutional effectiveness issues. In contrast, recommendations on strategy are for the most part already completed.

Recommendations on environmental and social matters also took time to implement, but most are now completed.

Recommendations on institutional effectiveness issues are also getting older and require further attention. Moreover, the majority of those recommendations had ratings of low, highlighting that learning from what works and what does not also remains an area requiring further attention by MIGA. IEG-MIGA is helping MIGA set up a self-evaluation pilot.

The Management Action Tracking Record could be improved by having a results framework for each recommendation that articulates its intended outcome and how IEG's recommended actions are linked to achieving the outcome. Such a framework would normally be spelled out in the original IEG evaluation, but it is lost in the presentation of the Management Action Tracking Record. Thus, a set of cogent and strongly motivated recommendations sometimes comes across as missing rationale. A results framework would also help clarify how much a given recommendation "matters"—what will be gained by implementing it.

Selected International Practices on Recommendation Follow-Up

A review of follow-up processes in multilateral development banks, international development organizations, and national agencies[18] and the existing literature on evaluation utilization show that a variety of approaches to recommendation follow-up exists. That review brought out the following as key elements to an effective follow-up system that balances accountability and learning.

> Four aspects of international practice on evaluation follow-up are worth noting.

- **Standards/guidelines for recommendations:** A set of characteristics and/or a checklist for good recommendation practices can help guide evaluators in finding the balance between specificity and generalization in crafting recommendations based on evaluation findings.
- **Management ownership of recommendations:** Early and continuing engagement with management, while preserving the evaluator's independence, is important to create ownership of evaluation findings and recommendations, strengthen accountability, and encourage learning.
- **Quality control during the tracking process:** Both the evaluation unit and management should ensure the quality of their ratings, assessments, and responses during the tracking process. Clear responsibilities and accountabilities are important during this process. Automated systems can greatly increase the efficiency in comparison to manual follow up.
- **Disclosure and utilization of implementation data:** Disclosure can be an important incentive for the diligence of all actors involved in the follow-up process. However, the implementation data have to be carefully analyzed, interpreted, and fed back to the oversight body, management, and the interested development community in a straightforward manner. Establishing a link between the analysis of previous actions by management in response to evaluation recommendations and future decisions can be a helpful step in developing a follow-up system that serves as a decision-making tool and fosters learning.

> IEG's approach tends to emphasize compliance more than management ownership.

Although no system incorporates all the elements, the Asian Development Bank (ADB) and Mexico's National Council for the Evaluation of Social Policy provide examples for consideration when improving follow-up. ADB's Independent Evaluation Department is working to improve the quality of its recommendations, being specific without being too prescriptive, and has classified its recommendations to provide a link to ADB's effectiveness.[19]

ADB reviews and publishes the implementation of its recommendations in its *Annual Report on Acting on Recommendations.* Mexico's National Council for the Evaluation of Social Policy promotes implementing agency ownership and ensures utilization of recommendations by engaging the agencies in prioritizing evaluation findings and recommendations and developing a plan for following-up. The ADB and the National Council for the Evaluation of Social Policy experiences are described in appendix C.

In comparison, IEG conducts very detailed validation of management's reporting on the adoption in IEG recommendations, but not on their utilization or effects on Bank effectiveness. IEG's approaches tend to emphasize compliance with recommendations more than management ownership or learning from implementation.

In addition, IEG could benefit from clear guidelines or standards for recommendations that address the balance between specificity and broad applicability of a recommendation. Finally, IEG (along with the other organizations) faces the challenge of establishing a clear link between the adoption of specific recommendations and its contribution to the development effectiveness of an organization like the World Bank Group.

Conclusion

Evaluation can and should play an important role in strengthening the World Bank Group's overall effectiveness. Evaluations, and the recommendations emerging from them, are an important instrument with significant potential to add value. In this chapter, for the first time, IEG reviewed recommendation follow-up across the World Bank, IFC, and MIGA. Based on the current processes and methods, there is a strong potential for win-win reforms.

IEG is committed to reforming what is known as the Management Action Record/Management Action Tracking Record process. Emphasis will be on enhancing the impact and value added from evaluations. This analysis points to directions for improving the way in which IEG provides recommendations to management, follows up on their implementation, and assesses their impact on development effectiveness.

A number of ideas can be drawn from the different approaches and experiences within the World Bank Group and its relevant comparators. However, more comprehensive work has to be carried out. Most important, any reform effort must be fully shared with management, as the constructive interaction between IEG and the Bank Group entities is essential.

Nevertheless, some principles for reform emerge. First, reforms must preserve the independence and accountability of IEG, while fostering openness and transparency. Second, reforms must move in the direction of a more harmonized system across the World Bank, IFC, and MIGA at the same time they accommodate inherent differences across the institutions.

Third, reforms need to be considered comprehensively, from formulation of recommendations, to prioritization, to follow-up processes. Fourth, emphasis needs to move toward the substantive content of the follow-up process, with linkages to institutional learning and knowledge strategies. Finally, criteria for successful reforms include the impact on IEG's credibility and contribution to accountability and transparency of the World Bank Group; the value added for the managements of the Bank, IFC, and MIGA; and the support to their respective Boards in fulfilling their oversight role.

The three chapters that follow discuss some selected drivers of development outcomes at the Bank Group. Highly relevant is an analysis of evidence regarding decentralization and development outcomes at the World Bank, based on the experience of the past decade. Chapter 4 presents an analysis of external and internal risk factors and controls for IFC, exploring the role of overall work quality and quality at entry. In chapter 5, the focus is on the quality of underwriting of MIGA projects, a key issue in MIGA's development effectiveness.

Part II SELECTED ISSUES RELATED TO RESULTS

Chapter 3

Photo by Curt Carnemark, courtesy of the World Bank Photo Library.

EVALUATION HIGHLIGHTS

- Decentralization at the World Bank has been in process for a decade.
- There are many possible effects of decentralization. IEG examines one dimension: the association between staff location and development outcomes.
- The location of the task team leader is not significantly associated with project outcome ratings.
- Quality Assessment Group data also show that there is no association between task team leader location and quality at entry or quality of supervision.
- Decentralization is associated with better CAS outcomes if country directors are located in the country overseen, though not when the Director is in a nearby hub.
- More systematic Bank data and analysis are needed.

World Bank: Decentralization and Outcomes

Decentralization of World Bank staff has been ongoing for a decade. Enhanced field presence is intended to increase responsiveness to client demand, improve country ownership and partnership, and enhance the cost-effectiveness of Bank support. Decentralization is intended to integrate global and local expertise.

Many factors are relevant to an assessment of the benefits or effects of decentralization. Some include the strength of relationships with clients and other stakeholders, potential reduction of costs, and other efficiency gains in the delivery of services (box 3.1).

The impact on development outcomes as seen in project ratings is only one element, albeit an important one, of an overall assessment. An initial review of intermediate and final outcomes of Bank-financed operations does not provide evidence that the decentralization of task team leaders in the field is associated with better development outcome ratings. In contrast, decentralization of country directors into country offices is associated with improved outcome ratings in Bank country programs, but only when the director is located in the country overseen, rather than a nearby hub.[1]

Context

For more than a decade, the World Bank has decentralized its staff from a headquarters model to a model with greater field presence, while allowing staff to retain close contact with headquarters for regional, Bank-wide, and cross-cutting issues. (IFC started decentralizing more recently; see box 3.2.) There are four objectives for this decentralization: to increase responsiveness to client demands; to integrate global and local knowledge; to improve country ownership and strengthen partnerships; and to improve the cost-effectiveness of Bank support.

The Bank has been decentralizing for more than a decade.

Each of these objectives was expected to contribute to improving development results. An earlier assessment of the Bank's decentralization notes that "closer proximity to clients was expected to enhance substantially the impact of the Bank's assistance. Increased delegation of authority, functions, and staff to country offices was intended to give the Bank a better understanding of conditions and concerns in

BOX 3.1 Decentralization Tensions

In a transport project in India in which the team leader was based in Delhi, frequent supervision allowed for an effective response to financial management issues. The project team was able to coordinate well with other agencies working in the same sector and address challenges as they emerged. In contrast, there were other implementation challenges for the project, and the team found it difficult to develop innovative solutions. Such solutions would have been more likely to arise if the project had both a better presence in Washington, DC, and the chance to interact with teams supervising similar transport projects elsewhere.

This vignette of the Bank's experimentation with the decentralization of its staff and decision-making authority highlights an important tension: a deep presence in the field allows for close supervision of project implementation and direct interaction with clients, but possibly at the expense of global expertise and careful management oversight. In addition, decentralization may have positive or negative effects on staffing patterns and on pressures for timely project preparation and implementation.

Which forces dominate, and with what overall impacts? These are important questions that deserve careful empirical analysis to guide future decision making.

Source: IEG ICR Reviews.

client countries, and thus to act as a powerful tool for greater development effectiveness" (World Bank 2001, pp. 29–30).

A central feature of the 1997 Strategic Compact, a Bank-wide strategy to create a more agile and efficient institution, was the decentralization of staff and decision-making authority from Washington (World Bank 1997, p. 1). By 2001, an assessment of the Compact found that the number of internationally and locally recruited staff based in country offices

BOX 3.2 Decentralization at IFC

Decentralization efforts at IFC are more recent than those at the World Bank. In 2006, IFC's management group announced the formation of the Global/Local IFC Working Group. This group was to identify the major issues, constraints, opportunities, and costs associated with a change to a client-centered organizational model. This was the first step toward forming a decentralization policy that would place more staff and decision-making authority in IFC's field offices and therefore closer to its clients. The efforts of the working group crystallized as IFC's Vision 2010 Initiative. To date, the percentage of staff in the field has increased from 32 percent in fiscal 2001 to 54 percent in 2009.

Management launched its IFC 2013 Initiative in 2010 as the next step in decentralization "to ensure that IFC's organizational structure, processes, and incentives are aligned with its strategic priorities" (IFC 2010). One of the four key areas of focus of the IFC 2013 Initiative is the shifting of regional and industry portfolios to regional operating centers. Global industry groups will be based both in Washington, DC, and in regions. As a part of this initiative, IFC's Istanbul office is to be converted from a regional hub to a multiregional operations center. This conversion will include the relocation of senior staff, including one vice president to lead the transition.

Although an integrated strategic approach to decentralization is a relatively recent phenomenon in IFC, a decentralized model for delivery of IFC advisory services has evolved over the years and has been a reality for quite some time. At present, IFC has a more decentralized delivery model for its advisory services than for its investment services. As of the end of fiscal 2009, more than three-quarters of IFC advisory services staff were based in field offices, versus 37 percent of investment staff. There are more advisory services than investment services staff in the field in developing countries.

IEG has taken a preliminary look at the role that location of the task team leader plays in the development effectiveness of IFC advisory services. In its first review of IFC advisory services, IEG found that advisory services projects that were led from the field tended to perform somewhat better than projects led from headquarters (78 percent and 65 percent development rating of high, respectively). The update of this analysis, which covers more recent advisory services projects, does not, however, find a statistically significant difference in performance depending on the location of the task leader (development outcome ratings are 62 percent and 60 percent, respectively, for field based and headquarters based).

Development Effectiveness of IFC's Advisory Services and Task Leader Location

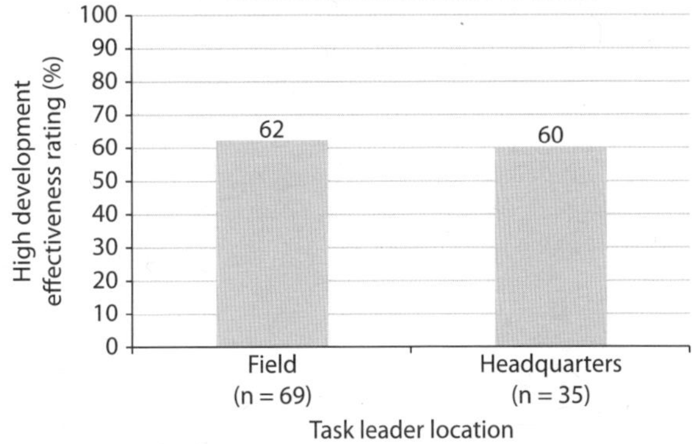

Sources: IEG-IFC Project Completion Report review data for fiscal 2008–09; IFC advisory services database as of December 31, 2009.

Note: Excludes projects where no development effectiveness rating was possible and where task leader location was not available. High development effectiveness ratings refer to projects rated mostly successful or higher.

had increased by a third.[2] Figure 3.1 shows that decentralization has continued apace since that time, among both team leaders and country directors.

A 2001 assessment found slightly better project results in decentralized locations, but those results could not be attributed to decentralization.

The Bank is further exploring different stylized options to complement its decentralized structure. The extent and nature of decentralization are clearly relevant to many other Bank goals—among others, the knowledge strategy, given the Bank's role as a global connector of knowledge and the importance of field staff access to global knowledge (World Bank 2010). Several internal papers about transformation to a global Bank discuss the benefits of decentralization to date. They indicate that the ability of Bank staff who are based in countries to coordinate with important stakeholders or to provide a rapid response when a critical window of opportunity opens has enhanced the Bank's ability to deliver results tremendously. [3]

These papers discuss client preferences and trends in increased decentralization over time in parallel with improved Bank performance. However, there is little evidence of causality or impact, or of attempts to account for the benefits of decentralization. It is noted that "there remains a need for more systematic evaluation of these benefits." The last of the three stylized options proposes that the Bank expand its decentralized structure and potentially scale down the Washington, DC, headquarters and supplement it with three to seven regional hubs.

Although papers about transforming the Bank claim benefits of decentralization, there is little evidence of or direct accounting for those benefits.

Select aspects of the relation between decentralization and development outcomes are explored below. Findings are preliminary and necessarily within the context of the current model of decentralization. Data on the degree of decentralization are limited; for example, the Bank does not currently compile a readily accessible database on the location of a task team leader at the time of preparation or after approval of a loan, only at the end of a project. One cannot determine from the presently available database whether a task team leader is internationally recruited and placed in the field or recruited locally. Information on the team complementing each task team leader is also not readily accessible. Aspects such as cost-effectiveness are not addressed here, and benefits such as improved quality of dialogue may be difficult to quantify.

The determination of where to locate the management of an operation may not be independent of the extent to which its objectives are likely to be easily achieved; this may lead to potential for endogeneity in the relation between task manager location and project outcomes. However, subject to these and other caveats, results suggest that decentralization is not associated with improved project development outcome ratings in all circumstances, and it may be appropriate to give deeper consideration to different aspects and circumstances.

FIGURE 3.1 Shares of Field-Based Staff and Country Directors since 2000

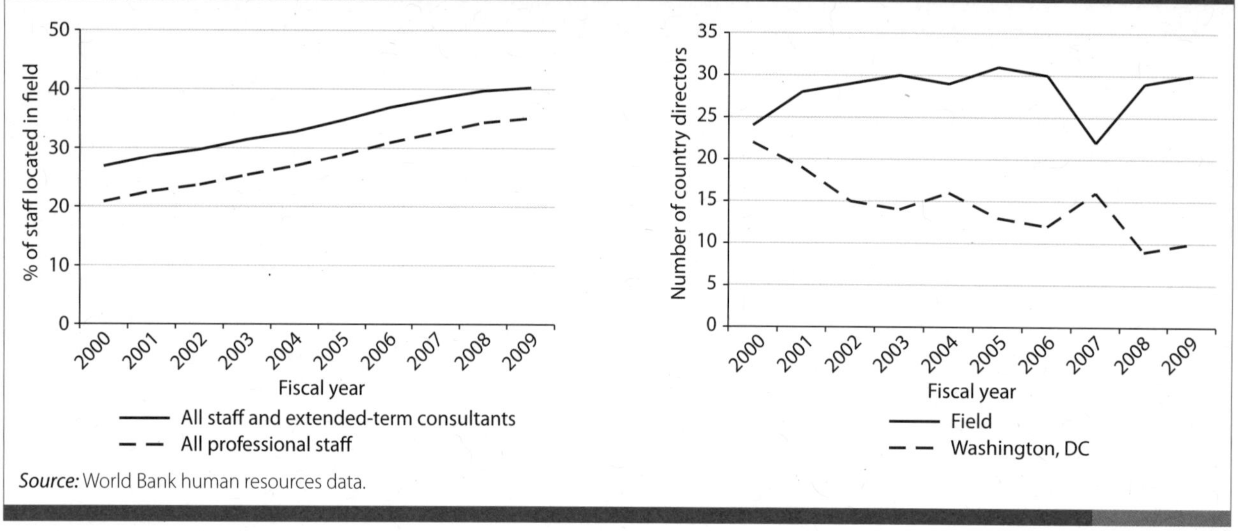

Source: World Bank human resources data.

Findings

Team leader location and intermediate outcomes

The person primarily responsible for individual operations is the task team leader, who prepares the operation in consultation with the client and with Bank management, undertakes its appraisal, and monitors and supports implementation.

How might outcomes be improved by locating a task team leader in the field? The objectives of decentralization can be distilled into at least three mechanisms for improvement: better project design (integrated global and local knowledge), better project supervision (increased responsiveness), and better donor coordination (stronger partnerships). Although cost-effectiveness is among the objectives for the global Bank, data were not readily available and are not considered at present. The results chain in figure 3.2 details these mechanisms.

The presence of a task team leader in the field does not appear to affect the quality of project design.

On the quality of design, the two indicators available suggest there is no difference whether a task team leader is based in the field. First, QAG assesses the quality at entry of a random sample of active operations 6–18 months after they have been approved by the Bank's Board, using a six-point rating scale. QAG data from Quality at Entry assessments for 225 operations approved since fiscal 2004 indicate that there is no statistically significant difference in the quality of design between headquarters-based operations (92 percent moderately satisfactory or better) and field-based operations (95 percent).[4] These data consider the location of the task team leader *at the time the project is designed*. Results from this and the following analyses are summarized in table 3.1.

Second, IEG evaluations include an assessment of the quality at entry[5] of closed operations. These data show that 77 percent of operations closing between fiscal 2005 and 2009 in which the task team leader is based in the field *when the project closed* were rated moderately satisfactory or better for their Quality at Entry. This compares with 74 percent for those based in headquarters (a difference not statistically significant among the universe of 876 operations).

As with the quality of project design, two indicators assess the quality of the Bank's supervision. QAG's Quality of Supervision reports that assess a random sample of 260 operations during implementation that were active at the start of fiscal 2005 and 2007 did not show a statistical difference in the quality of supervision of operations with a task team leader based in the field *during implementation* compared with headquarters-based task team leaders, even when controlling for a number of other factors. Nor was this the case among 849 IEG evaluations of operations closing between fiscal 2005 and 2009, which are based on the location of the task team leader *at the time an operation closes.*

Quality of supervision and the quality of partnership during supervision appear unaffected by the team leader's location.

FIGURE 3.2 Results Chain for Bank Decentralization

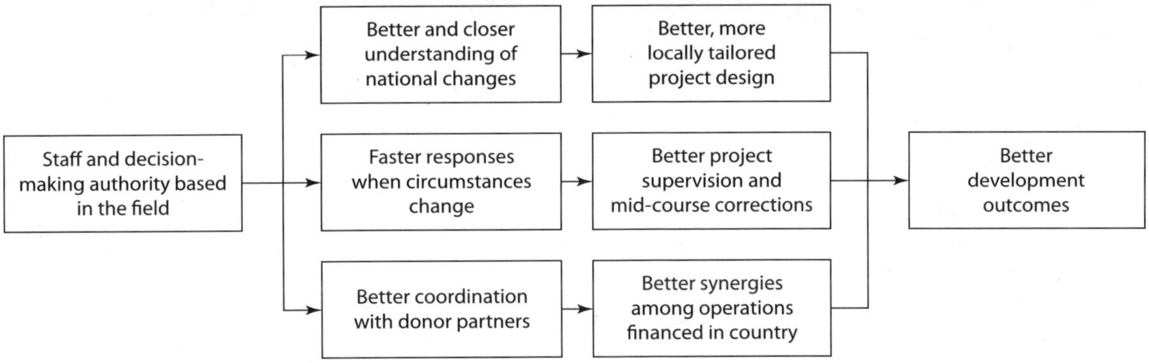

Source: IEG.

TABLE 3.1 Effects of Field-Based Task Team Leaders on Operations Design, Supervision, and Partnerships

	Simple tabulation (% moderately satisfactory or better)		Regression analysis[a]	
	Task team leader in field	Task team leader in headquarters	Coefficient (times 100)	Significance
Quality at Entry				
QAG QEA	94.7	92.0	–4.4	No
IEG	77.4	74.3	1.8	No
Quality of Supervision				
QAG QSA	86.5	90.9	–5.4	No
IEG	77.7	74.3	2.3	No
Partnerships				
QAG QSA	86.5	90.9	–5.4	No

Sources: World Bank internal database; QAG database.

Note: QAG = Quality Assurance Group; QEA = Quality at Entry Assessment; QSA = Quality of Supervision Assessment.
a. Regression refers to five separate two-stage least square regressions with percent rated moderately satisfactory or better as the dependant variable (for the five different ratings), and using distance from Washington as an instrumental variable for task team leader based in the field. Regressions control for Country Policy and Institutional Assessment, growth of per capita gross domestic product, year of approval, and dummy variables indicating whether the operation is a development policy operation, the region of the country and network of the operation, and whether the country is fragile or eligible for IDA finance or blended finance between IDA and IBRD.

Finally, QAG Quality of Supervision reports also assess the effectiveness of relationships with in-country partners, including clients, donors, and other stakeholders. Using the same sample and regression techniques, there is no statistically significant difference in the quality of partnerships between operations with a task team leader based in the field *during supervision* and those with a task team leader based in headquarters.

Team leader location and final outcomes of operations

Operations with field-based task team leaders at the time of closing do not consistently outperform those whose leaders are based in headquarters in terms of final outcome ratings. Among 981 operations exiting the portfolio between fiscal 2005 and 2009, of which 19 percent had task team leaders based in the field at closing, 82 percent of those with task team leaders located in the field were rated moderately satisfactory or better in IEG's independent evaluations, compared with 79 percent that had leaders based in headquarters (table 3.2).[6] Although average outcome ratings were slightly higher in the case of in the case of field-based task team leaders for most relevant subgroups, these differences were not statistically significant when controlling for other factors.

> Operations that have field-based team leaders do not consistently perform better than those that do not.

Regression analysis undertaken to test the relevance of these differences added controls for the institutional environment of the country (proxied by the Country Policy and Institutional Assessment); pace of development (measured by growth of per capita gross domestic product); year of project approval; nature of the lending instrument; Bank region and network of the operation; and whether the country is fragile, eligible for IDA finance, or blend finance between IDA and IBRD.[7] A two-stage least squares regression was used to test for any selection bias (tables 3.3 and 3.4).[8]

Overall, regression results suggest that there is no statistically significant difference in outcome ratings whether the task team leader is based in headquarters or the field at closing (tables 3.3 and 3.4 and appendix C).

Country director location and outcomes of Bank country programs

In addition to staff, the Bank has also moved decision-making authority to the field. The country director serves as the face of the institution to the client, leading overall dialogue and holding primary decision-making authority over the nature of the Bank's country program and its operations and strategies, rather than focusing on the implementation of individual operations. As shown in figure 3.1, the share of country directors based in the field has grown from about half in fiscal 2000 to three-quarters in 2009.[9]

TABLE 3.2 Field-Based Operations Outcomes versus Those Based in Headquarters

	Frequencies percent moderately satisfactory or better	
	Task team leader in field	Task team leader in headquarters
Overall	**82.4**	**79.0**
By types of operations		
Investment Operations	81.3	77.8
DPLs	90.0	84.3
IBRD loans	88.7	84.2
IDA credits	77.8	74.8
By type of country		
Fragile situations	66.7	68.1
Nonfragile	83.8	80.8
MICs	84.0	82.6
LICs	79.8	73.7

Source: World Bank internal database.

Note: DPL = development policy loan; IBRD = International Bank for Reconstruction and Development; IDA = International Development Association; LIC = low-income country; MIC = middle-income country.

TABLE 3.3 Determinants of the Location of Task Team Leader at Closing (first-stage regression)

Dependent variable	Coefficient
Distance from Washington (in thousands of km)	0.016***
CPIA control	0.016
GDP per capita growth control	−0.843*
Exit fiscal year	0.010
IDA country dummy	−0.035
Blend country dummy	0.129***
Fragile state dummy	−0.090**
DPL dummy	−0.061
FPD network dummy	−0.053
HDN dummy	0.089***
PREM dummy	0.008
SDN dummy	(omitted)
Observations	882
Pseudo R^2	0.078

Source: World Bank.

Note: Regression uses ordinary least squares model with percent of outcomes rated moderately satisfactory or better as the dependent variable. FPD = finance and private sector development; HDN = Human Development Network; PREM = Poverty Reduction and Economic Management Network; SDN = Sustainable Development Network.

TABLE 3.4 Determinants of IEG Outcomes (second-stage regression)

Dependent variable	Coefficient
Based in field (instrumented dummy)	0.174
CPIA control	0.111***
GDP per capita growth control	0.497
Exit fiscal year	−0.021
IDA country dummy	−0.052
Blend country dummy	−0.001
Fragile state dummy	−0.034
DPL dummy	0.145***
FPD network dummy	−0.115**
HDN dummy	−0.145***
PREM dummy	−0.114**
SDN dummy	(omitted)
Observations	882
Pseudo R^2	0.052

Source: World Bank internal database.

Note: Regression uses distance from Washington as instrument for location of task team leader in the field. Percent rated moderately satisfactory or better by IEG is the dependent variable. CPIA = Country Policy and Institutional Assessment; DPL = Development Policy Loan; FPD = finance and private sector development; GDP = gross domestic product; HDN = Human Development Network; IDA = International Development Association; PREM = Poverty Reduction and Economic Management Network; SDN = Sustainable Development Network.

The share of country directors in the field has grown from half to three-quarters.

Do programs overseen by field-based country directors have better outcomes than those with country directors based in headquarters? Country directors often oversee programs in more than one country but necessarily are based in only one. Do country programs with a country director located in the country of the operation perform better than those with a country director based in a nearby country?

Outcomes are better among country programs with country directors located in country rather than in a nearby hub.

IEG conducts CAS Completion Report Reviews, which evaluate the outcomes of Bank country programs and typically cover a period of three to four years.[10] On the left side of table 3.5, a simple tabulation of 67 such ratings covering country program periods that end after fiscal 2005 (and thus a period during which the policy to decentralize country directors had been well established) indicates that outcomes were better among country programs with country directors located in the country rather than a nearby hub.

Using regression analysis to control for relevant factors, no significant difference was found between outcomes of country programs based on the location of the country director. However, the difference in outcomes between country directors based in country and in a nearby hub is nearly statistically significant at 90 percent confidence (p value = 0.11), and the coefficient indicates that outcomes are 25 percentage points more likely to be moderately satisfactory or better. The level of significance may be affected by the relatively small sample size.

It is important to note, as discussed in relation to project task team leaders, that causation may run in either direction—there may be some systematic process by which those country directors located in Washington oversee countries with well-performing portfolios, and country directors who oversee a number of countries may choose a better performer as the hub. Indeed, reverse causation is arguably more likely to be a factor for country programs than for projects, and thus the positive association between country director decentralization and country program outcome should not be interpreted as causation one way or the other without further evidence.

Among the projects for which data were available, decentralization does not appear to be either a positive or negative attribute of operations in any systematic way.

Distance

Does distance matter? An internal Bank document notes that the farther a country is from Washington the stronger the rationale is for transferring authority or duties of staff.[11] In more distant countries, missions from headquarters are long and costly, both for the Bank and for those going on

TABLE 3.5 Country Program Outcomes When Director Is In-Country versus at Headquarters

	Outcomes of Bank country programs CASCRRs covering periods ending in fiscal 2005 or later	
Country director location	**Percent moderately satisfactory or better** (number of observations)	**Regression coefficient[a] times 100** (standard error)
In country	84.0 (25)	(omitted)
In field, not country	54.6 (33)	−25.1 (16.0)
In headquarters	70.0 (20)	−11.6 (22.9)

Source: World Bank internal database.

Note: CASCRR = CAS Completion Report Review.

a. Regression refers to "dprobit" regression with the dependent variable a dummy for country programs that are rated moderately satisfactory or better in CASCR Reviews. Coefficients in the table are not statistically significant at 90 percent confidence.

TABLE 3.6 Importance of Location of Team Leader by Regions

	Simple tabulation (% moderately satisfactory or better)		Regression analysis[a] ($n = 882$)	
Region	**Task team leader in field**	**Task team leader in HQ**	**Coefficient (times 100)**	**Significance**
AFR	69.0	67.7	6.4	No
EAP	92.0	87.0	–5.9	No
ECA	87.0	84.1	1.7	No
LCR	66.7	85.3	**–21.4**	95%
MNA	57.1	79.2	–12.4	No
SAR	88.4	69.1	**21.3**	95%

Source: World Bank internal database.

Note: AFR = Africa Region; EAP = East Asia and Pacific Region; ECA = Europe and Central Asia Region; LCR = Latin America and the Caribbean Region; MNA = Middle East and North Africa Region; SAR = South Asia Region.

a. Regression refers to six separate dprobit regressions with the dependent variable a dummy for operations that are rated moderately satisfactory or better by IEG. The coefficient in the table is the coefficient on an interaction term between a dummy for the TTL based in the field and a dummy for each individual region. Controls for CPIA, growth of per capita GDP, year of closing, and dummy variables indicating whether the operation is a development policy operation, the region of the country and network of the operation, and whether the country is fragile, eligible for IDA finance, or blended finance between IDA and IBRD. In nonlinear models, the interaction effect is the cross-partial derivative of the expected value of ***y***. This is not accurately estimated in the dprobit model. Using the interaction effects model, the table above corrects for this error. For more information, see http://www.unc.edu/~enorton/NortonWangAi.pdf.

the trip, and could drive differences in outcomes between operations overseen by headquarters- and field-based task team leaders.

Distance from headquarters results in a significant difference in outcome for only two regions.

Regression analysis demonstrates that differences are only significant in two Bank regions, as shown in table 3.6.[12] In South Asia, where decentralization is most advanced, outcomes are 21 percentage points better for operations with a task team leader based in the field at closing; in Latin America and the Caribbean, where fewer staff are based in the field, outcomes are 21 percentage points better for operations with a task team leader based in headquarters at closing. There are no statistically significant differences among operations in Sub-Saharan Africa, East Asia and the Pacific, Europe and Central Asia, or the Middle East and North Africa.

The regression does not provide much evidence that distance from Washington matters, as there is a positive correlation between decentralization and outcomes in only one of the three farthest regions (South Asia, but not Africa or East Asia and Pacific). Even this result is sensitive to the precise specification. There are undoubtedly many factors other than distance that influence both regional patterns of decentralization and project outcomes. For instance, one region may decentralize by placing internationally recruited staff in the field, whereas another may recruit more local staff. Further work would be required to unbundle the primary cause of any differences in outcomes.

In none of the four sectors for which analysis was done was there a significant difference in outcome based on task team leader location.

Type of operation

Does the impact of decentralization differ by sector? When considering simple tabulations of frequencies, there appear to be better outcomes among field-based task team leaders in the Sustainable Development Network and Poverty Reduction and Economic Management operations.

But regression analysis similar to those conducted above does not confirm this, as shown in table 3.7. The coefficients of the regression are interpreted as the relative performance of operations with a task team leader based in the field at closing (versus task team leaders based in headquarters) within a given network, measured in percentage points. In none of the four networks is there a significant difference in

TABLE 3.7 Importance of Location of the Team Leader in "Scattered Site" Projects

Sector	Tabulation (% moderately satisfactory or better)		Regression analysis[a] (*n* = 882)	
	Task team leader in field	Task team leader in headquarters	Coefficient (times 100)	Significance?
SDN	92.6	84.1	25.0	No
PREM	89.5	77.4	−5.0	No
FPD	75.0	75.4	−18.9	No
HDN	67.7	71.1	−27.5	No

Source: World Bank internal database.

Note: FPD = financial and private sector development; HDN = Human Development Network; PREM = Poverty Reduction and Economic Management Network; SDN = Sustainable Development Network.

a. Regression analysis refers to two-stage least squares regression using distance from Washington as the instrument for whether the task team leader is based in the field. Regression controls for Country Policy and Institutional Assessment, growth of per capita gross domestic product, year of closing, and dummy variables, indicating whether the operation is a development policy operation, for IDA or blend status, status as a fragile state, region, and network.

outcomes between operations with task team leaders based in the field at closing and those based in headquarters.

Qualitative evidence from assessments

What does qualitative evidence show? Among 46 recently closed projects for which both IEG evaluations and QAG supervision assessments are available, decentralization does not appear to be considered a positive (or negative) attribute of operations in any systematic way. Assessments for 24 of the 46 projects specifically mention the staff location as a material factor directly affecting project outcomes. Of these, 14 had field-based task team leaders. In 4 cases, this was considered a detraction from the success of the project, and in 10 cases it was considered a contribution.

For ten projects identifying staff location as important (those in which the task team leader was based in headquarters), the lack of a field presence was said to hamper performance of the project in seven cases, but management at headquarters was considered a positive attribute in the other three.

Conclusions

Overall, there is little evidence that decentralization is associated with improved development outcome ratings. Controlling for key variables, there is no clear evidence of superior outcomes for operations led by task team leaders based in field *at closing*, except for in one particular region (South Asia). Likewise, evidence does not suggest that better design is associated with the location of the task team leader in the field *during preparation*; better supervision when the leader is located in the field *during implementation*; or better partnerships with clients, donors, and other stakeholders when the leader is located in the field *during implementation*. In contrast, outcomes of country programs appear to be better when country directors are based in the country of operation, rather than in a nearby hub.

These findings come with many caveats. Data that would enable more precise measurement—such as whether the task team leader is internationally or locally recruited, the extent of his or her experience to date, and his or her location over the entire lifespan of an operation—are not readily available. There are avenues for deeper analysis that could reveal a more nuanced understanding of when decentralization works and when it does not.

Finally, there may be other benefits from decentralization. Further analysis is needed to weigh costs and benefits carefully.

Chapter 4

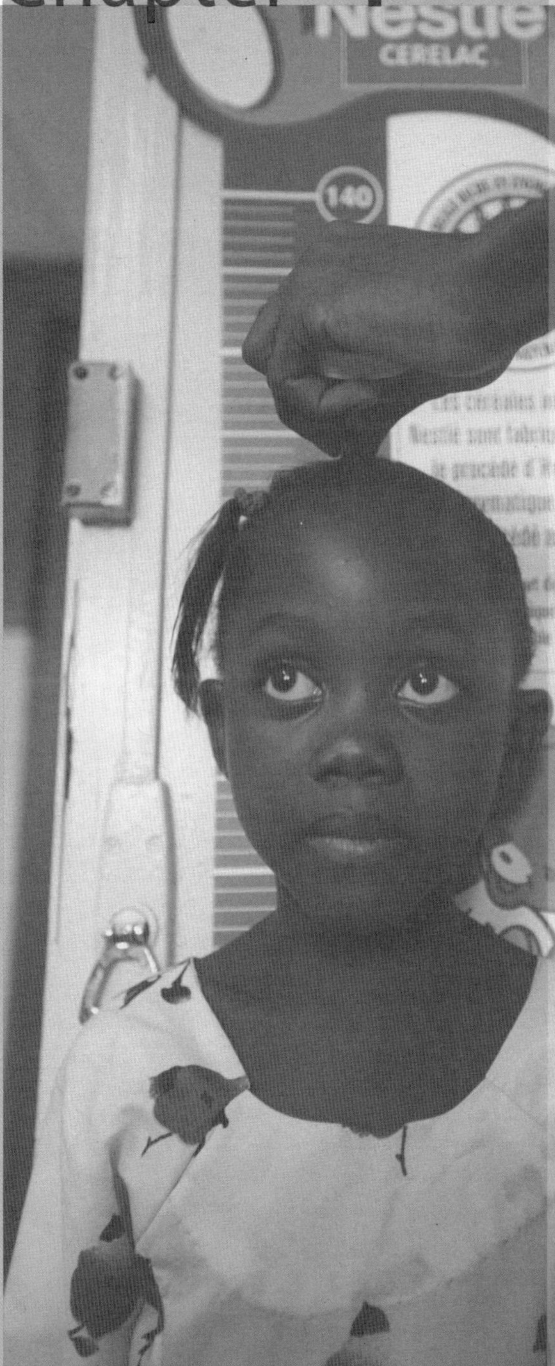

Photo by Ami Vitale, courtesy of the World Bank Photo Library.

EVALUATION HIGHLIGHTS

- IFC's project results hinge significantly on internal and external risk factors.
- IFC has a significant degree of control over project development outcomes through its work quality.
- Deterioration in the investment climate is likely to contribute to a decline in IFC's project development outcome ratings.
- IFC's overall work quality has continued a two-year gradual improvement, but supervision quality has declined recently.
- Client contributions to advisory services tend to enhance development effectiveness ratings.
- When linked to an investment project, advisory services projects have enhanced development effectiveness.
- Sensitivity analysis is the weakest area in IFC project appraisal and due diligence.

IFC: Key Factors Affecting Performance

Current external conditions pose significant challenges to IFC's mission to fight poverty through support to private sector development in socially and environmentally sustainable ways. As IFC carries out its strategy to increase its focus on frontier markets, it must manage the associated risk found in difficult and less developed environments. Factors within IFC's control, such as work quality at entry, are critically important as IFC expands its reach for greater development impact.

IFC Development Impact: Factoring in Project Risks

The project development outcome of IFC-supported investments is measured by their financial, economic, and environmental and social performance, as well as by their contributions to private sector development. Project evaluation and in-depth analyses show that project development outcomes hinge significantly on two types of factors: those external to IFC—notably, changes in country business climate risk, sponsor risk, market risk, and project-type risk—and those internal to IFC—the quality of IFC's work in project appraisal and structuring, project supervision, and additionality (see box 4.1).

Experience suggests that, in general, more difficult external conditions can be offset in part by strong IFC work quality, although the frequency of successful development outcome ratings still tends to be lower in more difficult external environments. The distinction between external and internal factors is not absolute. Rather, it is a matter of degree, as IFC still exercises considerable discretion as to the types of countries and clients it decides to engage with. In addition, IFC has the mandate and the instruments to contribute to improvements in countries' investment climates and client capacities. Over the short to medium term, however, these can be viewed as parameters in IFC's decision-making process (figure 4.1).

Trends in external factors

Evaluation results demonstrate that development outcome ratings are affected by whether country risk improves or worsens during the life of a project. For the period 1996–2009, projects operating in countries with improved risk profiles tended to have higher development outcome ratings than projects in countries with steady and/or worsening risk.

> Projects operating in countries with improved risk profiles tended to have higher development outcomes.

The Institutional Investor Country Credit Rating (IICCR) attempts to measure the quality and trends in a country's investment climate.[1] According to this measure, economic conditions were stable and/or improving through calendar year 2008. However, the effects of the global financial crisis have been quickly reflected in the IICCR country risk ratings. Most regions show a decline in the quality of their investment climate as of the end of 2009, with Central and Eastern Europe experiencing the largest drop. Investment climate risk remained stable in the South Asia and Sub-Saharan Africa Regions, the two regions where most of the poor live, creating opportunities for IFC to expand its activities.

> The effects of the financial crisis have been reflected in country risk ratings.

The deterioration in the investment climate is likely to contribute to a decline in IFC's project development outcome ratings. Historical trends indicate that IEG's evaluation ratings are lagging indicators[2] and manifest the effects of increased risk resulting from economic or financial crises with some delay.

Figure 4.2 highlights the timing and magnitude of changes in IFC's development outcome ratings against those of reserves in IFC's loan portfolio, which reflect perceived increased risks related to various regional and country-specific crises. The Asian crisis, for example, began in 1997, but the effects did not translate into declining development outcome ratings until about a year later. Similarly, the crises experienced in Argentina occurred in 2001, with effects emerging in 2003. This pattern seems to hold in the present circumstances, as we have not yet seen the impact on the crisis manifested strongly in IFC's development outcome ratings.

> The decline in investment climate is likely to contribute to a decline in IFC's development outcome ratings.

In addition to the investment climate, partner quality, market conditions, and project risks are important determinants of development outcome ratings. Newer projects (those approved between 2005 and 2008) had lower sponsor risk but tended to have higher risk relating to project type. That reflects a growing trend in increasing exposure to new, greenfield, or early stage businesses. Increased competition, liquidity, and high valuations before the crisis also contributed to

BOX 4.1 External and Internal Factors Affecting IFC Development Outcomes

External Factors

Changes in country business climate—This includes changes in the Institutional Investor Country Credit Risk score between approval and evaluation. A higher value indicates a larger improvement in the business environment. An improving business environment creates more and distributes better investment and growth opportunities, rewards entrepreneurial efforts, facilitates business growth, and is therefore expected to translate into more jobs, higher community impact, and greater tax revenues.

Sponsor/partner quality—This factor captures the sponsor's experience, financial capacity, commitment to the project, and governance/business reputation. If the sponsor is rated low in these dimensions, sponsor quality is deemed to be low. This factor is based largely on assessment of project documentation and, where available, public information and field visits/interviews. IFC is delivering development impact through partners, typically private enterprises. Therefore, their capacity, integrity, and commitment are an important factor of development impact. However, IFC's additionality may mitigate the risks arising from low sponsor quality. The variable is measured at time of approval.

Market risks—This factor captures the project's underlying competitiveness in the market in which it is operating and any market distortions such as high tariff protection, degree of the presence of state-owned enterprises in the sector, artificial monopoly positions, and other distortions that typically result in low competitiveness. Clearly demonstrated market competitiveness improves a venture's ability to meet business adversity and survive its early years to reach its development potential. Economic rates of return and development impact in general tend to be lower in distorted market environments. Distortions are normally unsustainable over the long term, creating financial risks if a particular enterprise benefits financially from market distortions. The variable is measured as of time of approval.

Project type—This factor indentifies a project as greenfield or otherwise. Greenfield projects involve new plant construction and new operations and thus pose higher risks than expansions of existing plants and operations. They pose the greatest challenge to structuring and risk sharing.

Internal Factors

Screening, appraisal, and structuring—This is an indication of the extent to which IFC followed good practice standards. For example, did IFC identify key risk factors, mitigate them as far as possible, and arrive at realistic expectations for project and company performance? Actual results are compared to expectations, and the main reasons for variance are analyzed to assess whether IFC's assumptions were well grounded in good practice due diligence and structuring, and the extent to which differences in actual results were the result of extraneous effects such as recognized but uncontrollable risks.

Supervision and administration—Following approval and commitment, and through to eventual closure, this indicator assesses how well IFC supervised an investment. For example, was IFC able to detect emerging problems and respond expeditiously with appropriate and effective interventions?

IFC role and contribution—This indicator describes the extent to which IFC played a catalytic role in an investment and made a special contribution. This is the closest proxy for IFC's additionality.

Source: IEG.

FIGURE 4.1 High IFC Work Quality Effects on Business Environments

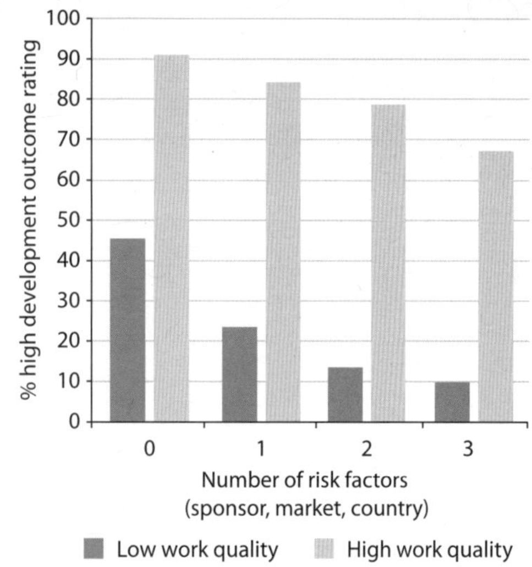

Source: IEG-IFC project evaluation database.

project-type risk. Market risk, although recently declining, remains high (figure 4.3).

Trends in internal factors

Although external factors are important determinants of performance, IFC exercises a significant degree of control over development outcomes through its work quality. IEG measures IFC work quality as a synthesis of three separate subindicators: *screening, appraisal, and structuring*; *supervision and administration*; and *IFC role and contribution* (figure 4.4). IFC's overall work quality has continued a two-year gradual upward trend, but there has been a recent decline in supervision quality. The decline is more evident in the year-on-year analysis, which shows a drop in the rating from 89 percent in calendar year 2008 to 76 percent in 2009.

> IFC's work quality has continued a two-year gradual upward trend, but supervision quality has declined recently.

FIGURE 4.2 Loan Reserve Balances versus Development Outcome Ratings

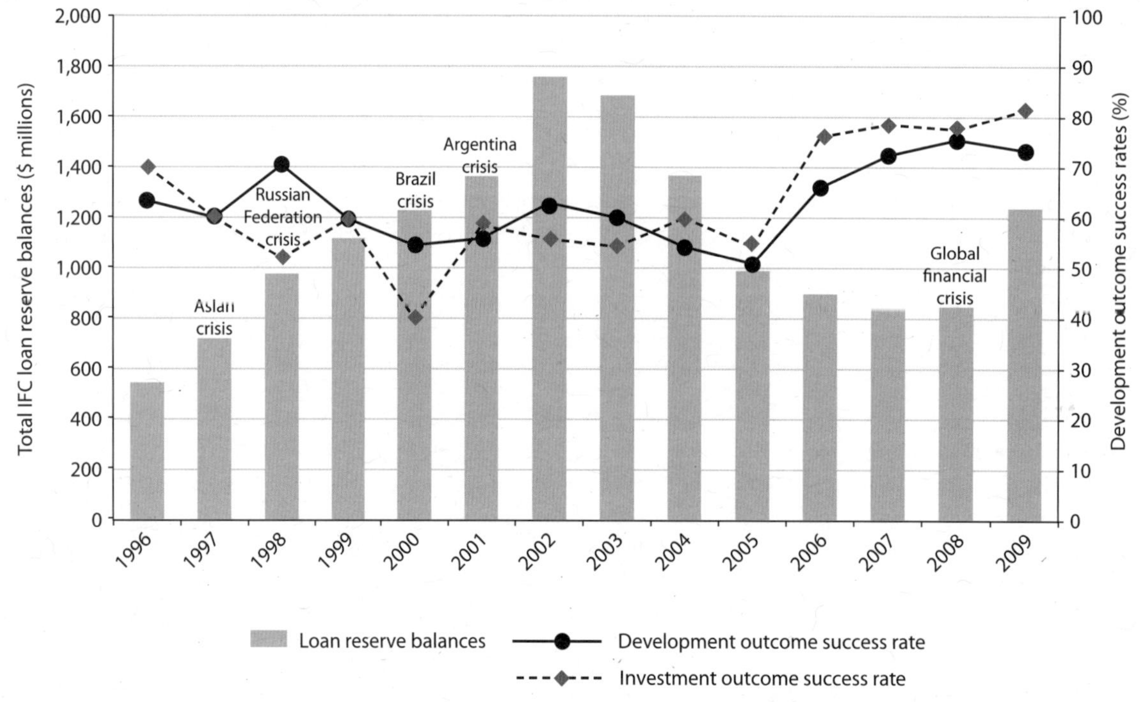

Sources: IFC annual reports and IEG-IFC XPSR ratings database.

Note: Loans are written off when IFC has exhausted all possible means of recovery by reducing the reserve against losses on loans. Such reductions in the reserve are offset by recoveries associated with previously written-off loans. Loan provisions are plotted by approval fiscal year. Development and investment outcome success rates, where the percentage of successful projects is those that are mostly successful or higher on a six-point scale, are plotted by calendar year.

The Asian financial crisis gripped much of Asia beginning in July 1997. In 1998, the Russian Federation experienced a financial crisis. The next year saw the effects of Brazil's currency crisis; in 2001 the Argentine currency crisis and debt default occurred.

The global financial crisis of September–October 2008 is a major ongoing financial crisis, the worst of its kind since the Great Depression.

The decline in supervision quality appears to reflect several important dimensions that can potentially impact supervision quality: (i) stretched resources in trying to respond to an increased volume of troubled accounts resulting from the crisis; (ii) internal changes related to decentralization and the IFC 2013 Initiative;[3] and (iii) organizational changes that have resulted in diffusion of portfolio function among cluster managers and the absence of concentrated responsibilities for the portfolio at the vice presidential level.

FIGURE 4.3 Project Risk versus Sponsor and Market Risk

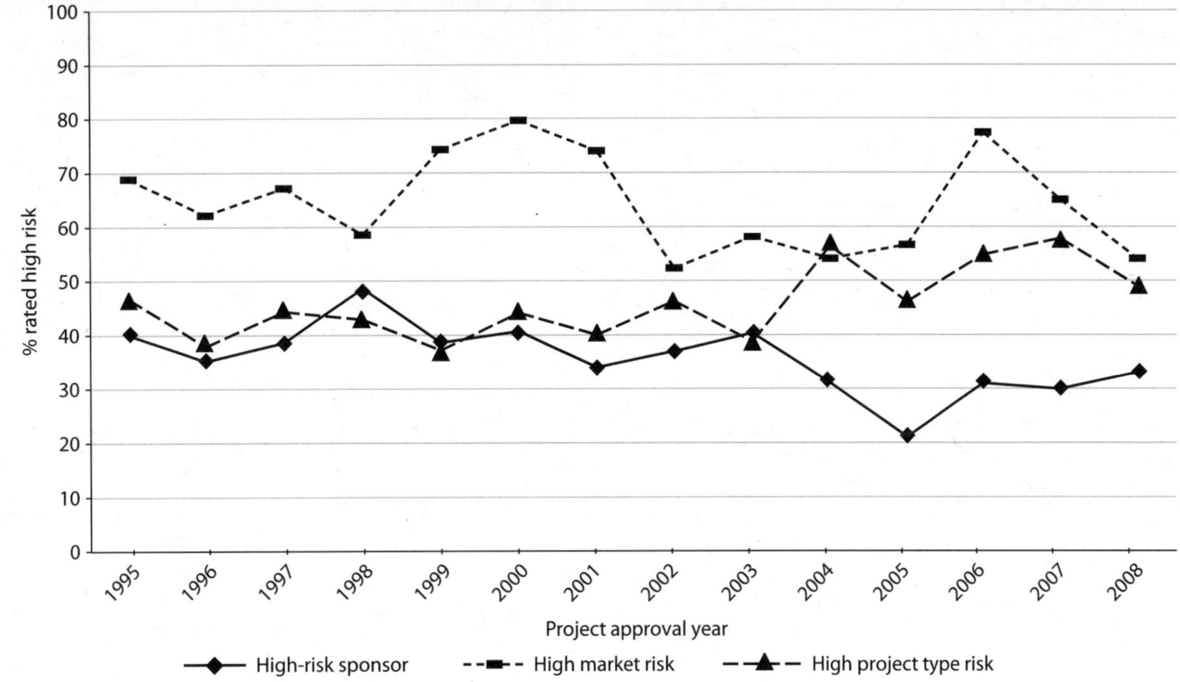

Source: IEG.

Note: 2005 and beyond are a representative sample of projects approved that have not yet reached maturity.

FIGURE 4.4 Overall Work Quality versus Supervision Quality

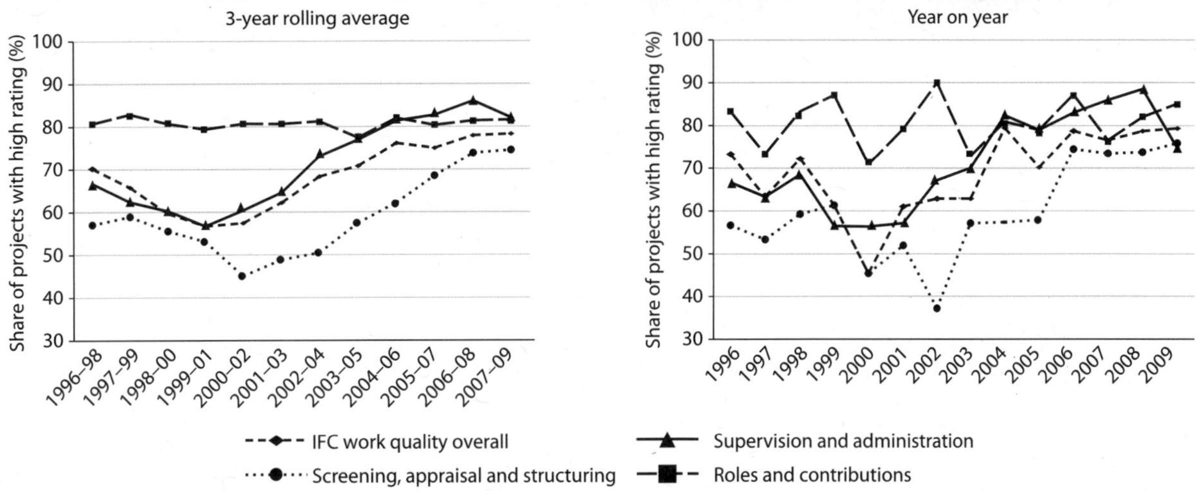

Source: IEG.

Note: Three-year moving averages and year-on-year.

Project evaluation data indicate that the decline in supervision quality is concentrated in financial market projects mostly located in the Europe and Central Asia and Latin America and the Caribbean Regions. The need to pay strong attention to work quality and portfolio risk management is particularly acute under the current circumstances, when the global economy is fragile and IFC is undergoing profound institutional changes.

A Review of IFC's Work Quality at Entry

IEG-IFC conducted a Quality at Entry review of 2008 investment approvals to assess the quality and depth of IFC's *screening, appraisal, and structuring.* The sample of projects was selected using a stratified random sampling method and is statistically representative of the 2008 approvals. It consists of 93 projects.

The purpose of the Quality at Entry study is to assess whether recent due diligence work follows IFC's Credit Review Guidelines (CRG) and internal procedures related to additionality and development impact. There are two main reasons for this.

First, as IFC's investment volume grows and decentralization continues, it is essential to assess whether credit and related due diligence policies are intact and are consistently followed. Second, as IEG analyses have repeatedly demonstrated, IFC work quality is strongly correlated with project outcome. Therefore, the quality at entry assessment can provide insight into a project's prospect for success and help management address any emerging issues in the most effective and informed manner.[4]

FIGURE 4.5 Role of Client Contributions to Development Effectiveness Ratings in Advisory Services Projects

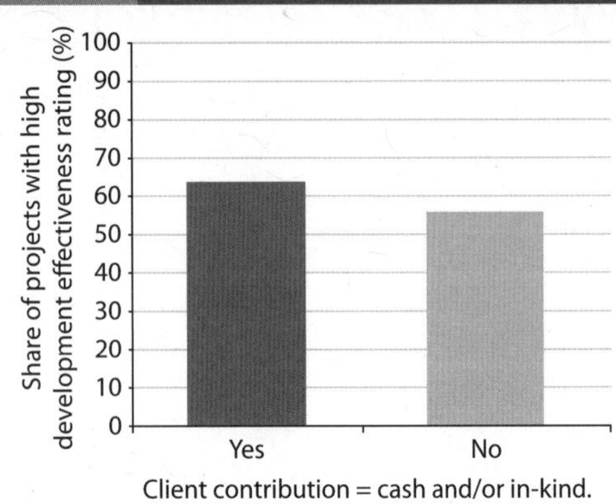

Source: IFC advisory services database as of December 31, 2009.

Note: Excludes projects that were backfilled, dropped, cancelled, or terminated or that started prior to fiscal 2005. High development effectiveness ratings refer to projects rated mostly successful or higher, on a six-point scale. Client contribution = cash and/or in-kind.

When benchmarked against the high standards of the CRG, many nonfinancial institution projects show some deficiencies, though these shortcomings do not reflect serious contraventions. In contrast, most financial institution projects are close to full compliance, reflecting a high degree of standardization within the sector.

Sponsor commitment

IFC delivers development impact through its partners. Therefore, a sponsor's commitment to a project is a key factor for successful development outcomes. The CRG mandates that the sponsor's motivations and—more specifically—how its incentives are aligned with the project's performance be identified in the due diligence process.

IEG found that this information is largely present, although there are several exceptions. Sponsors expect significant gains from activities that are related but auxiliary to the project, such as marketing of IFC's investee company products, sale of sponsors' equipment, rent for assets used by the investee company (land on which new plant is located), and management fees or fees for other services provided to the investee company. Based on the review, such calculations either are seldom made or go unreported.

> Advisory services projects that have some level of client contribution tend to achieve higher development effectiveness ratings.

In advisory services operations, client commitment is also key for achieving development results. IEG findings show that, in general, advisory services projects that have some level of client contribution tend to achieve higher development effectiveness ratings (IEG-IFC 2009). The implication is that client contributions will strengthen project development outcomes (figure 4.5).

In 2007, IFC revised its framework for an advisory services pricing policy.[5] Central to this policy is the principle that IFC does not seek client contributions to maximize revenue, cost recovery, or profits. Rather, pricing is used as a tool to help strengthen client commitment to implementation and to ensure that any subsidy is justified by the public benefits involved. IFC has stated that management considers client contributions an essential component of the advisory services' funding model and sustainability (IFC 2010).

Management has estimated that on average, client contributions will amount to 25 percent of total project costs from its fiscal 2008 approvals and 35 percent from 2009 approvals (IFC 2010). Based on estimates made at project approval, there are expectations that levels of client contributions from the Latin America and the Caribbean Region will rise. Other regions, such as South Asia and the Middle East and North Africa, have declining estimates. This may be a reflection of the strategic focus or design of advisory services projects in the particular region (that is, public versus private sector focus).

Company analysis

Benchmarking analysis is not only important for IFC's work quality, but is often expected from clients who choose to engage with IFC because of the added value they expect from a development financier with deep industry knowledge and global reach. The CRGs indicate as a good practice the comparison of the IFC client company to others in the industry in several areas: competitive strength and comparative advantage, profitability, and financial structure. Such comparative analyses are at times not carried out in great detail. The practice is better in the case of IFC's engagement with banks, but the routine use of comparators in bank appraisals should be extended to funds and other collective investment vehicles.

> Comparative analysis of client companies with others is sometimes not done in great detail, and basic information on simple questions can be hard to find.

Such a comparison requires an understanding of the accounting standards being used. The CRGs stipulate that the client company's accounting standards, systems, and audits be scrutinized. But it is difficult to find answers to simple questions in the reports, such as (i) what accounting system (local, International Financial Reporting Standards, or generally accepted accounting principles) was used in the preparation of a company's financial statements, (ii) how it compares to International Financial Reporting Standards; and (iii) whether the corresponding accounts are audited, and if so, whether the auditors' opinion was qualified and why. A company could produce strikingly different financial statements depending on what particular accounting system was followed, so it is essential to assess the quality of earnings and whether they are based on reasonable assumptions.

> Sensitivity analysis is the weakest area in appraisal and due diligence.

Sensitivity analyses

In uncertain and volatile economic conditions, and as IFC moves to more risky frontier markets, high-quality risk analysis—including sensitivity analysis—is an important factor for achieving expected development results. The purpose of sensitivity analyses is to identify factors that are critical to the project's success and/or influence its performance. This is the weakest area in the appraisal and due diligence stage. This review has identified deficiencies with respect to sensitivity analyses:

- The percent up/percent down approach is still commonly used, even though the breakeven approach should be the norm.
- The impact of combined factors, rather than focusing on one factor at a time, is rarely analyzed.
- The factors identified as the main reasons for a project's competitiveness are not tested in the sensitivity analysis.
- Although most loans bear variable interest rates, the impact of rate increases is almost never tested in nonfinancial institution projects.

> The comprehensiveness of country analyses is questionable, leaving some doubt about whether certain aspects were overlooked, unreported, or irrelevant to the specific project.

Commodity price trends and volatility have a major impact on related projects' performance. Commodity prices are typically sensitivity tested through percentage variations from their current levels, rather than testing the project's performance at the inflexion points in the commodity price cycle.

Country analysis

A good understanding of the country conditions in which IFC-supported projects operate is essential for achieving development impact. IFC's country analysis is commonly limited to the economic risks from a broadly macro "International Monetary Fund perspective" (economic growth, inflation, balance of payment, risk of currency devaluation, and the like). This is the case more with real sector projects than other types.

IFC's good practice notes suggest going far beyond this level of analysis to the political, legal, business, and regulatory risks that may be relevant for the particular project. Regarding these types of risks, IFC as a member of the World Bank Group is expected to have a comparative advantage in understanding and managing them. Mitigation of these risks is often an integral part of IFC's additionality to clients.

However, there are questions regarding the comprehensiveness of these analyses in IFC, which leaves some doubt as to whether these important aspects were overlooked, unreported, or irrelevant to the specific project. Financial institution projects fare better in this area, because a detailed review of the banking sector and relevant regulations is normally part of the appraisal due diligence.

IFC additionality

IFC's additionality is the extent to which IFC brings to the market products and services that are uniquely beneficial, or additional to those provided by other financiers (IEG-IFC 2008a). Clarity on IFC's additionality is not only important for reporting purposes but is critical for the success of IFC's business development efforts. A good understanding of IFC's additionality should be at the center of IFC's engagement with a client from the very beginning, as it is essential for articulating IFC's competitive advantage and value proposition to a client.

> There have been improvements in the articulation of additionality, but weaknesses persist.

This review noticed improvements in articulating additionality in project approval documents. The introduction of an "Additionality Primer" for IFC investment officers appears to have helped the project teams to focus on additionality. However, weaknesses persist in identifying and justifying IFC's additionality in investment projects:

- There is a tendency to assume that it is self-evident that IFC has definite, albeit undefined, additionality in a project. The justification provided is insufficient in most cases and is occasionally nonexistent.
- Although most additionality could be described as an IFC role, not all IFC roles constitute additionality. There is insufficient differentiation between roles that could be performed by IFC or other players, and roles/contributions that are unique to IFC (additionality).
- There are often instances when a project's developmental impact is used in lieu of additionality. Staff often do not differentiate between the two.

Figure 4.6 shows the frequency of the various types of additionality addressed in project development and approval documents based on IEG's ex ante project review.[6] Box 4.2 describes additionalities observed by clients, as well as gaps in achievement.

IFC considers its ability to provide and combine advisory and investment services a unique competitive advantage over institutions engaged in private sector development (IFC 2010). IFC advisory services are often heavily subsidized, thereby giving IFC flexibility as to how, where, and when a project will be implemented and focused. Linking advisory services to investment operations is viewed by IFC management as a strategy for leveraging IFC's knowledge and financial resources, with the goal of maximizing development impact by enhancing the project's quality and effectiveness. IEG has found that when linked to an investment project, advisory services

FIGURE 4.6 IFC Additionality by Type: Financial/Nonfinancial

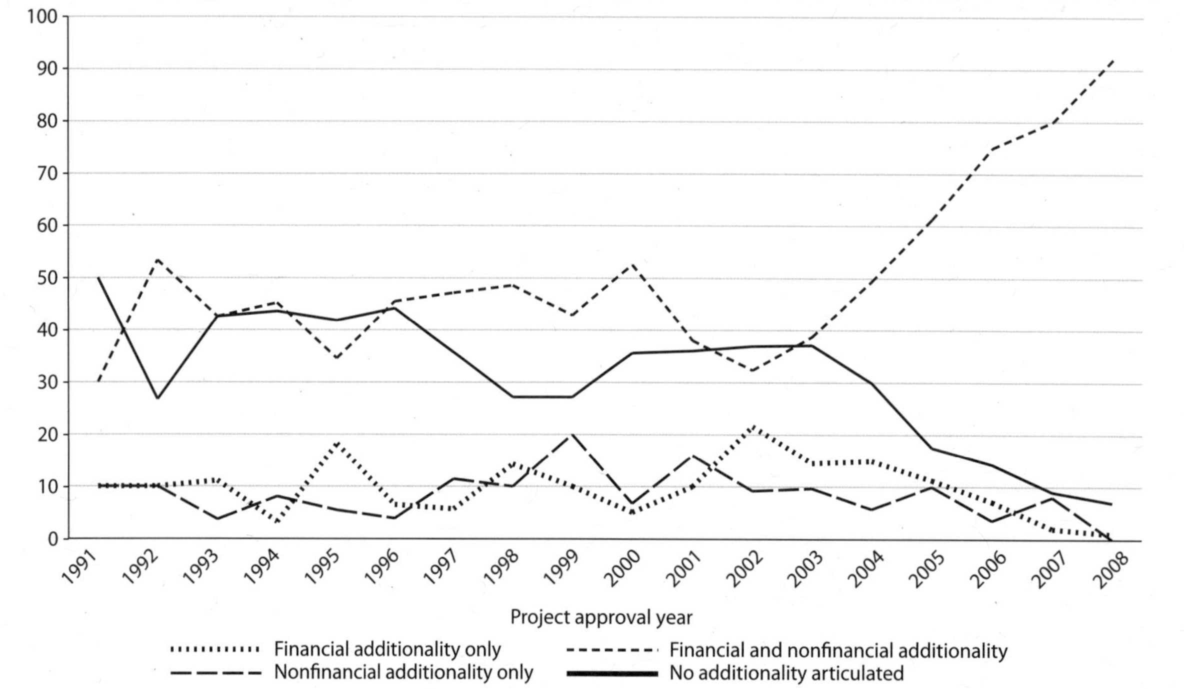

Source: IEG-IFC.

projects enhance development effectiveness (see figure 4.7).

When linked to an investment project, advisory services projects have enhanced development effectiveness.

In fiscal 2009, 23 percent of all new advisory services approvals were linked to investment projects, and approximately 35 percent had expectations for being linked to an investment project within three years of project approval. When advisory services projects, such as those focused on advice to governments are excluded, this number is much higher. As advisory services and investment operations have begun to share a more integrated strategy, it is reasonable to expect more systematic collaboration and coordination.

Developmental impact

With the introduction of the Development Outcome Tracking System (DOTS), greater attention is being paid to anticipated development outcomes in project preparation and follow-up.

FIGURE 4.7 Advisory Services Projects Linked to Investments versus Those with No Linkages

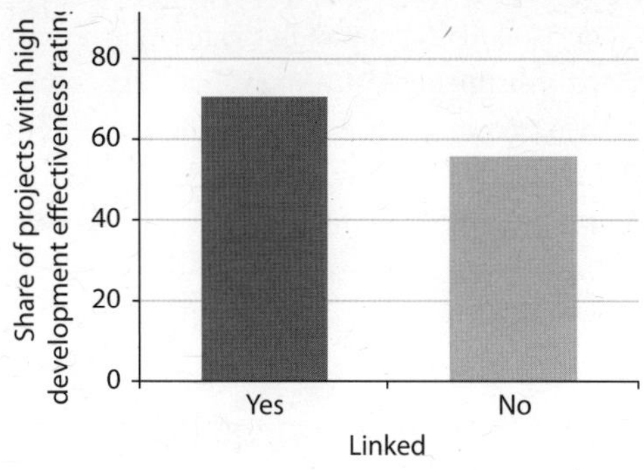

Sources: IEG-IFC Project Completion Report review data, fiscal 2008–09; IFC advisory services database as of December 31, 2009.

Note: Excludes projects where no development effectiveness rating was possible. High development effectiveness ratings refer to projects rated mostly successful or higher, on a six-point scale.

BOX 4.2 Examples of Observed Additionalities and Gaps in Achievement

Observed Additionalities

- The client attributes its strong E&S performance to IFC's guidance and performance requirements.
- The World Bank-IFC performance standards for resettlement were adopted in relation to the possible infrastructure extension. IFC has also helped the company respond to nongovernmental organization concerns regarding resettlement issues with the infrastructure extension at a different site that was not part of the original project.
- IFC provided guidance on obtaining international accreditation and on corporate governance, reporting, and accounting standards.
- IFC undertook a market benchmarking exercise to help analyze the company's competitiveness for its products in the global market.

Observed Gaps between Ex Ante and Ex Post Statements

- IFC had started to develop a pilot-linkage program between the client company and its suppliers, but failed to make any progress during the project period of 18 months.
- IFC provided a credit line to increase a bank's mortgage and small- and medium-size enterprise lending portfolio. However, this was not supported by any advice or knowledge transfer from IFC.
- Although the client company has raised the bar in terms of the operational standards, environment, and cleanliness of retail stations, this capacity already existed within the company. IFC's additionality in terms of E&S standards was therefore marginal.
- The client financial institution had an existing environmental management system, thanks to earlier IFC interventions. There was no incremental impact arising from the last project.
- The owners—international companies—implemented their own high standards of governance and environmental stewardship. There was limited opportunity for IFC to add value.

Source: IEG.

Yet the challenge of mainstreaming development impact considerations in project work remains. Financial performance is the starting point of looking at development impact, but often the analysis does not go much beyond financial performance. Economic performance is the most frequently emphasized aspect of developmental impact in the projects reviewed. But often the only distinction between expected economic and financial performance is tax payments, and project effects on other stakeholders are rarely quantified. The distributional impacts of IFC's projects are also rarely being reviewed.

> Although financial analysis is the starting point for examining development impact, the analysis often does not go much further.

An important development with the introduction of DOTS is identification of monitorable development impact indicators during project preparation. Several weaknesses were found in the identification and monitoring of the developmental impact or a project:

- Some of the proposed indicators are not incremental. They appear to commingle the performance of the project with that of the preproject company. An increase in these indicators may not be solely a result of the project.
- The use of business performance measures is at times presented as sufficient evidence of a project's development impact.
- The targets for some indicators were less demanding than goals the company had been able to achieve in the past. This is counterintuitive, as IFC's involvement should help the company achieve higher standards.
- Baseline data supporting the development impact indicators are often missing.

IFC achieves its development impacts through its influence on partners' activities. It also relies to a large extent on client reporting to monitor development impact. The data for monitoring development impacts may not be readily available, as the legal documentation often does not include a clause requiring the sponsors to provide the necessary information. Some loan documents do mention developmental impact as one of the items to be provided by the sponsors in their annual reports to IFC. However, IEG found no further indication of what specific data are required.

> Early review reports for the projects examined usually described the lessons learned.

Inclusion of lessons from past investments

With few exceptions, the early review reports for the projects reviewed fully described the lessons learned pertaining to the specific projects, and the findings were fully reflected in the design, risk mitigation, or other relevant aspects of the projects. Specifically, out of a sample of 93 projects, 84 percent had comments about lessons learned. And more than 80 percent of these projects had the lessons reflected in the appraisal due diligence and/or project structuring. However, the quality and appropriateness of the lessons selected needs to be strengthened.

Looking Ahead

Newer projects (those approved between calendar year 2005 and 2008) had lower sponsor risk but tended to have higher risk relating to project type; this reflects a growing trend in increasing exposure to new greenfield or early-stage businesses. Market risk, although recently showing a downward trend, remains high. The changes in IICCR scores—indicators used for measuring the changes in a country's business climate—deteriorated sharply in recent years.

Taking the above dynamics in risk factors, the expected development outcome ratings are likely to be lower in coming years. The shifts in risks have been significant in the agribusiness and health and education sectors, where drops in development outcomes can be expected if risks and work quality assumptions are taken into account. In Sub-Saharan Africa and the Middle East and North Africa Regions, newer projects were not significantly influenced by the risks, but work quality must improve for outcomes to reach levels observed in other regions (see appendix F).

Summary

The external environment in which IFC is operating has become more difficult with continued global economic fragility. IFC is also taking on more risks as it moves into frontier markets and countries. These trends require an increased focus on work quality, especially given IFC's ongoing decentralization efforts.

IFC's upfront review process is mature and sophisticated. However, weaknesses exist in key areas related to assessing client commitments, understanding political and regulatory risks at the country level, and fully integrating and mainstreaming additionality and development impact considerations into the project cycle.

Chapter 5

Photo by Edwin Huffman, courtesy of the World Bank Photo Library.

EVALUATION HIGHLIGHTS

- To deliver more effectively on its developmental mandate and to improve the development outcome ratings of its guarantee projects, MIGA must strengthen its quality of underwriting.
- MIGA's country and political risk assessment during underwriting has been good.
- Just over half of evaluated guarantee projects had satisfactory or better development outcome ratings.
- Inadequate quality of underwriting was often behind the weak development outcome performance of MIGA's guarantee projects.
- The most recurrent shortcoming in quality of underwriting was inadequate analysis of projects' expected financial viability, including failure to assess commercial risks to project viability.

MIGA: Development Outcome and Quality of Underwriting

Evaluations are often associated with assessment of project outcomes or impacts—that is, the "downstream" side of the project cycle. Increasing evidence, however, indicates that the quality of workmanship at the beginning of the project cycle—that is, during "upstream work" and project implementation—is crucial for delivering development results.

This chapter explores linkages between MIGA project development outcome ratings and the quality of its "upstream work," that is, MIGA's quality of underwriting. During underwriting, MIGA selects, assesses, underwrites, and monitors projects and thus lays the foundation for the development outcomes of its projects.[1]

The main finding of this chapter is that for MIGA to deliver more effectively on its developmental mandate and improve project development outcome ratings, strengthening the quality of underwriting is crucial. The discussion[2] of MIGA's quality of underwriting indicator is presented in the context of enabling MIGA to more effectively pursue its development mandate and strengthen its position as a full-service provider of political risk insurance, capable of encouraging investment into the least-served parts of the market.

The findings presented in this chapter are based on IEG's project evaluation database of 33 ex post evaluations of MIGA guarantee projects (see appendix G for IEG's ex post project evaluation methodology for MIGA). The 33 projects were underwritten by MIGA between fiscal 1996 and 2006 and evaluated by IEG between fiscal 2004 and 2010. The evaluation findings and lessons thus relate to an era when the current MIGA management team was not in place. They also reflect MIGA's then-prevailing underwriting procedures and practices (although the relevance of these findings and lessons would appear to extend beyond that period). Appendix H provides a complete list of projects evaluated for this report.

IEG also analyzed two "subclusters" of project evaluations within the overall population of 33 project evaluations for this report. In the cluster of 12 recently evaluated projects (evaluations completed in fiscal 2010 and referred to henceforth as the "recently evaluated projects" or the "fiscal 2010 cluster"), all but one were underwritten by MIGA between fiscal 2000 and fiscal 2006.[3] Findings of these 12 recently evaluated projects are being presented in an aggregated manner for the first time in this report. In an earlier cluster of 12 projects evaluated in fiscal 2006 (and referred to henceforth as the "fiscal 2006 cluster"), all but one were underwritten between fiscal 1997 and fiscal 1999.[4] The fiscal 2010 cluster of project evaluations was used to analyze more current trends in project performance, and comparisons are made with findings from the earlier fiscal 2006 cluster, when IEG-MIGA last reported on project performance (IEG-MIGA 2006).[5]

The next section first presents a high-level overview of development outcome ratings of MIGA projects and then discusses in more detail MIGA's quality of underwriting and its importance for achieving better project development outcomes.

Development Outcome

Development effectiveness is part of MIGA's mandate and "product brand" and relates to MIGA's role as a catalyst of "high-quality" foreign direct investment (FDI) flows—FDI that sees value in MIGA's environmental and social safeguards and its developmental orientation. Development outcome measures aim to capture a project's overall economic and social impacts and reflect how well a project has contributed to fulfilling MIGA's mission of facilitating FDI that promotes sustainable growth and development.

In considering the results below, it is important to remember that in the case of MIGA, project-level results cannot be extrapolated to the level of the portfolio, as the sample of Project Evaluation Reports is too small for statistical inference. For this reason, conclusions cannot be drawn on MIGA's overall portfolio performance.

Just over half (58 percent) of recently evaluated projects had satisfactory or better development outcome ratings,[6] that is, were rated excellent or satisfactory.[7] Similar development outcome performance was found in the cluster of projects evaluated in fiscal 2006 (figure 5.1).

> Just over half of recently evaluated projects had satisfactory or better development outcome ratings.

Development outcome is a synthesis of four separate dimensions of project performance. The four subdimensions of development outcome show a range of performance. The recently evaluated projects generally performed well with regard to the contribution to private sector development—83 percent were rated satisfactory or better on the indicator. A large proportion of recently evaluated projects (67 percent) also performed well in terms of their economic sustainability. Performance was not as good on business performance, where only 58 percent of recently evaluated projects were rated satisfactory or better. In contrast, performance on E&S effects was generally weak—only a third of recently evaluated projects performed well, that is, were rated satisfactory or better. Similar patterns were found in the earlier cluster of projects evaluated in fiscal 2006, except that in that cohort, a smaller share of projects performed well on the contribution to the private sector development indicator.

> Projects generally performed well on their contribution to private sector development but were weak on E&S effects.

Projects with low[8] development outcome ratings had several features in common. The most important factor was low quality of underwriting. Why quality of underwriting matters for achieving development results is explained in the next section. A full discussion of project performance and quality of underwriting is in IEG-MIGA's report, *Achieving Value-Driven Volume—MIGA's Development Results and Institutional Effectiveness—2010* (IEG-MIGA 2010).

> Inadequate quality of underwriting was often behind weak performance.

Quality of Underwriting

MIGA's quality of underwriting has been good in the area of country and political risk assessment. IEG found that in most of the evaluated projects, country (political) risk assessment had been thorough, and many of the identified risks have been borne out by subsequent events. MIGA's design of project-level risk mitigants has also generally been good. However, other aspects of underwriting quality have been weak, especially—but not only with respect to—the ex ante assessment of project development outcomes. Overall, MIGA's quality of underwriting is weak.

> Quality of underwriting has been good on country risk assessment.

Over half (58 percent) of recently evaluated projects had less than satisfactory quality of underwriting, that is, were rated partly unsatisfactory and unsatisfactory on this dimension. This performance level was marginally better than the fiscal 2006 cluster (only one more satisfactory-rated project than in the fiscal 2006 cluster, figure 5.2).

The quality of underwriting, taking together all 33 projects evaluated by IEG-MIGA, shows a similar pattern. Seventy percent of all evaluated projects were rated less than satisfactory, that is, partly unsatisfactory or unsatisfactory.

FIGURE 5.1 Project Development Outcome Ratings in Both Clusters

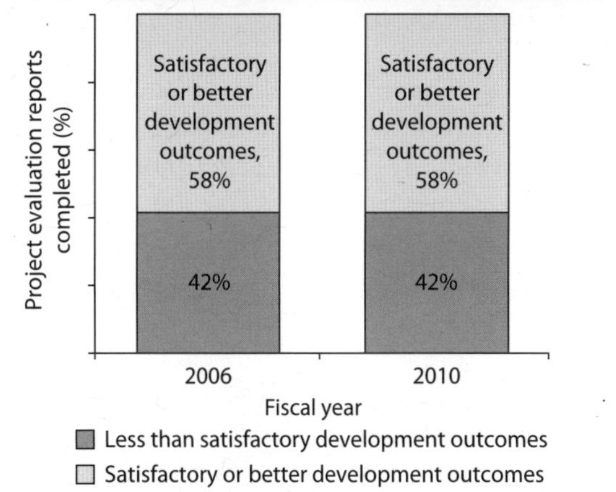

Source: IEG-MIGA project evaluation database.

FIGURE 5.2 MIGA's Quality of Underwriting in Both Clusters

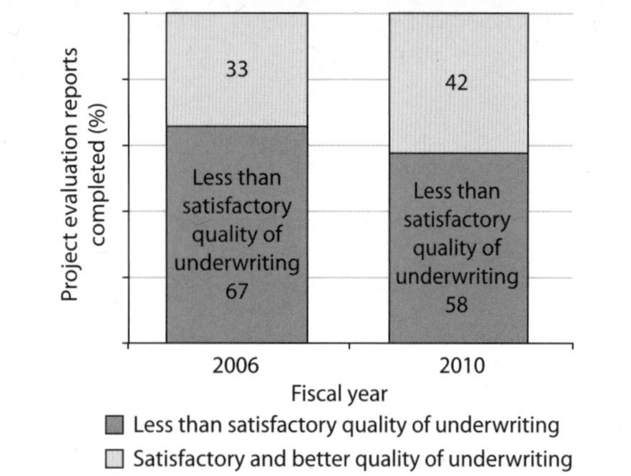

Source: IEG-MIGA project evaluation database.

FIGURE 5.3 Quality of Underwriting and Development Outcome

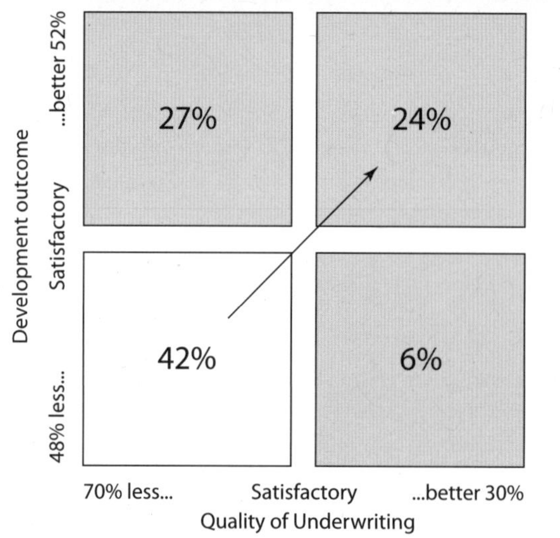

Source: IEG-MIGA project evaluation database.

Including the earlier-evaluated projects (those underwritten by MIGA between fiscal 1996 and fiscal 1998) with those evaluated in fiscal 2006 and fiscal 2010 does not materially change the quality of underwriting results. This suggests that quality of underwriting has been a persistent problem for MIGA.

Poor quality of underwriting and development outcome ratings went hand in hand. Of the 16 evaluated projects with low development outcome ratings, 14 of them (88 percent) also had poor quality of underwriting ratings. This association between poor quality of underwriting and low development outcomes is worrisome, as quality of underwriting has been a persistent problem for many years—and one that is fully under MIGA's control.

> MIGA could improve its development outcome ratings by improving its quality of underwriting.

Improving MIGA's quality of underwriting could improve guarantees' development outcome ratings. The majority of guarantees with low quality of underwriting also have low development outcome ratings (60 percent).[9] In contrast, the overwhelming majority of projects with high quality of underwriting also have high development outcome ratings (80 percent) (figure 5.3).[10] Thus, MIGA could improve the development outcome ratings of its guarantees by improving its quality of underwriting.

The most recurrent quality of underwriting shortcoming was inadequate analysis of the project's financial viability, including MIGA's failure to assess commercial risk. Why does this matter? First, financial viability is critical for a project's development outcome. Good financial performance is required for positive development impact—a project cannot be a commercial failure and have a satisfactory development outcome. Second, failure to analyze commercial risk has negative consequences for MIGA's own business—projects with poor business performance tend to cancel early and incur more investment disputes and preclaims. Thus, commercial risk does not matter to MIGA as a political risk insurer because commercial risk can quickly turn into political risk.

> The most common shortcoming was inadequate analysis of the project's financial viability.

IEG's Project Evaluation Reports indicate that MIGA often failed to verify investor representations of the project's financial viability. In the majority of projects evaluated, MIGA did not verify profitability forecasts provided by the sponsors, nor did it check their soundness against industry norms (box 5.1).

> MIGA's underwriting failed to verify investor representations or to check their realism.

Inadequate monitoring of Category B projects (projects with potential limited adverse social or environmental impacts) was another serious quality of underwriting issue. For Cat-

BOX 5.1 Analyzing Project Financial Viability Is Key to Underwriting Quality

MIGA has often relied on investor representations about project viability without confirming sponsors' forecasts through its own due diligence. As a result, MIGA unwittingly underwrote projects with poor ex ante business performance and development outcomes. Some examples from evaluations include the following:

- A MIGA underwriting paper presented a 120 percent financial rate of return for an infrastructure project. This was based on investor representations and many multiples of that industry's best ever performance. The project, underwritten on that basis, was soon cancelled, as it quickly proved unviable.
- MIGA underwrote a complex infrastructure concession based on investor representations about the project's scope. The guarantee contract based on those representations did not reflect the actual project as described in the concession contract. The evaluation found no evidence that the concession contract itself had been reviewed.
- An underwriting paper documented project financial soundness based on investor representations of yearly revenue flows that turned out to have annualized the peak revenue month of the year. The project has been in dispute because of commercial problems from the outset and was very costly to MIGA in terms of provisioning and mediation work.

Source: IEG.

egory B projects, monitoring of their E&S effects would be essential to ensure that ex ante defined performance standards are met. Further issues with respect to applying performance standards to financial intermediary guarantees are highlighted in box 5.2.

Poor documentation and record keeping was identified as another fundamental quality of underwriting issue. The fiscal 2010 cluster of project evaluations confirms that key underlying project documents were missing from MIGA's files, including concession agreements, environmental impact assessments, project financial models, and the like.

The quality of underwriting issues noted here were highlighted in previous IEG-MIGA annual reports, and specific recommendations were made. However, follow-up has been partial, and several recommendations issued between 2004 and 2009 relating to quality of underwriting remain outstanding.[11]

BOX 5.2 Quality of Underwriting: Assessing Banks' Environment and Social Management Systems

MIGA's 2007 performance standards require that financial intermediaries' Environment and Social Management Systems be assessed. However IEG found this was done only half the time—an important gap. Financial intermediary guarantees are important for MIGA, and many such guarantees support shareholder loans to subsidiaries' lending to sectors that involve significant environmental and social risks.

MIGA's due diligence currently focuses only on the bank headquarters—not on any subsidiary supported by MIGA's guarantee. Given the likelihood of significant differences between a parent bank's environment and social management system with that of its subsidiaries, this approach may not provide an accurate assessment of the subsidiary's compliance with performance standards.

Because MIGA has not received monitoring reports on its financial intermediary projects' E&S performance, it has no information on the impacts of subsidiaries' loans and no basis for knowing if the bank headquarters' environment and social management system reflects that of its subsidiaries.

MIGA needs to focus its due diligence for financial intermediary projects on the developing country subsidiaries projects' environment and social management systems, rather than the parent institutions.

Source: IEG.

Summary

For delivering improved development results, the quality of MIGA's workmanship in selecting, assessing, underwriting, and monitoring of projects—defined collectively as quality of underwriting—is crucial. With respect to project results (development outcomes), just over half (58 percent) of recently evaluated MIGA projects had satisfactory or better development outcome ratings. Those projects with low development outcomes, that is, those rated partially unsatisfactory or unsatisfactory with regard to development outcome, had low quality of underwriting as the most important factor in common.

Quality of underwriting has been a persistent problem for MIGA for many years. MIGA has done well in assessing country and political risks, one aspect of quality of underwriting. However, other aspects of underwriting quality have been weak. This has led to poor quality of underwriting overall—more than half (58 percent) of recently evaluated MIGA projects had low quality of underwriting. The most recurrent shortcoming was inadequate analysis of projects' financial viability, including MIGA's failure to assess commercial risk. For example, MIGA often failed to verify investor representations of projects' financial viability, as indicated in IEG's Project Evaluation Reports and "quality at entry analysis." Inadequate monitoring of Category B projects was another serious quality of underwriting shortcoming, as was poor documentation and record keeping. Although IEG-MIGA issued recommendations to address these quality shortcomings in previous IEG-MIGA annual reports follow-up by MIGA management appears partial.

In conclusion, to deliver on MIGA's development mandate and improve MIGA's project development outcome ratings, strengthening MIGA's quality of underwriting is crucial—and achievable—as it is fully under MIGA's control.

APPENDIX A

IEG Evaluation Frameworks

This appendix describes select elements of the evaluation systems in the World Bank, the International Finance Corporation (IFC), and the Multilateral Investment Guarantee Agency (MIGA) that are the basis for this report. They illustrate intrinsic differences in evaluation practices at the Independent Evaluation Group (IEG), for the World Bank, IFC, and MIGA. These differences explain the difficulties in drawing out common messages across the World Bank Group as a whole and are intended to form a prelude to a more comprehensive review of evaluation methodology at IEG.

The World Bank, IFC, and MIGA differ in their fundamental business. The Bank conducts investment and policy-based lending operations in support of economic and social development and offers policy and technical support to shape development agendas and build capacity. The Bank works largely with governments and public sector entities. IFC finances private sector investment by mobilizing capital in international financial markets and providing advisory services to businesses and governments. MIGA promotes foreign direct investment (FDI) by providing political risk insurance for foreign investments. Each institution has an evaluation system tailored to its different foci, clients, and services.

In each organization, the evaluation system comprises different components—self-evaluation, independent evaluation, and validation of self-evaluation, as described in table A.1.

TABLE A.1 World Bank Group: Self-Evaluation and Independent Evaluation

Type of evaluation	World Bank	IFC	MIGA
Management systems			
Results-based monitoring system for investment/guarantee operations	Yes, Results Secretariat	Yes, DOTS	No
Requirement for supervision reports for investment/guarantee operations	Yes	Yes	No
Quality at entry review	Yes, QAG	Yes, credit review	No
Self-evaluation of investment/guarantee operations	Yes, ICRs	Yes, XPSRs (managed by IEG)	Being piloted (one project evaluation report completed to date)
Results-based monitoring system for advisory services/AAA	No, but discussing	Yes	NA
Requirement for supervision reports for advisory services/AAA	Yes (ACS)	Yes	NA
Independent systems			
System for reviewing self-evaluations of investment operations	Yes, ICR Reviews	Yes, EvNotes	Yes (one validation to date underway)
System for reviewing self-evaluations of advisory services/AAA	No, but discussing; do technical assistance evaluation for sector studies and piloting in PPARs	Yes, PCR Reviews	NA
Conduct of independent evaluations	Yes	Yes	Yes

Source: IEG review.

Note: AAA = analytic and advisory activities; ACS = Activity Completion Summary; DOTS = Development Outcome Tracking System; ICR = Implementation Completion and Results Report; NA = not applicable; PCR = Project Completion Report; PPAR = Project Performance Assessment Review; QAG = Quality Assurance Group; XPSR = Expanded Project Supervision Report.

The project evaluation methodologies and frameworks in the World Bank, IFC, and MIGA are consistent with the Good Practice Standards established by the Evaluation Cooperation Group (ECG) Working Groups for Public Sector Evaluation and Private Sector Evaluation, which aim to harmonize evaluation standards of multilateral development institutions' public and private sector operations. In the private sector, each of the independent evaluation systems is regularly benchmarked against these standards. The most recent benchmarking exercise of private sector evaluation was just concluded. IFC and MIGA were benchmarked at 93 percent and 73 percent compliance with the standards, respectively.

The three independent evaluation entities were established at different times—IEG-World Bank was created in 1973, IEG-IFC in 1996, and IEG-MIGA in 2002—and have quite different institutional histories, as their evaluative functions evolved over time to respond to changes in their host institution and the interests of the Committee on Development Effectiveness. Their work programs and staffing are accordingly also very different; each is broadly scaled to its respective institutional host. For example, IEG-MIGA's core business is evaluation of guarantee projects, as MIGA just began to pilot self-evaluation of its guarantees in 2010. In contrast, IEG-World Bank and IEG-IFC concentrate more on validation, given the mature self-evaluation systems in those institutions. Clearly, therefore, the fundamental priority for MIGA is completing the current self-evaluation pilot and rolling out a project self-evaluation system across the agency, rather than fine-tuning of evaluation systems.

Project Evaluation Frameworks across IEG

Projects (including guarantee projects) are the World Bank Group's main vehicle for delivering development results. Accordingly, IEG focuses in large part on performance at the project level. Project evaluations serve as the building blocks for higher-level sector, thematic, country, global, and corporate evaluations. Increasingly, and in response to Board requests, IEG evaluation reports on these higher-level topics reflect findings and lessons across the World Bank Group.

Project-level completion reporting

The World Bank self-evaluates 100 percent of completed investment operations, with some 250 Implementation Completion Reports (ICRs) prepared per year. World Bank operational staff carry out self-evaluation of closed projects. IEG conducts desk reviews of all ICRs, primarily to validate ratings, and prepares an ICR Review for each.

IFC self-evaluates of around 50 percent of its projects that are reaching early operating maturity, 80 a year on average. IEG independently desk reviews all self-evaluations and field evaluations (Expanded Project Supervision Reports [XPSRs]), producing an Evaluation Note on each. Until 2005, when IFC management introduced the Development Outcome Tracking System, a monitoring system for investment operations, outcome information and self-review for many projects that were not randomly selected for self-evaluation were incomplete.

Since 2002, IEG has drawn a random sample of 50 percent of MIGA guarantee projects that MIGA had underwritten three years earlier for evaluation. It conducts select field validations of sampled projects, producing a Project Evaluation Report (PER) on each. MIGA has just begun to pilot self-evaluation of its guarantee projects—the first PER was completed in fiscal 2010—and IEG has recently developed a validation methodology and system similar to IFC's to do an independent desk review of these. MIGA is expected to self-evaluate a growing number of guarantee projects, but mainstreaming this pilot, with MIGA self-evaluating all sampled guarantee projects, will take a number of years. Until then, IEG will have major ongoing responsibilities for direct project evaluation, while also validating all MIGA's self-evaluations.

All three World Bank Group organizations review projects that fail to fully implement—projects that cancel early (World Bank); early cancellations (MIGA); and, in IFC's case, projects with early cancellations. This is important, as the respective project samples would otherwise suffer from systemic bias. In the World Bank, these are separate shorter self-reviews, known as Notes on Cancelled Operations. IEG reviews them before they go to the Board. For MIGA, IEG includes all guarantees, including early cancellations, in the population to be sampled, and evaluates any that are selected (one in 2010); in the future, it will validate those self-evaluated by MIGA.

IFC and MIGA evaluate projects at early operating maturity, defined as generating 18 months of revenues for the company and having one set of audited financial statements. Financial projects are selected from those that are least 30 months from final IFC disbursement. These comprise the sampling population. The average age of XPSR projects, therefore, is not very different in age from World Bank projects at evaluation, which are evaluated after closure—on average at five years.[1]

Comparisons of investment/guarantee project rating systems at IEG

As noted earlier, each institution has an evaluation system tailored to its specific foci, clients, and services. Given that IFC and MIGA both evaluate private sector projects and are both consistent with the harmonized Good Practice Standards of the ECG, these two systems are very comparable, although MIGA still relies primarily on independent evaluation rather than on self-evaluation. The World Bank evaluation system differs in key ways, consistent with its public sector orientation (projects' business performance, and their financial profitability to the institution are not measured, for example).

In each case, the overall project development outcome is a synthesis rather than a numerical average of ratings. The Bank and IFC use a six-point scale (see box A.1); MIGA uses a four-point scale. Elements of the aggregate rating systems differ across IEG. IFC summary development outcome ratings exclude project investment returns to IFC as well as IFC performance (see box A.2). IFC views the relevance of project objectives as the responsibility of its staff, and relevance is thus a measure of IFC's own performance or effectiveness. In the World Bank system, however, project relevance is rated separately from Bank performance, as the outcome rating considers whether,

BOX A.1 IEG's Ex Post Project Evaluation Methodology for MIGA Projects

IEG uses a standard benchmark-based methodology for its evaluation of MIGA guarantee projects. It rates projects in three dimensions:

Development outcome aims to capture the project's overall impact on a country's economic and social development and is thus important as an implicit proxy for how well the project has contributed to MIGA's purpose and mission. It is evaluated across four subdimensions:

- *Business performance* measures the guarantee project's actual and projected financial impact on the project financiers—its lenders and equity investors.
- *Economic sustainability* measures whether the project has contributed to the country's development.
- *Environmental and social (E&S) effects* measures a project's performance in meeting MIGA's environmental and social requirements, as well as its actual E&S effects.
- *Private sector development* aims to capture the effects of the guarantee project on the development of productive private enterprise beyond the project and relates to MIGA's mandate to enhance the flow of private foreign investment to developing countries.

MIGA's effectiveness captures MIGA's work quality in assessing, underwriting, and monitoring its guarantee projects and the value added MIGA brings to the client or project. It is assessed across three subdimensions:

- *Strategic relevance* refers to the degree of consistency of the guaranteed project with the development priorities of the host country and the Bank's country strategy.
- *MIGA's role and contribution* relates to the benefits or value added that MIGA brings as a development institution. The contribution may be catalytic (in facilitating FDI in economically sound and sustainable businesses) in encouraging the development of the political risk industry or in conveying additionality.
- *MIGA's quality of assessment, underwriting, and monitoring* assesses the extent to which the project's expected development outcomes were adequately assessed, key material risks were identified and mitigated, and whether MIGA's underwriting policies and guidelines were adhered to, and whether MIGA took adequate remedial action if country or project conditions changed subsequent to issuing the guarantee.

Contribution to MIGA's financial results relates to the financial contribution by MIGA of guarantee projects it underwrites.

A four-point scale is used for rating projects: excellent, satisfactory, partly unsatisfactory, and unsatisfactory.

Source: IEG-MIGA.

BOX A.2 How IFC Assesses Project Outcomes

Project Development Performance ratings are assigned in the following dimensions:

Project Business Success: Returns relative to a company's cost of capital (real sector); associated subportfolios or asset growth contribution to an intermediary's profitability, financial condition, and business objectives (financial sector).

Economic Sustainability: Economic rate of return (real sector). This indicator also takes into account job creation, net gains or losses by nonfinanciers, nonquantifiable indicators, and contributions to widely held development objectives; economic viability of the financial institution and its subprojects, and contribution to improving living standards (financial sector).

Environmental and Social Effects: Consistency with IFC requirements; net impact, of the project or subprojects, in terms of pollution loads, conservation of biodiversity and natural resources, and, in a broader context, social, cultural, and community health aspects, as well as labor and working conditions and workers' health and safety.

Private Sector Development Impacts (beyond the project): Demonstration effect in creating sustainable enterprises capable of attracting finance, increasing competition and linkages, and bringing about improvements in regulation.

These ratings are then synthesized (not averaged) into a single **development outcome** rating on a six-point scale from highly successful to highly unsuccessful.

IFC Investment Outcome: Assessments are based on the following:

- *IFC investment return ratings:* These are based on the gross profit contribution quality of an IFC loan and/or equity investment (without taking into account transaction costs or the cost of equity capital).
- *Loans:* These are considered satisfactory provided they are expected to be repaid in full, with interest and fees as scheduled (or prepaid or rescheduled without loss).
- *Equity:* This is considered satisfactory if they yield an appropriate premium on the return of a loan to the same company (a nominal internal rate of return greater than or equal to the fixed loan interest rate, plus an instrument risk premium).

Source: IEG.

and how efficiently, the operation's major relevant objectives were achieved.

In each case, IEG looks for the return on the investment—ideally, the economic rate of return. In the World Bank's goal-based approach, the ex post economic rate of return is compared with the original estimate. For IFC and MIGA projects, the benchmark for a satisfactory rating is equal to or greater than 10 percent. (In MIGA, if an economic rate of return or a tax-adjusted financial rate of return cannot be calculated, qualitative evidence is requested.)

In the IFC and MIGA rating frameworks, IEG gives prominence to environment and social (E&S) effects of projects as a separate rating dimension. For IFC and MIGA, an unsatisfactory rating on this dimension would generally result in a less-than-satisfactory synthesis rating for the development outcome. However, in IEG's rating framework for the World Bank, environmental and social performance is not a separate dimension, but one of many factors to be taken under consideration. However, since 2006, IEG has begun to rate the World Bank on the quality of project monitoring and evaluation, based on such factors as design, utilization, and dissemination.

For the World Bank, with its focus on public sector projects, borrower performance is separately rated. Indeed, guidance calls for the borrowers to submit their own completion reports. Additionally, self-evaluators are to take into consideration the performance of cofinanciers and other partners. Comments on the draft completion report are sought from the borrower, cofinanciers, and other partners, and the final completion report is publicly disclosed.

Consistent with the proprietary information on which they are based (client data are subject to confidentiality restrictions), IFC and MIGA do not disclose XPSRs, PERs, Evaluation Notes, and so forth, nor do they share the self-evaluation outside of IFC or MIGA. However, the perspectives of investors and other financial stakeholders are routinely gathered as input to the evaluation.

Additionally, IEG provides ratings of the quality of the self-evaluation completion report. The ratings are based on factors such as quality of the analysis and strength of the evidence.

Overall lessons learned are a common feature of the ICRs, XPSRs, and MIGA PER pilot self-evaluations and are reviewed by IEG. Formats for the lessons are the same in IFC and MIGA, whereas the Bank reports on different aspects, using an objectives-based system. IFC and MIGA's project rating systems are based on quantitative and qualitative benchmarks rather than on achievement of specific development outcomes.

Advisory Services

Only IFC's self-evaluation template asks for the details of any advisory service projects linked to investment operations. And only IFC has a self-evaluation system for all advisory service operations that can be independently reviewed by IEG. IEG's review of IFC advisory services self-evaluations has focused on the evaluative substance of Project Completion Reports, the sufficiency of the evidence produced, and the correctness of ratings assigned, largely via desk review. Selective field-based validations have also been conducted.

This is a young system for IFC and noteworthy in that it reflects a results-based approach. IFC has supplementary external reviews and "rigorous" evaluations of specific projects and programs.

The World Bank requires an Activity Completion Summary (ACS) to be prepared for all analytic and advisory activities, within six months of delivery to the client. The information therein is largely mechanical and does not lend itself to evaluation, and the rate of noncompletion is significant. IEG has not routinely reviewed the ACS; as discussed above, it is piloting the review of technical assistance components of projects as part of Project Performance Assessment Reviews (PPARs). IEG is discussing evaluation of analytic and advisory activities, including nonlending technical assistance, with World Bank management.

Comparison of Direct Project-Level Evaluations in the Field

The core business of the IEG-MIGA group is direct evaluation of projects randomly selected for independent evaluation. Almost all these evaluations involve a field visit. Although MIGA is expected to self-evaluate a growing number of guarantee projects, mainstreaming the pilot—with MIGA self-evaluating all sampled guarantee projects—will take a number of years. Until then, IEG-MIGA will continue to undertake a large number of direct project evaluations, in parallel with validating MIGA's self-evaluations

For the Bank and IFC, IEG selects about 20–30 percent of evaluated and reviewed projects for field reassessments (PPARs for the World Bank). The assessment ratio is set by the Bank's Committee on Development Effectiveness. PPARs are typically conducted three years after program completion. IEG criteria for identifying projects for project-level field reviews include those that offer good potential for further learning because of particularly good or bad performance and those related to sectors, thematic areas, or countries that are soon to be evaluated, where PPARs can be inputs for those evaluation tools.

PPARs are increasingly clustered by issue or topic to reduce their cost and increase their learning impact. PPARs rate projects in terms of their outcome (taking into account relevance, efficacy, and efficiency), sustainability of results, and institutional development impact. Beyond this, an established field methodology has not been developed.

IEG field reviews of IFC projects do not have clearly defined criteria, but in practice they frequently are undertaken to validate the environmental and social performance of projects selected for IEG studies and/or where there are major disagreements on these or other ratings between IFC investment staff and IEG.

Larger-Scale Evaluations

Project evaluations serve as the building blocks for higher-level evaluations—sector, thematic, country, global, and corporate. Increasingly, and in response to Board requests, such IEG reports reflect findings and lessons across the World Bank Group.

Country-level evaluations

All World Bank Country Assistance Strategies (CASs) are now required to include a self-evaluation of the Bank's country program, called a CAS Completion Report. IEG conducts a desk review of the CAS Completion Report to validate the self-evaluation and makes its assessment available to the Board before the presentation of a related CAS. If the CAS is a joint Bank-IFC document, IFC contributes to the report a third of time. IEG also reviews IFC's performance.

Given the growth of this report, IEG has decreased the number of more expensive field-based evaluations of the performance of country programs. These evaluations are called Country Assistance Evaluations (CAEs) when Bank country programs are evaluated and Country Impact Reviews when evaluating IFC activities in a country. For CAEs in countries where IFC does not have a significant role, IEG prepares a brief Country Evaluation Note. IEG views itself as having moved toward more of a continuum approach to country program evaluations to meet the different needs for information. The one end of the continuum is CAS Completion Reports and the other is the full CAE.

Country performance is not the focus of strategy and accountability for IFC. The client is not the country, but rather private companies. IEG reflected on this issue in its *Biennial Report on Evaluation 2008* (IEG-IFC 2008a).

Other areas of evaluation

Sector and thematic reviews examine performance and experience in a lending sector, such as agriculture or transport, or a thematic area, such as investment climate or gender. More often, IEG seeks to review and provide the experience of the World Bank Group as a whole in the sector and thematic studies.

Evaluations of global partnership programs have grown in prevalence and importance in IEG's Bank evaluations. Global partnership programs represent collective actions to achieve common development objectives. The evaluations correspondingly address global or regional issues that cross national boundaries. These global partnership evaluations have not extended to IEG's IFC work.

IEG also conducts evaluations focused on World Bank, IFC, and MIGA instruments and/or organizational and development effectiveness. Recent IEG reports on the World Bank have addressed the Bank's engagement with client countries, internal management, and the strengths and weaknesses of different Bank instruments. IEG has focused separately on IFC advisory services in Eastern Europe and Central Asia and on IFC's additionality. IEG prepares separate annual reports on MIGA's organizational and development effectiveness and has also assessed the design and implementation of MIGA's strategy.

Finally, efforts are being made to pay more attention to the "theory of change," or to give midstream attention to implementation, for example, moving away from an exclusively ex post, downstream strategy. Management use of real-time systems such as IFC's Development Outcome Tracking System and appreciation of ongoing real-time evaluations at the World Bank (for example, on crisis response) confirm the value of this direction. IEG plans to determine how to engage more in prospective and implementation evaluations without compromising independence.

APPENDIX B

Recent Trends in World Bank Project Performance

Because year-to-year variations in project performance by sector are not statistically significant or representative of any particular trend, the analysis of sectoral results in this report compares actual values of average sector board performance scores for fiscal 2009 with those predicted on the basis of data on performance outcomes from 1993 to 2008.

In table B.1, a regression analysis is first undertaken on data over fiscal 1993–2008 to measure sector- or region-specific performance differences, controlling for instrument type, and adding a time trend. Column A is the regression coefficient obtained for each sector and region, which gives the performance of each sector and region relative to the top performing sector

TABLE B.1 World Bank—Recent Trends in Project Performance

Projected and actual values for fiscal 2009 (fiscal 1993–2008 regression)					Fiscal 2000–04		Fiscal 2005–09	
Variable	A. Est. effect coefficient	B. Relative impact	C. Predicted fiscal 2009	D. Actual fiscal 2009	E. Est. effect coefficient	F. Relative impact	G. Est. effect coefficient	H. Relative impact
Exit year	**0.02**	0.29			–0.01		**–0.05**	–0.21
Transport (reference sector)			4.64	4.27				
Agriculture and rural dev.	**–0.43**	0.04	4.25	4.11	**–0.53**	–0.01	–0.21	
Economic policy	**–0.56**	0.01	4.21	4.57	**–0.81**	–0.02	–0.21	
Education	**–0.22**	0.00	4.41	3.85	–0.26		**–0.38**	0.00
Energy and mining	**–0.52**	0.06	4.21	4.10	**–0.61**	0.04	**–0.43**	–0.01
Environment	**–0.38**	–0.02	4.27	4.09	**–0.77**	0.01	–0.13	
Financial and private sector dev.	**–0.60**	0.00	3.99	4.30	**–0.65**	0.01	**–0.48**	0.02
Health, nutrition, population	**–0.56**	–0.04	4.01	3.11	**–0.61**	–0.01	**–0.82**	0.02
Public sector governance	**–0.67**	–0.01	4.06	3.90	**–0.69**	0.01	**–0.68**	0.02
Social protection	**–0.24**	–0.01	4.45	4.00	**–0.34**	–0.01	**–0.43**	0.00
Urban development	**–0.34**	0.01	4.34	4.14	**–0.50**	0.00	–0.02	
Water	**–0.47**	–0.01	4.17	4.07	**–0.54**	–0.01	–0.13	
Total sector		0.02				0.01		0.04
East Asia and Pacific			4.54	4.10				
Africa	**–0.63**	0.06	3.86	3.83	**–0.36**	0.02	**–0.46**	0.00
Europe and Central Asia	–0.06		4.43	4.22	0.16		–0.06	
Latin America and Caribbean	–0.09		4.37	4.06	0.02		–0.12	
Middle East and North Africa	**–0.43**	0.02	4.13	3.86	–0.19		**–0.46**	0.00
South Asia	**–0.27**	0.00	4.27	4.31	0.10		–0.23	
Total region		**0.08**				**0.02**		**0.00**
DPLs	**0.32**	**0.00**	4.35	4.15	0.22	**0.00**	0.21	**0.00**
Constant	**-34.58**	0.00			29.74		**109.87**	0.00
World Bank average			4.27	4.04				
Total sector, region, DPL		**0.094**				**0.029**		**0.035**

Source: IEG.

Note: Average performance among sectors is estimated relative to transport; among regions, relative to East Asia and Pacific; among lending instruments, relative to investment operations. Only regions with significant performance effects are included in columns B, F, and H. Three small sectors are excluded due to their small sample size. Columns B, F, and H give the estimated effects from the regression—that is, the average increase (on the six-point rating scale) in project performance relative to the reference sector or region. Bold values are statistically significant. DPL = Development Policy Loan.

and region over that time period, and in the case of Development Policy Loans (DPLs), relative to investment loans.

Weighting sectoral performance by the change in the share of each sector in the Bank's portfolio over the same period, column B shows estimates of the relative contribution of these shifts to the change in overall Bank portfolio performance. Based on the coefficients of the regression over the period fiscal 1993–2008, the predicted performance of each sector and region in fiscal 2009 is estimated (column C). Column D gives actual values for average sector and regional performance in fiscal 2009.

The comparison of columns C and D shows the difference between actual performance in fiscal 2009 and predicted performance, based on data from fiscal 1993 to fiscal 2008. It shows that many sectors have performed below trend values.

Actual and predicted values are presented in terms of scores per sector or region averaged on a six-point scale. As shown in the World Bank's previous *Annual Report on Development Effectiveness* (IEG 2009a), there can be a difference between ratings measured by the percentage of satisfactory (that is, moderately satisfactory or better) versus unsatisfactory projects on the one hand and an average along the six-point scale on the other. In this alternative metric, performance is averaged over the six categories from 1 (or highly unsatisfactory) to 6 (or highly satisfactory). Using this metric, the Health, Nutrition, and Population Sector Board, for example, has a predicted average performance score of 4.01, compared with an actual average of 3.11. Transport, which was the leading performer for 2008, with an expected average performance on a six-point scale of 4.64, had an actual value of 4.27.

In a separate exercise, given the long period from 1993 to 2008 and the possibility that there may have been shifts in trends in more recent years that have been masked by the long-term trend, an examination of performance over more recent years was separately undertaken, comparing the last five years, 2005–09 (columns G and H), with the previous five-year period (columns E and F). These regressions each include sectors, regions, the type of loan (DPLs or investment lending), and a time trend (the exit year); this is similar to the regression undertaken for the entire period fiscal 1993–2008.

A first finding is that, although there was a positive overall time trend over the entire time period (0.02 points per year), the trend over time has been negative over the last 10 years. This is evident in both subperiods from fiscal 2000–04 (0.01 points per year) and fiscal 2005–09 (0.05 points per year). Yet, despite the decline in average ratings in the latter period, there was a positive contribution in terms of compositional effects by sector, amounting to 0.01 points in the first five-year period (fiscal 2000–04) and 0.04 points in the second five-year period (fiscal 2005–09); regional shifts had no net effect. The overall decline is therefore caused by deteriorating outcomes within sectors, not compositional effects.

Columns E and G in the table show performance relative to the leading sector over the period 1993–2008 (transport), which also remained the leading sector in the recent five-year subperiods, and the leading region (East Asia and the Pacific, looking only at coefficients that are significant). For example, column G confirms that the worst performer in 2005–09 is the health, nutrition, and population sector, which achieved an average rating 0.82 points below the transportation sector. Public sector governance and finance/private sector development were rated 0.68 and 0.48 points, respectively, more poorly than the reference sector. The urban sector performed .02 points worse than transportation in the last five years. Health, nutrition, and population was a poorer performer in the previous period (0.61 points below the transportation sector), but it deteriorated further (to 0.82 points lower). Another statistically significant relative deterioration, compared with the leading sector, was in social protection (from –0.34 to –0.43).

Coefficients for agriculture, environmental lending, economic policy, urban development, and water suggest improvement between the two five-year subperiods, but the coefficients are not significant in the second period. There was, however, a clear improvement in the energy and mining sector, from –0.61 to –0.43. Financial sector and private sector development, although a poor performer in 2005–09, also improved relative to the previous period, from –0.65 to –0.48. Overall, the results suggest that apart from some consistently good or poor performing sectors (transport/urban compared to health, nutrition, and population), relative performance of other sectors varies over time.

In terms of regional performance, in the first subperiod (fiscal 2000–04) Africa was the weakest. The Middle East and North Africa Region appears the second worst, but its coefficient is not significant. In the second subperiod (fiscal 2005–09), these two regions performed comparably. Other regional changes were not statistically significant.

APPENDIX C

Follow-Up to Evaluation in Other Institutions

Asian Development Bank

One of the examples for progress in the area of follow-up to recommendations has been the Asian Development Bank (ADB) Independent Evaluation Department (IED). IED is working to improve the quality of its recommendations by taking into consideration the need to be more specific regarding suggestions and avoid being too prescriptive. In its 2009 reports, IED has addressed this dual approach by cross-referencing the recommendations with those paragraphs that provide specific suggestions for implementation.

IED has also made arrangements to enhance the skills of its staff in writing recommendations and plans to dedicate a section of its new guidelines to suggestions for developing evaluation recommendations (ADB 2009). Moreover, the IED has also classified its recommendations and published a comprehensive review of their implementation in its annual report on acting on recommendations.

The newly developed automated Management Action Record System allows IED to input its recommendations after the circulation of a particular evaluation report. Subsequently, ADB management-nominated focal points from implementing and operating departments include the relevant action plans and action completion target-dates in Management Action Record System. The electronic processing of the information provided by management eliminates time-consuming manual processing.[1]

IFAD

The International Fund for Agricultural Development's (IFAD) Agreement at Completion Point (ACP) process is a time- and resource-intensive but interesting example regarding the use of informal processes, management ownership, and the utilization of evaluation findings (Bandstein and Hedblom 2008). The ACP process is designed to build ownership and stakeholder commitment to taking action on agreed Office of Evaluation recommendations both in IFAD and in country. IFAD's Office of Evaluation facilitates the ACP process by holding large, in-country stakeholder workshops to reach agreements expressed in the ACP. The ACP process and related monitoring of the status of implementation through the President's "Report on the Implementation Status of Evaluation Recommendations and Management Issues" promote the use of evaluation findings and make it more difficult for evaluations to be ignored.

IFAD management is responsible for implementing evaluation recommendations as agreed in the ACP and Office of Evaluation comments on management's record of responding to evaluation recommendations when the "Report on the Implementation Status of Evaluation Recommendations and Management Issues" is considered at the evaluation committee (IFAD 2009). A recent peer review of IFAD's Office of Evaluation and Evaluation Function, however, has recommended that responsibility for the ACP would be more appropriately placed with the Programme Management Department.

CONEVAL

On the national level, Mexico's National Council for the Evaluation of Social Policy (CONEVAL) presents an interesting approach with regard to management ownership and the focus on developing follow-up to recommendation mechanisms that help ensure quality, categorization, prioritization, and utilization of evaluation findings.[2] CONEVAL places the emphasis on the ministries' ownership of evaluation findings and recommendations. Once an evaluation is cleared by the program or agency, recommendations are selected in terms of its relevance and feasibility of implementation (figure C.1).

Recommendations are then classified by the type of actor involved in the solution, depending on their scope of influence, and prioritized in terms of importance. Based on these steps, an implementation plan, which outlines the activities and timeline for the introduction of recommendations at the program and the institutional level, is requested by the programs.

Once a plan is prepared, its dissemination on the responsible ministry's Web site is encouraged (evaluation units within line ministries are expected to be responsible for

FIGURE C.1 **CONEVAL's Follow-Up to Evaluation Recommendations**

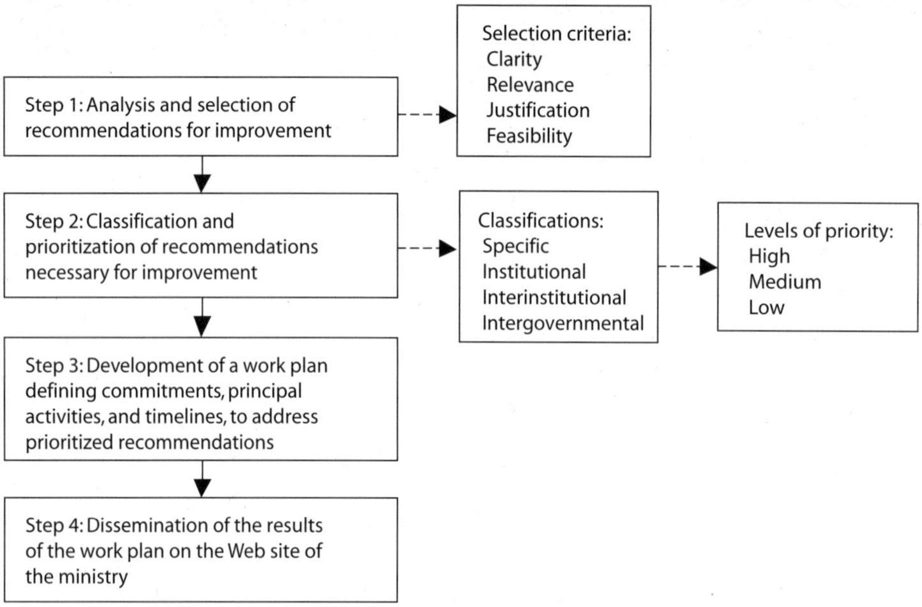

Source: IFC.

Note: CONEVAL = National Council for the Evaluation of Social Policy (Mexico). Follow-up mechanism to potential improvements identified by external evaluations of federal programs, México D.F., October 14, 2008.

this process) and the National Audit Institution also monitors and reports on the use of those recommendations.

Even though CONEVAL's follow-up system was only introduced in 2008, there are already promising examples of evaluation findings that have led to shifts in budgetary and programmatic priorities (Castro and others 2009). CONEVAL's emphasis on the ownership of the ministries for making evaluation findings and recommendations useful, and the attention that the national media has been paying to evaluation results, have been important factors in the current success of Mexico's monitoring and evaluation system.

APPENDIX D

Further Details of Regression Analysis—World Bank Decentralization

Effect of Location of Task Team Leader on Final Outcomes

To tease out potential selection bias, a two-stage least squares regression was used. In the first-stage regression, distance from Washington, DC, is shown to be a strong candidate as an instrument for location of a task team leader in the field. With a greater than 99 percent confidence (and an *F*-score of 37, exceeding a rule-of-thumb value of 10), distance appears to predict whether the Bank chooses a field-based task team leader to oversee an operation (at least in its final stages). Operations in health, education, and social protection (the human development network) are 9 percentage points more likely to have a task team leader based in the field than those in the infrastructure, agriculture, or environment sectors (sustainable development network).

The second-stage regression, in which distance serves as an instrument for a task team leader based in the field, does not find any evidence that the location of the task team leader at project closing has an effect on outcomes of operations.

When individual regions are considered separately, this instrumental variable does not hold power, that is, when considering the marginal effects of locating a task team leader in the field for each individual region. This is because the instrument exhibits too much collinearity with dummy variables for the regions. Instead, a series of simple "dprobit" regressions correcting for the same factors is detailed in table D.1. Focusing on the interaction term, the regression reveals that there are only statistically significant effects in South Asia, where a task team leader located in the field at closing has a positive effect on outcomes, and in Latin America and the Caribbean, where a task team leader located in the field at closing has negative effects on outcomes.

Location of country director and outcomes of Bank country programs

Does the location of the country director affect outcomes of Bank country programs? The dprobit regression detailed in table D.2 uses outcome of country program as the dependent variable and the usual controls. There is no appropriately powerful instrumental variable available, so the question of causality remains.

TABLE D.1 Determinants of IEG Outcomes by Regions

Variable	AFR	EAP	ECA	LCR	MNA	SAR
Based in Field (dummy)	0.031	0.059	0.043	0.079**	0.058	0.017
Field * [region] (interaction)[a]	**0.064**	**−0.059**	**0.017**	**−0.214***	**−0.124**	**0.213****
CPIA control	0.108**	0.109**	0.108**	0.111***	0.108**	0.109**
GDP per capita growth control	0.365	0.352	0.335	0.341	0.340	0.364
Exit fiscal year	−0.019*	−0.019*	−0.019*	−0.020*	−0.019*	−0.019*
IDA country dummy	0.008	0.007	0.009	0.013	0.013	0.013
Blend country dummy	0.054	0.053	0.055	0.063	0.054	0.053
Fragile state dummy	−0.042	−0.045	−0.046	−0.047	−0.042	−0.049
DPL dummy	0.113***	0.112***	0.112**	0.113***	0.112**	0.112***
AFR Region dummy	0.003	0.021	0.016	0.031	0.017	−0.086
EAP Region dummy	0.121**	0.135**	0.123**	0.128**	0.123**	0.052
ECA Region dummy	0.076	0.083	0.076	0.093*	0.085	−0.008
LCR Region dummy	0.073	0.079	0.077	0.111**	0.082	−0.017
MNA Region dummy	0.078	0.084	0.082	0.094	0.099	(omitted)
SAR Region dummy	(omitted)	(omitted)	(omitted)	(omitted)	(omitted)	−0.189**

(continued on next page)

TABLE D.1 Determinants of IEG Outcomes by Regions *(continued)*						
Variable	AFR	EAP	ECA	LCR	MNA	SAR
FPD network dummy	–0.128**	–0.126**	–0.124**	–0.121**	–0.126**	–0.127**
HDN dummy	–0.129***	–0.131***	–0.129***	–0.124***	–0.129***	–0.127***
PREM dummy	–0.117**	–0.117**	–0.115**	–0.110**	–0.113**	–0.115**
SDN dummy	(omitted)	(omitted)	(omitted)	(omitted)	(omitted)	(omitted)
Observations	882	882	882	882	882	882
Pseudo R^2	0.083	0.083	0.083	0.088	0.083	0.087

Source: World Bank internal database.

Note: **Regions:** AFR = Sub-Saharan Africa; EAP = East Asia and Pacific; ECA = Europe and Central Asia; LCR = Latin America and the Caribbean; MNA = Middle East and North Africa; SAR = South Asia. **Sectors:** FPD = finance and private sector development; HDN = Human Development Network; PREM = Poverty Reduction and Economic Management Sector; SDN = Sustainable Development Network. CPIA = Country Policy and Institutional Assessment; DPL = Development Policy Loan; GDP = gross domestic product; IDA = International Development Association.

a. In nonlinear models, the interaction effect is the cross-partial derivative of the expected value of ***y***. This is not accurately estimated in the dprobit model. Using the interaction effects model, the table above corrects for this error in the interaction term. For more information, see http://www.unc.edu/~enorton/NortonWangAi.pdf.

TABLE D.2 Determinants of Outcomes of Bank Country Program	
Variable	Coefficient
CD based in hub (dummy)	**–0.251**
CD based in headquarters (dummy)	**–0.116**
CD based in country (dummy)	**(omitted)**
CPIA control	0.357
GDP per capita growth control	5.12
IDA country dummy	0.099
Blend country dummy	–0.026
Fragile state dummy	–0.239
AFR dummy	0.081
EAP dummy	0.088
ECA dummy	0.015
LCR dummy	0.116
MNA dummy	–0.027
SAR dummy	(omitted)
Observations	67
Pseudo R^2	0.207

Source: World Bank internal database.

Note: Dummy for CASCRR rating Bank country program as moderately satisfactory or better is the dependent variable. The ***p*** value on the country director based in hub is 0.11, and thus not quite significant. **Regions:** AFR = Sub-Saharan Africa; EAP = East Asia and Pacific; ECA = Europe and Central Asia; LCR = Latin America and the Caribbean; MNA = Middle East and North Africa; SAR = South Asia. CPIA = Country Policy and Institutional Assessment; GDP = gross domestic product; IDA = International Development Association.

APPENDIX E

IFC Supplemental Data Tables

TABLE E.1 IEG-IFC Evaluation Methodologies

Evaluation activity	Focus	Main data sources
Meta analysis of IFC investment portfolio and new business	Results (relevance)	IFC investment operations database World Bank database
Meta analysis of secondary data on FDI investment	Results (relevance)	World Bank database; MDB annual reports
Evaluation of mature IFC investment operations	Results (outcomes) IFC additionality	Expanded Project Supervision Reports (214) and Project Completion Reports (40 projects from 2008 and 82 projects from 2009)
Risk profiling of mature and new IFC investment operations	Risk-adjusted expected development outcomes	679 IEG risk-layering reviews, completed between 2000 and 2009 Institutional Investor Country Credit Risk ratings
Project *case examples*	Results and IFC additionality	IEG EvNotes, country and sector studies, site visits

Source: IEG.

Note: FDI = foreign direct investment; MDB = multilateral development bank.

FIGURE E.1 Combined Project Development Outcome and IFC Investment Return Characteristics, 2007–09

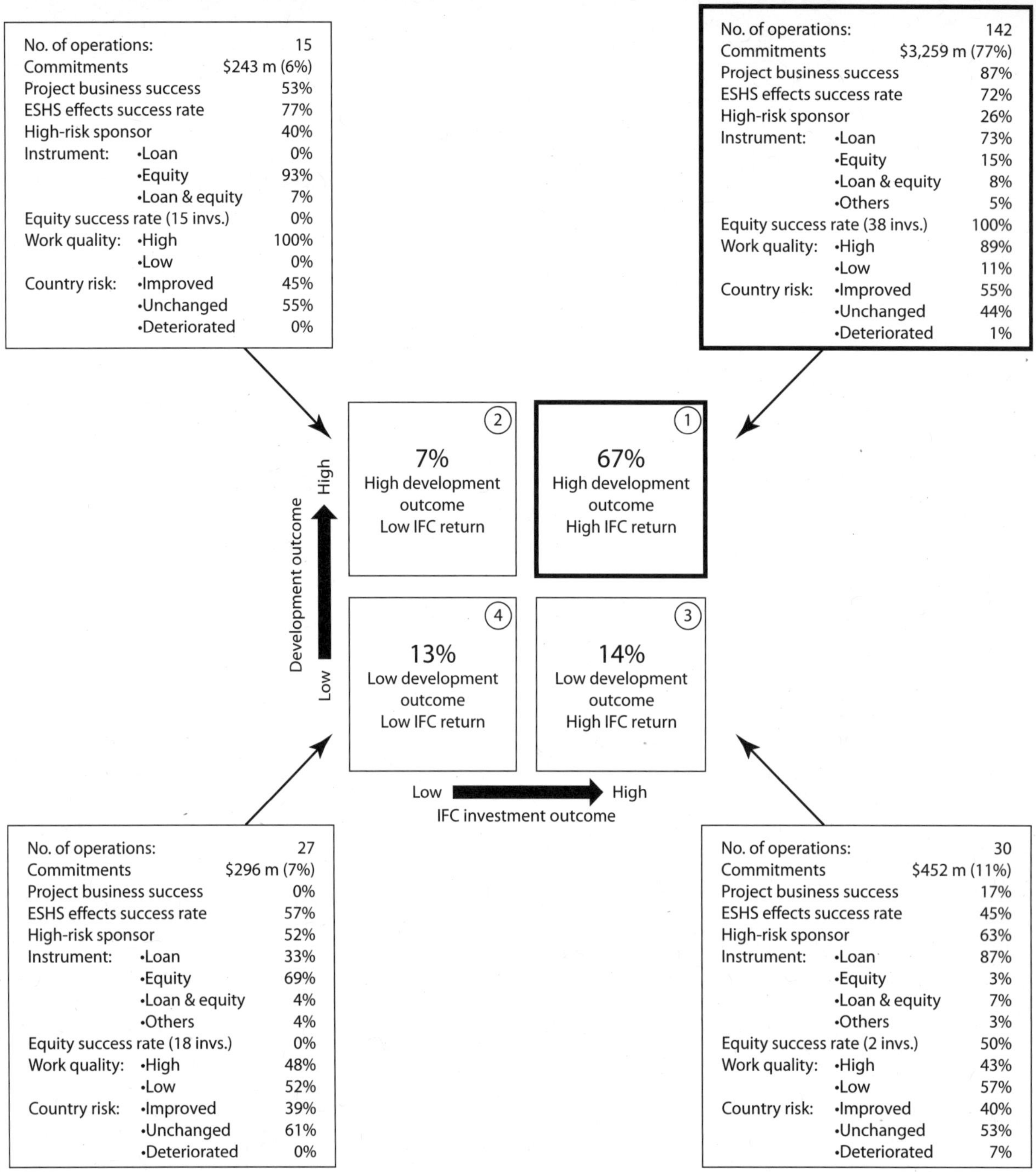

Source: IEG-IFC.

Note: ESHS = environmental, social, health, and safety; m = million.

TABLE E.2 IFC: Project Sample Representativeness—Investment Operations

	Number of investments					Value of investments ($ millions)				
	CY2007–09 XPSRs (a)		CY2002–04 NAP (b)		(c) = (a)/(b)	CY2007–09 XPSRs (a)		CY2002–04 NAP (b)		(c) = (a)/(b)
	Number	Percent	Number	Percent	Percent	Amount	Percent	Amount	Percent	Percent
	216	*100*	*424*	*100*	51	4,652	*100*	9,048	*100*	51
Net IFC										
Mean	—	—	—	—	—	22	—	21	—	—
Median	—	—	—	—	—	13	—	13	—	—
Investment size										
X = <4.66	42	*19*	85	*20*	49	92	*2*	193	*2*	48
4.66 < X = <38.02	137	*63*	264	*62*	52	2,203	*47*	4,194	*46*	53
X > 38.02	37	*17*	75	*18*	49	2,356	*51*	4,661	*52*	51
	216	*100*	424	*100*	51	4,652	*100*	9,048	*100*	51
Instruments										
Equity only	47	*22*	96	*23*	49	726	*16*	1,176	*13*	62
Other	169	*78*	328	*77*	52	3,926	*84*	7,872	*87*	50
	216	*100*	424	*100*	51	4,652	*100*	9,048	*100*	51
Sectors										
Financial markets	93	*43*	184	*43*	51	2,171	*47*	3,851	*43*	56
Nonfinancial markets	123	*57*	240	*57*	51	2,481	*53*	5,197	*57*	48
	216	*100*	424	*100*	51	4,652	*100*	9,048	*100*	51
Departments										
Agribusiness	14	*6*	27	*6*	52	319	*7*	565	*6*	56
Global Financial Markets Group	74	*34*	148	*35*	50	1,742	*37*	3,089	*34*	56
Global Inform. & Comm. Tech.	15	*7*	29	*7*	52	217	*5*	471	*5*	46
Global Manufacturing & Services	47	*22*	94	*22*	50	1,049	*23*	2,130	*24*	49
Health and Education	7	*3*	12	*3*	58	58	*1*	102	*1*	56
Infrastructure	26	*12*	51	*12*	51	503	*11*	1,206	*13*	42
Oil, Gas, Mining, and Chemicals	15	*7*	29	*7*	52	381	*8*	774	*9*	49
Private Equity and Investment Funds	18	*8*	34	*8*	53	384	*8*	712	*8*	54
	216	*100*	424	*100*	51	4,652	*100*	9,048	*100*	51
Regions										
Africa	19	*9*	41	*10*	46	109	*2*	585	*7*	19
Asia	54	*25*	105	*25*	51	1,103	*24*	2,065	*23*	53
Europe and Central Asia	66	*31*	127	*30*	52	1,581	*34*	2,639	*30*	60
Latin America and the Caribbean	58	*27*	114	*27*	51	1,566	*34*	3,191	*36*	49
Middle East and North Africa	15	*7*	29	*7*	52	225	*5*	421	*5*	53
World	4	*2*	8	*2*	50	67	*1*	148		
	216	*100*	424	*100*	51	4,652	*100*	9,048	*100*	51

(continued on next page)

TABLE E.2	IFC: Project Sample Representativeness—Investment Operations (*continued*)									
	Number of investments					Value of investments ($ millions)				
	CY2007–09 XPSRs (a)		CY2002–04 NAP (b)		(c) = (a)/(b)	CY2007–09 XPSRs (a)		CY2002–04 NAP (b)		(c) = (a)/(b)
	Number	Percent	Number	Percent	Percent	Amount	Percent	Amount	Percent	Percent
	216	*100*	424	*100*	51	4,652	*99*	9,048	*100*	51
Active/Closed										
Active	135	*63*	254	*60*	53	3,057	*66*	5,608	*62*	55
Closed	81	*38*	170	*40*	48	1,595	*34*	3,440	*38*	46
	216	*100*	424	*100*	51	4,652	*100*	9,048	*100*	51
Indicative performance (as of 06/30/2008) (i) *All investments:*[a]										
With loss reserves	3	*1*	6	*1*	50	17	*0*	36	*0*	47
Without loss reserves	213	*99*	418	*99*	51	4,635	*100*	9,012	*100*	51
	216	*100*	424	*100*	51	4,652	*100*	9,048	*100*	51
(ii) Equity only:[a]										
With loss reserves	0	*0*	0	*0*	—	0	*0*	0	*0*	—
Without loss reserves	47	*100*	96	*100*	49	726	*100*	1,176	*100*	62
	47	*100*	96	*100*	49	726	*100*	1,176	*100*	62
Countries (excluding regional):	65		82							

Source: IEG.

Note: NAP = National Action Program; XPSR = Expanded Project Supervision Report.

a. Amounts with loss reserves are the IFC approved investments that are affected by loss reserves (not the actual amount reserved).

FIGURE E.2 Implementation of IFC's Global Crisis Initiatives

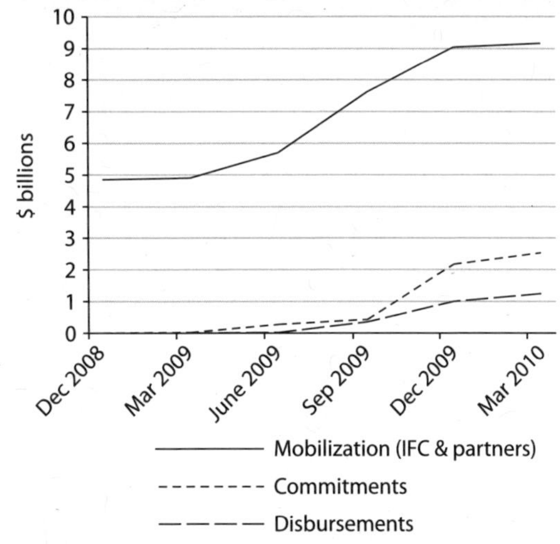

Source: IFC.

TABLE E.3 IFC Crisis Initiatives

Initiative	Funding: Target	Funding: Actual mobilization	Deployment: Target (by end fiscal 2010)	Deployment: Actual commitments (03/31/10)	Deployment: Actual disbursement (03/31/10)
Global Trade Finance Program	Program ceiling raised to $3 billion	N/A (supported by IFC capital base)	N/A (unfunded guarantee program)	$2.4 billion	N/A
Global Trade Liquidity Program	Up to $5 billion	$1.5 billion partners $1 billion IFC	$3 to $5 billion	$2.05 billion	$1.05 billion
IFC Capitalization Fund	Up to $5 billion	$2 billion JBIC $1 billion IFC	$1.6 billion	$81 million	$81 million
Microfinance Enhancement Fund	$500 million	$292 million partners $150 million IFC	$0.47 billion	$122 million	$92 million
Infrastructure Crisis Facility	Up to $10 billion ($8 billion debt and $2 billion equity)	$1 billion partners $300 million IFC	$0.48 billion[b]	$120 million	$6.5 million
Debt and Asset Recovery Program	$6–$8.5 billion	$300 million partners $1.6 billion IFC	$0.5 billion	$140 million	$5.3 million
Advisory services	$30 million (revised from $60 million)	$16.1 million partners	$20 million	$10.7 million	$2.7 million
Total new partnerships[a]	$26–$29 billion	$9.2 billion	$6.1–$8.1 billion	$2.5 billion	$1.2 billion
% of target		35		41	20

Source: IFC.

Note: Table does not include expected parallel financing in the case of GTLP ($3 billion) and the Infrastructure Crisis Facility ($3.5 billion). JBIC = Japan Bank for International Cooperation.

a. Excludes Global Trade Finance Program as an existing program that was expanded and given its unfunded guarantee nature.

b. The December 2008 Board approval paper for the facility (IFC/R2008-0345) describes a "satisfactory" result as 40 percent of committed capital invested within one year; $0.48 billion is 40 percent of $1.2 billion.

TABLE E.4 High and Low Development and Investment Success Rates (2007–09)

Development success ratings, 2007–09

	Low outcomes (%)			High outcomes (%)		
	Highly unsuccessful	Unsuccessful	Mostly unsuccessful	Mostly successful	Successful	Highly successful
Development outcome	***3***	***10***	***15***	***25***	***38***	***10***
		27			***73***	
(by commitment volume)	*1*	*5*	*12*	*29*	*41*	*12*
		18			*82*	

	Unsatisfactory (%)	Partly unsatisfactory (%)	Satisfactory (%)	Excellent (%)
Project business success	17	18	31	34
	35		65	
Economic sustainability	9	13	46	32
	22		78	
Environmental effects	6	26	62	5
	32		68	
Private sector development	6	16	54	24
	22		78	

IFC investment success ratings, 2007–09

	Unsatisfactory (%)	Partly unsatisfactory (%)	Satisfactory (%)	Excellent (%)
Investment outcome	***14***	***6***	***64***	***16***
	20		***80***	
(by commitment volume)	*7*	*6*	*64*	*23*
	14		*86*	
Loan	3	4	88	5
	7		93	
Equity	40	7	15	38
	47		53	

IFC work quality ratings, 2007–09

	Unsatisfactory (%)	Partly unsatisfactory (%)	Satisfactory (%)	Excellent (%)
IFC's overall work quality	***1***	***19***	***67***	***12***
	20		***80***	
(by commitment volume)	*0*	*18*	*67*	*15*
	18		*82*	
Screening, appraisal, structuring	2	23	61	14
	25		75	
Supervision and administration	0	17	71	11
	18		82	
Role and contribution	1	17	60	23
	17		83	

Source: IEG.

Note: IEG uses a binary interpretation of these evaluation results, which describes operations' ratings as either "high" or "low." By volume, figures are the percentages of the total committed IFC investment amounts in each outcome-rating group. The success rates are the percentages of all assigned ratings.

APPENDIX F

Risk-Adjusted Expected Development Outcomes at IFC

Model Specification

Years of evaluation and econometric testing show that project development results hinge significantly on two types of factors: those external to IFC—notably, country risk, sponsor risk, and product market risk—and those internal to IFC—the quality of IFC's work in project appraisal and structuring, project supervision, and additionality. It is important to note, however, that the so-called external factors also come within IFC's decision-making purview and that there can be interactions between external and internal factors. Distinguishing between the two and in general assessing the sensitivity of development outcomes to various factors nevertheless can potentially help in measuring, understanding, and rewarding performance. In general, risks can be offset by strong work quality, although project development outcomes still tend to be lower when risk is higher.

With this understanding, IEG developed an initial model to provide views of project performance that better consider country, sector, and product risk context and thereby enhance understanding about the quality of IFC's efforts in meeting different development challenges. The conceptual framework views development outcome of a project as a function of two sets of factors: external and internal (again noting possible interactions among them).

Development Outcome $_I$ = f (External Factors $_I$, IFC-controllable factors $_I$) + ε_I

The model includes the following external factors:

- *Changes in country business climate*—Changes in the Institutional Investor Country Credit Risk score between approval and evaluation. A higher value indicates a larger improvement in the business environment.
- *Sponsor/partner quality*—The variable captures the sponsor's experience, financial capacity, commitment to the project, and governance/business reputation. If the sponsor is rated low in these dimensions, sponsor quality is deemed to be low. This factor is rated on a binary scale, with 1 as high risk/low quality and 0 as low risk/high quality, based largely on assessment of project documentation and, where available, public information and field visits/interviews.
- *Market risks*—Captures the project's underlying competitiveness in the market in which it is operating, and any market distortions, such as high tariff protection, degree of presence of state-owned enterprises in the sector, artificial monopoly positions, and other distortions that typically result in low competitiveness. Rated on a binary scale, with 1 as high risk/low competitiveness and 0 otherwise.
- *Project type*—Rated on a binary scale, with 1 for a greenfield project and 0 otherwise. Greenfield projects involve new plant construction and new operations and thus pose higher risk compared to expansions of existing plants and operations. They pose "the greatest challenge to structuring and risk sharing" (IFC 1999, p. 29).

The model excludes some possible factors, such as whether the client is a new client or a repeat client, IFC sector experience, and project size, that are in some way highly correlated with factors that are already included in the model.

The set of IFC-controllable factors considered in the model are as follows:

- *Screening, appraisal, and structuring quality*—Rated on a binary scale, with 1 as satisfactory or better and 0 as less than satisfactory.
- *Supervision and administration quality*—Rated on a binary scale, with 1 as satisfactory or better and 0 as less than satisfactory.
- *IFC additionality*—Proxied by IFC's role and contribution rated on a binary scale, with 1 as satisfactory and 0 as less than satisfactory.

Table F.1 presents the analysis.

TABLE F.1 Summary Statistics for Key Variables: 2000–05, 2006–08, 2007–09

Variable	Average for 2000–05	Average for 2006–08	Average for 2007–09	Direction and magnitude of change (2006–08 versus 2007–09)	Average for 2000–05
Development outcome success (%)	0.57	0.72	0.74	Higher	0.57
Changes in country business climate	3.13	13.6	12.67	Lower (less improvement in business climate)	3.13
Sponsor risk	0.4	0.37	0.36	No significant change	0.4
Market competitiveness	0.68	0.60	0.55	Lower (improvement)	0.68
Project type	0.41	0.42	0.48	Higher (more risk)	0.41
Screening, appraisal, and structuring work quality	0.51	0.74	0.74	Same	0.51
Supervision and administration work quality	0.69	0.86	0.83	Lower	0.69
IFC role and contribution	0.79	0.82	0.84	Higher	0.79
No. of observations	361	173	210		361

Source: IEG.

TABLE F.2 Determinants of Development Outcome-Probit Regression Summary, 2000–09

Variable	2000–08 (IEDR 09)	2000–09 (RAP 2010)
Changes in country business climate	0.006**	0.004*
Sponsor risk	−0.09*	−0.127**
Market competitiveness	−0.14**	−0.135**
Project type	−0.10*	−0.067
Screening, appraisal, and structuring work quality	0.38**	0.327**
Supervision and administration work quality	0.35**	0.271**
IFC role and contribution	0.55**	0.497**
# Observation	517	602
Pseudo R2	0.444	0.378

Source: IEG.

Note: Coefficients displayed represent marginal changes in probability of successful development outcome due to unit change in explanatory variable, which for a discrete change of dummy variable is from 0 to 1; * significant at 10 percent; ** significant at 5 percent. IEDR = Independent Evaluation of Development Results; RAP = results and performance.

The external variables in the model are consistent with the consideration of risk in both the financial and development worlds. Financial theorists and practitioners distinguish among the following main types of risks: (i) country risk: the risk of loss on cross-border exposure due to government actions; (ii) credit risk: the risk of loss due to borrower's default; (iii) business risks: uncertainties in the revenues and expenses of a business associated with general industry trends, technological or regulatory changes; and (iv) market risks: risk of possible losses arising from changes in the market due to fluctuating or changing interest rates, foreign exchange rates, share prices, and prices in general.

Risks to development outcome are commonly considered in World Bank approval and evaluation documents. The risks most often identified in Bank project documents are similar to the risk factors included in the model: unfavorable changes in policies, or a law and order situation; and technical capacity and commitment of government partners and/or the implementing agency.

Regression results are presented in table F.2. All the coefficients except project type have the expected signs and are significant at the 5 or 10 percent level. It is clear from the results that factors controllable by IFC tend to dominate the external factors both in terms of statistical significance and statistical impact.

Preliminary Results

The results in table F.2 are used to estimate the impacts of risk and IFC-controllable factors on development outcomes by regional and industry departments. The point of departure is the realization that in an ideal situation of no risks and high work quality, the expected development success rate should be 100 percent.[1] The probability of success by regional and industry departments is then simulated with actual risk parameters and perfect work quality. This estimate of development outcome success rates is called "potential development outcomes" because it indicates what could be achieved with high work quality, given the actual risk profile of projects undertaken by the respective departments, that is, Potential DO = f (actual risks, perfect work quality). The difference between the risk-free 100 percent rating and the potential development outcome can therefore be attributed to the effect of the degree of risks taken.

From the basic regression in table F.2, predicted development outcome success rates are obtained by regional and industry departments, that is, predicted DO = f (actual risks, actual work quality). The difference between potential development outcome and predicted development outcome would then be due to gaps in work quality. Finally, the residuals—that is, the differences between predicted and actual development outcome success rate—are due to unexplained factors.

The results are presented in table F.3. Risk factors had the largest impact on performance in Sub-Saharan Africa and the Middle East and North Africa Regions, at 14 and 13 percent, respectively. For all departments, except Private Equity and Investment Funds and Health and Education, IFC-controllable factors tend to dominate external risk factors in terms of impact on development outcomes. The impact is particularly pronounced in the case of East Asia and the Pacific and Global Information and Communication Technologies.

In addition, in Africa and the Middle East and North Africa, even if risk is accounted for, the potential for success is higher but the potential is not achieved largely because of shortcomings in work quality. All departments and regions, except infrastructure, had unrealized potential in development outcome (which is the difference between potential and actual success rates). The gaps are large in global information and communication technologies and global manufacturing among the industries, and in Central and Eastern Europe and Sub-Saharan

TABLE F.3 IFC's Project Development Outcomes and Factor Attribution

	Development outcome				Difference between actual and maximum (100%)		
	Potential[a] (a) (%)	Predicted[b] (b) (%)	Actual (c) (%)	Unrealized potential (a–c) (%)	Due to risk (a-100%) (%)	Due to WQ (b–a) (%)	Unexplained (c–b) (%)
IFC 2007	91	72	72	19	-9	−19	0
IFC 2008	90	72	75	15	−10	−18	3
IFC 2009	90	72	74	16	−10	−18	2
IFC 2007–09	90	72	74	16	−10	−18	2
CAG	93	84	83	10	-7	-9	-1
CFN	89	73	72	17	−11	-16	-1
CGF	89	67	72	17	−11	-22	5
CGM	91	71	68	23	-9	-20	-3
CHE	89	79	86	3	−11	−10	7
CIN	92	86	96	–4	-8	-6	10
CIT	88	58	53	35	−12	-30	-5
COC	93	79	71	22	−7	−14	-8
Sub-Saharan Africa	86	65	58	28	−14	-21	-7
Asia	90	65	69	21	−10	-25	4
Europe and Central Asia	90	74	72	18	−10	-16	-2
Latin America & Caribbean	93	80	86	7	−7	−13	6
Middle East and North Africa	87	65	64	23	−13	-22	-1
World	88	74	75	13	−12	−14	1

Source: IEG.

Note: CAG = Agribusiness; CFN = Private Equity and Investment Funds; CGF = Global Financial Markets; CGM = Global Manufacturing and Services; CHE = Health and Education; CIN = Infrastructure; CIT = Global Information and Communication Technologies; COC = Oil, Gas, Mining, and Chemicals; WQ = work quality.

a. Risk-adjusted expected development outcome (RAEDO) assuming perfect work quality.

b. RAEDO with actual risk profile and actual work quality.

Africa among the regions. It appears that infrastructure had achieved high levels of work quality and realized the potential outcome given the projects' risks. It is evident, however, that there is room for improvement in almost all regions and sectors.

Predicted Results

Looking forward, newer projects (those approved between 2005 and 2008) had lower sponsor risk, but tended to have higher risk relating to project type. This reflects a growing trend in increasing exposure to new greenfield or early stage businesses. Increased competition, liquidity, and high valuations before the crisis also contributed to project-type risk. Market risk, although recently trending downward, remains high.

The crisis will dominate the outcome prospects of the newer projects. The changes in Institutional Investor Country Credit Rating scores, indicators used for measuring the changes country business climate, deteriorated sharply in recent years.

Considering the above dynamics in risk factors, the expected development outcome will be much lower, even if IFC achieved near-perfect work quality. The potential development outcome will not exceed 90 percent for 2010–13 evaluations (evaluation of 2005–08 approvals; table F.4). If average work quality of 2007–09 is assumed to continue in the future, predicted development outcome will be between 63 and 69 percent.

By department and regions, the shifts in risks are significant in agribusiness and health and education, where drops are predicted in expected development outcomes, taking the risks and work quality assumptions into account (table F.5). In Sub-Saharan Africa and the Middle East and North Africa, newer projects were not significantly influenced by the risks (as potential for newer projects are same or better than the XPSR of 2007–09), but work quality has to be better than the past or the outcome will be still lower than the overall average.

TABLE F.4 Potential and Predicted Development Outcomes by Year

	Potential (%)	Predicted by average work quality (2007–09) (%)
IFC 2010 (2005 approvals)	90	69
IFC 2011 (2006 approvals)	87	64
IFC 2012 (2007 approvals)	88	63
IFC 2013 (2008 approvals)	88	66
IFC 2010–12 (2005–08 approvals)	88	65

Source: IFC.

FIGURE F.1 Project Risk and Sponsor and Market Risk

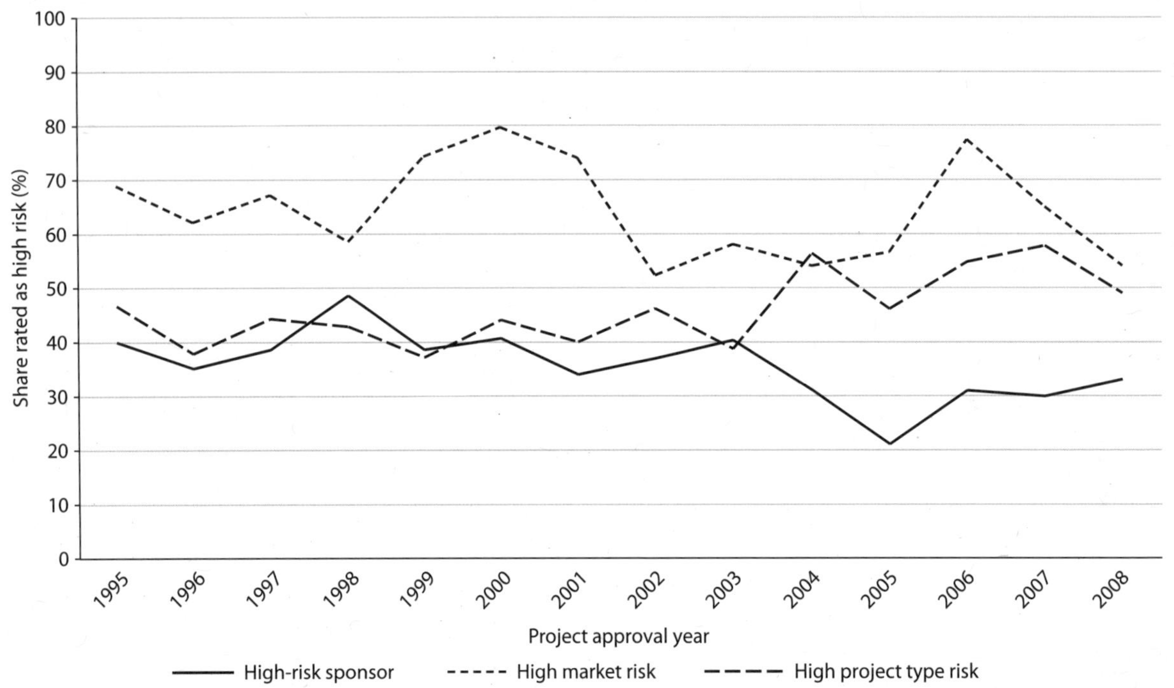

Source: IFC.

Note: 2005 and beyond are a representative sample of projects approved but have not yet reached maturity.

FIGURE F.2 Average Changes in IICCR Scores between Approval and Evaluation

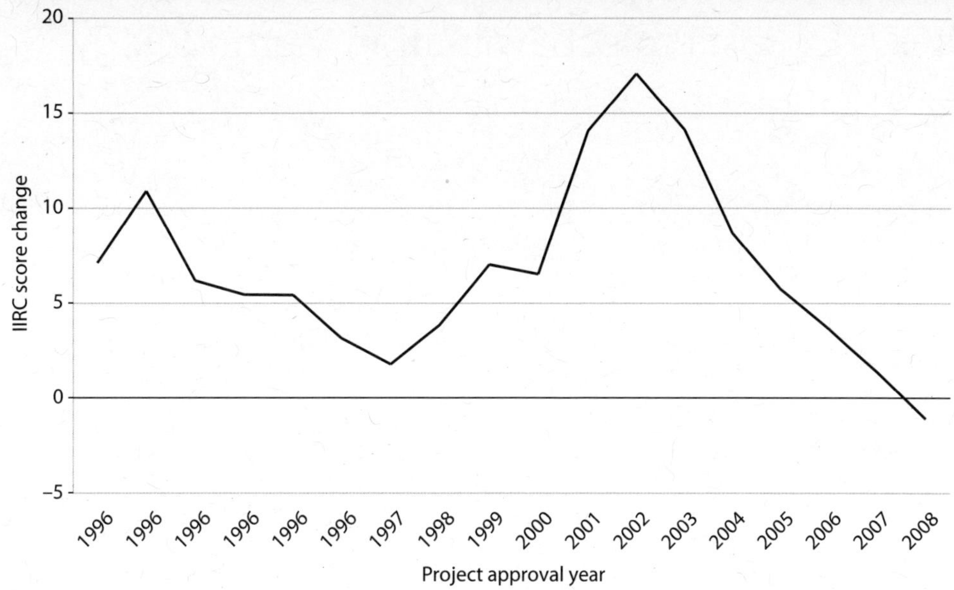

Source: IFC.

Note: Differences in IICCR scores between approval and most recent for projects that have not reached maturity (2005–08 approvals). IICCR = Institutional Investor Country Credit Rating.

TABLE F.5 Potential and Predicted Development Outcomes by Department and Region

Department	Potential 2007–09 (%)	Potential 2010–13 (%)	Department	Predicted 2007–09 (%)	Predicted 2010–13 with 2007–09 WQ (%)
CAG	93	88	CAG	84	58
CFN	89	89	CFN	73	68
CGF	89	89	CGF	67	62
CGM	91	89	CGM	71	63
CHE	89	85	CHE	79	56
CIN	92	90	CIN	86	81
CIT	88	88	CIT	58	68
COC	93	88	COC	79	80
Region					
Sub-Saharan Africa	86	87	Sub-Saharan Africa	70	66
South Asia	90	88	South Asia	63	57
Europe and Central Asia	90	88	Europe and Central Asia	80	72
Latin America and Caribbean	93	90	Latin America & Caribbean	69	59
Middle East and North Africa	87	87	Middle East and North Africa	76	62
World	88	88	World	77	75

Source: IFC.

Note: CAG = Agribusiness; CFN = Private Equity and Investment Funds; CGF = Global Financial Markets; CGM = Global Manufacturing and Services; CHE = Health and Education; CIN = Infrastructure; CIT = Global Information and Communication Technologies; COC = Oil, Gas, Mining, and Chemicals; WQ = work quality.

APPENDIX G

IEG-MIGA's Ex Post Project Evaluation Methodology

IEG-MIGA uses a standard benchmark-based methodology for its evaluation of MIGA guarantee projects. It rates projects in three dimensions: development outcome, MIGA's effectiveness, and contribution to MIGA's financial results. The methodology is consistent with Good Practice Standards established by the ECG Working Group for Private Sector Evaluation, an entity that aims to harmonize evaluation standards for private sector operations across multilateral development institutions.

Development outcome aims to capture a project's overall impact on a country's economic and social development and is thus important as an implicit proxy for how well the project has contributed to MIGA's purpose and mission. Development outcome is evaluated for each project on four dimensions: (i) project business performance, (ii) economic sustainability, (iii) E&S effects, and (iv) private sector development impact. Each of these measures rates a distinct aspect of the guarantee project's performance.

- *Business performance* measures the guarantee project's actual and projected financial impact on the project financiers—its lenders and equity investors.
- *Economic sustainability* measures whether the project has contributed to the country's development.
- *E&S effects* measures a project's performance in meeting MIGA's environmental and social requirements, as well as its actual environmental and social impact.
- *Private sector development* aims to capture the effects of the guarantee project on the development of productive private enterprise *beyond the project* and relates to MIGA's mandate to enhance the flow of private foreign investment to developing countries.

MIGA's effectiveness aims to capture MIGA's work quality in assessing, underwriting, and monitoring its guarantee projects, as well as the value added MIGA brings to the client or project. IEG assesses MIGA's effectiveness across three dimensions of operational performance: (i) strategic relevance; (ii) MIGA's role and contribution; and (iii) quality of MIGA's assessment, underwriting, and monitoring.

- *Strategic relevance* refers to the degree of consistency of the guaranteed project with the development priorities of the host country and the Bank's country strategy.
- *MIGA's role and contribution* relates to the benefits or added value that MIGA brings as a development institution. The contribution may be catalytic (in facilitating FDI in economically sound and sustainable businesses) in encouraging the development of the political risk industry or in conveying additionality.
- *Quality of MIGA's assessment, underwriting, and monitoring* assesses the extent to which the project's expected development outcomes were adequately assessed, key material risks were identified and mitigated, whether MIGA's underwriting policies and guidelines were adhered to, and whether MIGA took adequate remedial action if country or project conditions changed subsequent to its issuing the guarantee.

Contribution to MIGA's financial results relates to a guarantee's impact on MIGA.

Project ratings. IEG rates development outcome and MIGA's effectiveness and each of their dimensions using a four-point rating scale: excellent, satisfactory, partly unsatisfactory, and unsatisfactory.

Harmonization. The methodology and framework are consistent with the Good Practice Standards established by the ECG Working Group for Private Sector Evaluation, which aims to harmonize evaluation standards for private sector operations of multilateral development institutions.

APPENDIX H

MIGA Guarantee Projects Evaluated for This Report

TABLE H.1 MIGA Projects Evaluated

Project Evaluation Report completed	Fiscal year Issued	Number
Fiscal 2004		**4**
Manas Management Company	1998	
Romania Efes Brewery	1998	
Tilda Holdings Africa Limited	1998	
ZAO Knyaz Rurik Efes Breweries	1998	
Fiscal 2005		**5**
ABN AMRO Bank NV Istanbul Branch	1998	
Asia Power (Private) Limited	1998	
Light Servicos de Eletricidade	1997	
Philips do Brasil, Ltda.	1998	
PT Paiton Energy Company	1996	
Cluster—fiscal 2006		**12**
Banco WestLB do Brasil	1999	
Compania Hidroelectrica Dona Julia, S.R.L.	1998	
Grain Bulk Handlers Limited	1998	
Lima Airport Partners S.R.L.	2002	
Mozambique Aluminum Smelter	1998	
Nanjing Coastal Xingang Power Plant	1999	
Salvorhoteis Mozambique—Investimentos Turisticos, S.A.	1999	
Shanghai White Cap Ltd.	1999	
Suzhou Coastal Cogeneration Power Plant	1998	
Vidriera Centroamericana S.A.	1999	
Westdeutsche Landesbank Girozentrale Istanbul Branch	1999	
Wuxi Huada Gas Turbine Electric Power Company	1997	
Cluster—fiscal 2010		**12**
Barclays Bank of Ghana Limited	2006	
Cotecna Destination Inspection Ltd	2003	
Meridian Development Limited	2006	
SGS Scanning Nigeria Limited	2006	
HVB Bank Romania	2002	
JSBC Raiffeisen Bank Ukraine	2001	
Manila North Tollways Corporation	2002	
MINL Ltd	2005	
Ormat Momotombo Power Company	2000	
Hydelec BPA	2002	
Inertes de Cabo Verde, Lda.	2098	
OrPower 4 Inc. (Olkaria III)	2000	
Total		**33**

Endnotes

Chapter 1

1. Drawing on the speech by Robert Zoellick to the Woodrow Wilson Center, Washington, DC, April 14, 2010.
2. Not including guarantees, as is consistent with the Quality Assurance Group's Annual Report on Portfolio Performance. However, the $14 billion in IDA commitments mentioned in the World Bank annual report includes $0.4 billion in guarantees. Note that 2009 was an exceptional year in terms of crisis-driven patterns of activity. Relative scales of activity in this year do not reflect more normal periods.
3. Net exposure is what remains on MIGA's balance sheet after some of MIGA's (gross) guarantee exposure has been laid off via reinsurance.
4. Data for IFC before fiscal 2000 are estimated from IFC's management information system extract. The data from 2000–09 were obtained from IFC's management information system cubes.
5. IBRD and IDA new and supplemental loans only.
6. In fiscal 1998–99 relative to fiscal 1995–97.
7. Using the fiscal 2010 list of fragile states, based on the "Harmonized List of Fragile Situations FY10." Because the list typically changes annually, constructing a longer time series is difficult. The list also refers to "core" fragile states as those with a Bank CPIA rating of 3.0 or below. If this wider definition is used, based on country environment flags, World Bank support to core fragile states has kept pace with the average overall increase in lending with the crisis.
8. From 7 percent in fiscal 2004 to 19 percent in 2009.
9. Estimated on the basis of lending by sector board, which indicates an increase of 180 percent. Using sector allocations, the increase is 292 percent. Even if estimated on the basis of the finance and private sector development theme, the increase in fiscal 2009–10 relative to 2006–08 is 96 percent. There was also a large increase in the share of the financial sector in all lending compared to preceding years in the first half of fiscal 2010, whether coded by sector board (30 percent), sector (28 percent), or theme (36 percent).
10. Prior to fiscal 2009, only Colombia and Mexico had a deferred drawdown option DPL operation.
11. See OP/BP 13.20 on Additional Financing for Investment Lending, which replaces the policy on supplemental financing (former OP/BP 13.20, Supplemental Financing). From fiscal 2006, supplemental financing for investment loans was categorized as additional financing.
12. Subsequent to IEG's evaluation of financial intermediary loans, the Bank has taken steps to try to address these issues, adding a point person for ensuring compliance, together with indicators and system flags for monitoring purposes, and a Guidance Note. Capacity building of participating financial intermediaries is being incorporated in financial intermediary loan design.
13. This increased from approximately $370 million in 2006 to more than $2.35 billion by the end of 2009. In terms of its share in total new commitments, the Global Trade Finance Program's share grew from 11 percent in 2007 to 28 percent in 2009.
14. The 500 percent increase in social protection lending during the crisis refers to an annual average of fiscal 2009 and the first half of 2010, compared to the average of fiscal 2006–08, and is based on sector boards. If allocated by thematic codes, the increase in social protection for fiscal 2009–10 narrows to 234 percent. Other thematic contributions would also change. On a thematic basis, the Environment and Natural Resource Management theme in fiscal 2009–10 compared with 2006–08 increases by a smaller proportion: 106 percent.
15. If operations in social protection are measured by thematic code instead of sector board, a much larger number of operations and countries benefitted from social protection support. In fiscal 2009, there were 64 operations benefitting 43 countries. However, 31 of the 64 operations had only 25 percent or less allocated to the social protection theme. Measures by thematic code therefore complement rather than substitute for measures by sector board. Even if thematic coding is used, the observation on concentration remains: the top three loans with social protection components in fiscal 2009 were 50 percent of the total, and 52 percent in the first half of 2010; in contrast to 24 percent in 2008 and 25 percent in 2007.
16. By sector board, health and education managed to regain former levels in fiscal 2009; in contrast, classified by thematic code, new commitments increased by 113 percent in 2009 compared with the average of 2006–08.
17. In terms of the health and education sector board coding, the top five loans accounted for 33–36 percent of lending in fiscal 2006 and 2007, compared with more than 50 percent in 2008 and 2009.
18. The findings for MIGA are based on IEG-MIGA's project evaluation database of 33 ex post evaluations of MIGA guarantee projects underwritten between fiscal 1996 and 2006

and evaluated be IEG between 2004 and 2010. For this report, IEG analyzed and compared two subclusters of project evaluations. The cluster of 12 recently evaluated projects was underwritten by MIGA between fiscal 1998 and 2006; the earlier cluster of 12 projects, evaluated in 2006, was underwritten by MIGA between fiscal 1997 and 2002. The remaining nine project evaluation reports (not part of any cluster) were evaluated in 2003–04.

19. This analysis is based on the evaluation of 138 projects for fiscal 2009, which exceeds the 121 projects evaluated in the 2008 *Annual Report on Development Effectiveness.* This represents 47.8 percent of total exits for fiscal 2009, which is comparable to the 47.3 percent coverage that annual review based on 289 exits for 2009, compared with 256 for 2008.

20. If results are volume weighted, project performance shows an improvement over the past three years, from 80 percent satisfactory or better in 2007 to 89 percent in 2009. However, this is likely to be a reflection of compositional factors such as increasingly large DPLs. The 2009 *Annual Report on Development Effectiveness* did not estimate volume-weighted performance for this reason, and previous ARDEs have not tracked it systematically.

21. "Better" is defined as satisfactory or excellent—the top two ratings.

22. The 2009 *Annual Report on Development Effectiveness* reported that 80 percent of projects were satisfactory in 2008, compared with 78 percent for 2008. This is because the number of evaluated projects has now increased from 121 to 198.

23. IEG rates projects on a scale of 1–6, ranging from unsatisfactory to highly satisfactory. The traditional measure of performance, in aggregate, has been the percentage of projects that achieve levels of satisfactory or higher on this scale. Another metric is to assign ranks from 1 to 6 to outcomes, which permits the estimation of averages of outcomes for groups of projects, and more fully takes information into account.

24. "Sectors" in this analysis refer to the Bank's sector boards. Other definitions are possible: aggregation of relevant subsectors or thematic codes or aggregation of the percentage allocation to different sectors per project. Sector boards are used here as in previous *Annual Reports on Development Effectiveness.*

25. Based on a sector board classification. Using sector codings, the increase amounts to 67 percent. However, in the context of the overall increase in Bank lending over this period, the share of infrastructure in total lending did not increase and in fiscal 2009 and 2010 was lower than in 2007 and 2008, using either classification.

26. For purposes of this analysis, infrastructure includes the following: utilities, transport and warehousing, telecommunications, and power.

27. All but 12 of the Bank's 34 fragile states (2010) are in the Sub-Saharan Africa Region. As noted in the 2009 *Annual Report on Development Effectiveness,* the Sub-Saharan Africa Region has made efforts to improve results, including restructuring the weakest-performing portfolios, developing the Africa Results Monitoring System, which is now being rolled out as a Bank-wide system to track results for IDA credits, and providing training to task team leaders in the development of results-focused operations and programs.

28. These strategic priorities were outlined in *MIGA's Strategic Directions for FY05–08* and revalidated in *MIGA's FY09–11 Operational Directions* (see MIGA 200X , 200Y, 200Z). Complex infrastructure is defined by MIGA as infrastructure and extractive industries projects involving project finance, environment, or social issues.

29. Conflict-affected countries are one of MIGA's priority areas. This category includes some countries with very localized regional conflicts that would not affect performance of investments outside those localized regions; this to some extent explains the counterintuitive development outcome ratings encountered.

30. Direct costs of the service, including Bank budget funds and Trust Funds, to the extent they are reported in one internal Bank database.

31. Based on ESW and NLTA product line data. These estimates correspond with definitions used in the QAG Annual Report on Portfolio Performance.

32. In some countries, the Bank is promoting the increase of recipient-led analytical work and is making efforts to transfer core diagnostics to the government. There are examples in Vietnam, Indonesia, and Tanzania. Yet this is unlikely to account for a large part of the declines in numbers observed.

33. A simplified Activity Completion Summary was implemented in May 2004 with the introduction of ratings against development outcome indicators.

Chapter 2

1. Mandate of the Director-General, Evaluation, p. 1.
2. Mandate of the Director-General, Evaluation, p. 1.
3. The implementation indicators are not disclosed.
4. The *Annual Report on Development Effectiveness,* which looks at the Bank as a whole but does not make recommendations, Project Performance Assessment Reports, and Country Assistance Evaluations are not included in the Management Action Record and not systematically followed up with management, so they were excluded.
5. The current Management Action Record includes 55 recommendations from evaluations produced from 2006 onward and three recommendations held over from earlier evaluations.
6. The evaluations reviewed were (i) *From Schooling Access to Learning Outcomes: An Unfinished Agenda—An Evaluation*

of World Bank Support to Primary Education; (ii) *Engaging with Fragile States: An IEG Review of World Bank Support to Low Income Countries Under Stress;* (iii) *Financial Sector Assessment Program: IEG Review of the Joint World Bank and IMF Initiative;* (iv) the 2006 *Annual Report on Operations Evaluation;* (v) *Capacity Building in Africa: an OED Evaluation of World Bank Support;* and (vi) *Hazards of Nature, Risks to Development: An IEG Evaluation of World Bank Assistance for Natural Disasters.* The first four evaluations are scheduled to exit the Management Action Record in 2010. The evaluation on capacity building in Africa was the only evaluation with negligible ratings in the fourth year of implementation. The evaluation on hazards of nature had recommendations that were fully adopted by the Bank within three years.

7. Management and IEG use a four-point scale to rate adoption of recommendations: high (fully adopted); substantial (largely adopted but not fully incorporated into policy, strategy, or operations as yet); medium (adopted in some operational and policy work but not to a significant degree in key areas); and negligible (no evidence or plan for adoption, or plans and actions are in a very preliminary stage).

8. This is a change in trend for management, which rated only 25 percent of their first year recommendations as high and substantial for adoption in 2009 and only 32 percent in 2008.

9. The review includes all recommendations since 2003, both active and retired. Retired recommendations include ratings over four years. For evaluations of less than four years, only those years for which rating are available are included.

10. The extent to which the staff making the assessment are familiar with the topic and the issues behind the recommendation, which could be high if the original evaluator were making the assessment, but could be lower if there is staff turnover.

11. This is mainly due to the difference in treatment by IFC and IEG of recommendations that have been implemented: IFC categorizes them as inactive, whereas IEG keeps them for one more year.

12. Over the review period, IEG reports have included seven recommendations directed at IEG-IFC. Of these seven, the level of adoption for six is either substantial or high. Three of the seven recommendations are still active.

13. The *Independent Evaluation of IFC's Development Results* was formerly known as the *Annual Review of IEG's Evaluation Findings.*

14. The *Biennial Report on Evaluation,* formerly known as the *Annual Report on Operations Evaluation* in IFC, was produced annually until 2005.

15. In the current Management Action Tracking Record, most of the recommendations (19) are from the flagship annual reports (83 percent); only four are from joint thematic evaluations (*Guarantees and Extractive Industries*), where MIGA is selectively covered.

16. Implementation ratings are: low (MIGA's actions or plans for adoption are at a very preliminary stage or just beginning); medium (MIGA has taken some steps to adopt the recommendation and incorporate it into policy, strategy or operations, but has not incorporated it to a significant degree or not incorporated it in key areas); and completed (MIGA has fully adopted the recommendation and broadly incorporated/mainstreamed it into policy, strategy, and operations).

17. The results framework is spelled out in the IEG evaluation where the recommendation was first made, but is not specified in the Management Action Tracking Record itself.

18. This section is based on a review of the evaluation literature and on rounds of consultations and discussions on these topics with practitioners and evaluation experts on international evaluation recommendation follow-up systems, all of which were conducted by Osvaldo Feinstein.

19. See ADB (2009). ADB management has already indicated that it considers the first results of the Management Action Records "positive and encouraging."

Chapter 3

1. Some Country Directors oversee programs in multiple countries, but are located in just one.

2. From an internal Board document, "Decentralization—Location of Work: A Strategic Tool for Strengthening the Bank's Development Effectiveness," March 9, 2001.

3. Internal papers—"Toward a Global Bank: Discussion Note," October 6, 2008; "Toward a Global Bank: An Update," June 19, 2009; and "Toward a Global Bank: Second Update," February 3, 2010—are not for external review.

4. The finding on statistical significance is based on regression analysis with distance from Washington as an instrumental variable in place of task team leaders based in the field. Regression controls for Country Policy and Institutional Assessment, growth of per capita gross domestic product, year of approval, and dummy variables indicating whether the operation is a development policy operation, the region of the country and network of the operation, and whether the country is fragile, eligible for IDA finance, or blended finance between IDA and IBRD.

5. Quality at entry refers to the extent to which the Bank identified, facilitated preparation of, and appraised an operation such that it was most likely to achieve planned development outcomes and was consistent with the Bank's fiduciary role.

6. Tests of significance for differences in means were undertaken as a prelude to the regression analysis. Differences were not found to be significant.

7. Distance from Washington (in km) is a good predictor for presence of the task team leader in the field (z score = 4.18

and *F*-score = 36.99 on that coefficient in an OLS first-stage regression that includes all the explanatory variables), and is unlikely to affect outcomes of operations except through this mechanism.

8. In addition to other factors that affect outcomes, there may be a selection bias—managers may choose to base a task team leader in the field or in headquarters in part because of expected positive results. For instance, recurring financial management issues may be seen as a high risk, so the manager may presume that a field-based task team leader would be best placed to address them. But these risks in themselves may be what make outcomes of an operation unsatisfactory, not the location of the task team leader. To address any potential selection bias, a two-stage regression analysis was used with an instrumental variable. Distance from Washington (in km) is a good predictor for presence of the task team leader in the field (*z* score = 4.18 and *F*-score=36.99 on that coefficient in an OLS first stage regression that includes all the explanatory variables) and is unlikely to affect outcomes of operations except through this mechanism. In the first-stage regression, distance from Washington is used to predict whether the Bank chooses a field-based task team leader to oversee an operation (at least in its final stages). This instrumental variable is unlikely to affect development outcomes (or any other omitted variables) in any way except through its effect on the location of the task team leader. The second-stage regression, in which distance serves as an instrument for a task team leader based in the field, does not find any evidence that the location of the task team leader at project closing has an effect on outcomes of operations.

9. Accounting for 80 percent of operations and 86 percent of commitments made over fiscal 2008–10, as of January 25, 2010. In contrast, only 4 percent of sector managers, who directly oversee team leaders and staff working on day-to-day preparation and supervision of operations, were based in the field in fiscal 2009 (up from 2 percent in fiscal 2000).

10. Country Assistance Evaluations go into greater depth and cover a longer period of country program activity but have few observations over the period because decentralization expanded; these evaluations are not considered here.

11. "Toward a Global Bank: Discussion Note," October 6, 2008, internal report.

12. The coefficient multiplied by 100 should be interpreted as the relative performance of operations based in the field, compared with those based in headquarters within a given region, measured in percentage points.

Chapter 4

1. IICCR refers to the Institutional Investor Country Credit Risk Rating. A country is considered high risk if its IICCR score is below 30.

2. Lagging indicators are those that literally lag behind the actual events but that have high correlations. For instance, in this case, it is known that the financial crisis is having a negative effect on IFC's investments; however, it is not expected that XPSR ratings will reflect the effects of the crisis for at least another year.

3. The IFC 2013 Initiative is a multiyear, multiphase initiative begun in 2009 to redesign IFC processes management structure to allow IFC to increase its proximity to the client so that development outcome and relevance are enhanced. Decentralization and relocating decision makers to the field is a core component of the initiative.

4. A similar quality at entry review was conducted in 2004 to assess the influences of various quality enhancement measures during 1999–2003. The review compared fiscal 2002–03 approvals to the calendar year 1995–96 approvals. One of the important factors is the establishment of a credit department, introduction of credit notes, and training, as well as the separation of portfolio team (supervision) and origination (new business). The review found that newer project approvals have better risk profiles and improved work quality across all dimensions than the evaluated projects at that time (1995–96).

5. The initial steps of addressing how to price advisory services date back as far as the 1980s. The 2007 policy has been and continues to be supplemented by business line-specific guidelines.

6. Ex ante review refers to the articulation of additionality in the approval documents most commonly found in the Board documents.

Chapter 5

1. "Quality of underwriting" assesses the quality of MIGA's own work in selecting, assessing, underwriting, and monitoring its guarantees. It is not a rating of the project's performance, but of MIGA's own performance in underwriting.

2. For a comprehensive discussion of MIGA results and performance, see the IEG-MIGA (2010).

3. The exception was Inertes de Cabo Vertes, underwritten in fiscal 1998.

4. The exception was Lima Airport, underwritten in fiscal 2002.

5. Furthermore, when interpreting these findings and results, it is essential to note that unlike for the World Bank and IFC, it is inappropriate to attribute statistical significance to the project-level findings. Project-level results cannot be extrapolated to MIGA's overall portfolio of guarantees. The available sample size of Project Evaluation Reports yields a confidence interval that is too wide for statistical inference. For this reason, the report does not draw conclusions on MIGA's overall portfolio performance. Rather, the analysis

draws on qualitative assessments (content analysis of project evaluation findings) and quantitative analysis of project ratings to identify "common patterns," "enabling conditions," and "success factors."

6. IEG-MIGA evaluates project development outcome across four different dimensions: (i) project business performance; (ii) economic sustainability; (iii) its environmental and social effects; and (iv) private sector development impact. Each of these indicators measures a distinct aspect of the guarantee project's performance and is assessed separately, and "development outcome" is a synthesis of them. A project's development outcome rating thus encompasses all its effects (positive and negative) on economic and social development.

7. The cluster of 12 projects evaluated in fiscal 2006 was underwritten between fiscal 1997 and 2002, whereas the cluster of projects evaluated more recently (2010) was underwritten between fiscal 1998 and 2006.

8. Projects are referred to as having performed "low" or "less than satisfactory" (for example, with regard to the development outcome rating or quality of underwriting) when they were rated partly unsatisfactory or unsatisfactory. Conversely, projects are referred to as having performed high or satisfactory or better when they were rated satisfactory or excellent.

9. This was calculated as 42 percent over 70 percent, that is, those projects that have low quality of underwriting and low development outcomes divided by all projects that have low quality of underwriting.

10. This was calculated as 24 percent over 30 percent, that is, those projects that have high quality of underwriting and high development outcomes divided by all projects that have high quality of underwriting.

11. See discussion of the MIGA Management Action Track Record of this report.

Appendix A

1. Masking, however, wide differences in average project duration for adjustment and investment loans.

Appendix C

1. ADB management has already indicated that it considers the first results of the MARS "positive and encouraging" (ADB 2009).

2. CONEVAL played an important role in Mexico's shift in 2005 from a sectoral to a government-wide M&E system and the institutionalization of evaluation and a results focus at the federal government. In 2007, CONEVAL introduced new evaluation guidelines in response to low usage of the evaluation findings and to overcome the lack of awareness of the role that evaluation could play in improving government programs (Castro and others 2009).

Appendix F

1. The historical likelihood of default as ranked by Moody's, for example, shows over a normal five-year period only 0.1 percent of AAA US corporate bonds default (see Credit and Default Risks on http://personal.fidelity.com/products/fixedincome/risks.shtml).

Bibliography

ADB (Asian Development Bank). 2009. *2008 Annual Report on Acting on Recommendations.* Manila: Independent Evaluation Department, Asian Development Bank.

Bandstein, Sara, and Erik Hedblom. 2008. *IFAD's Management Response System—The Agreement at Completion Point Process,* Karlstad, SADEV.

Castro, Manuel Fernando, Gladys Lopez-Acevedo, Gita Beker Busjeet, and Ximena Fernandez Ordonez. 2009. "Mexico's M&E System: Scaling Up from the Sectoral to the National Level." ECD Working Paper Series No. 20, World Bank, Independent Evaluation Group, Washington, DC.

IEG (Independent Evaluation Group). 2010a. *Gender and Development: An Evaluation of World Bank Support 2002–2008.* Washington, DC: World Bank.

———. 2010b. *Poverty Reduction Support Credits: An Evaluation of World Bank Support.* Washington, DC: World Bank.

———. 2010c. *Water and Development: An Evaluation of World Bank Support 1997–2007.* Washington, DC: World Bank.

———. 2009a. *Annual Report on Development Effectiveness: Achieving Sustainable Development.* Washington, DC: World Bank.

———. 2009b. *The World Bank Group Guarantee Instruments 1990–2007.* Washington, DC: World Bank.

———. 2008a. *Environmental Sustainability: An Evaluation of World Bank Group Support.* Washington, DC: World Bank.

———. 2008b. *Independent Evaluation of IFC's Development Results 2008.* Washington, DC: World Bank.

———. 2008c. *Using Knowledge to Improve Development Effectiveness: An Evaluation of World Bank Economic and Sector Work and Technical Assistance 2000–2006.* Washington, DC: World Bank.

———. 2007. *Development Results in Middle-Income Countries: An Evaluation of the World Bank's Support.* Washington, DC: World Bank.

———. 2006a. *Annual Report on Operations Evaluation.* Washington, DC: World Bank.

———. 2006b. *Engaging with Fragile States: An IEG Review of World Bank Support to Low-Income Countries under Stress.* Washington, DC: World Bank.

———. 2006c. *Financial Sector Assessment Program: IEG Review of the Joint World Bank and IMF Initiative.* Washington, DC: World Bank.

———. 2006d. *From Schooling Access to Learning Outcomes: An Unfinished Agenda—An Evaluation of World Bank Support to Primary Education.* Washington, DC: World Bank.

———. 2006e. *Hazards of Nature, Risks to Development: An IEG Evaluation of World Bank Assistance for Natural Disasters.* Washington, DC: World Bank.

———. 2006f. *World Bank Lending for Lines of Credit: An IEG Evaluation.* Washington, DC: World Bank.

———. 2006g. *The World Bank in Turkey 1993–2004: An IEG Country Assessment Evaluation.* Washington, DC: World Bank.

———. 2005. *Capacity Building in Africa: An OED Evaluation of World Bank Support.* Washington, DC: World Bank.

———. 2003. *Power for Development: A Review of the World Bank Group's Experience with Private Participation in the Electricity Sector.* Washington, DC: World Bank.

———. 2001. *Information Infrastructure: The World Bank Group's Experience—A Joint Operations Evaluation Department–Operations Evaluation Group Review.* Washington, DC: World Bank.

IEG-IFC (Independent Evaluation Group–International Finance Corporation). 2009. *Independent Evaluation of Development Results: Knowledge for Private Sector Development.* Washington, DC: World Bank.

———. 2008a. *Biennial Report on Evaluation: IFC's Results Measurement for Better Results.* Washington, DC: World Bank.

———. 2008b. *Independent Evaluation of IFC's Development Results.* Washington, DC: World Bank.

IEG-MIGA (Independent Evaluation Group–Multilateral Investment Guarantee Agency). 2010. *Achieving Value-Driven Volume—MIGA's Development Results and Institutional Effectiveness—2010.* Washington, DC: World Bank.

———. 2006. *Independent Evaluation Group-MIGA 2006 Annual Report.* Washington, DC: World Bank.

IFC (International Finance Corporation). 2010. *IFC Road Map FY11–13.* Washington, DC: World Bank.

———. 1999. *Project Finance in Developing Countries.* Lessons of Experience Series, Vol. 7. Washington, DC: World Bank.

IFAD (International Fund for Agricultural Development) Office of Evaluation. 2009. *Evaluation Manual: Methodology and Processes.* Rome: IFAD.

World Bank. 2010a. "The Bank's Non-Lending Technical Assistance Program: A QAG Learning Review." Quality Assurance Group Synthesis Report, World Bank, Washington, DC.

———. 2010b. "Transforming the Bank's Knowledge Agenda: A Framework for Action." Board Report, April 12, World Bank, Washington, DC.

———. 2009. "World Bank Response to Financial Crises: The Special Development Policy Lending Option." Operations Policy and Country Services Corporate Finance and Risk Management, July 29.

———. 1997. "The Strategic Compact: Renewing the Bank's Effectiveness to Fight Poverty." World Bank, Washington, DC.